URBANITY
Twenty Years Later
Projects for Central European Capitals

centre for central european architecture

URBANITY
– TWENTY YEARS LATER

–
PROJECTS FOR CENTRAL EUROPEAN CAPITALS

007 **CENTRAL EUROP**
011 **WORKSHOP** 015 **E**
023 **LIEVEN DE CAU**
045 **BERLIN** ACTION
071 **BRATISLAVA** CI
093 **BUDAPEST** A_VO
115 **LJUBLJANA** LIV
143 **PRAGUE** LEGIBL
SLOW CAPITAL 199
PARKOUR 223 **LEARN**

AGAIN

IA ZENGHELIS

ER Ø29**CITIES**

SEED

Y OF TESTS

D TO BUILD

NG IN THE CITY

 CITY 165**VIENNA**

ARSAW CITY

NG FROM FUTURE

BERLIN

BRATISLAVA

BUDAPEST

005

LJUBLJANA

PRAGUE

VIENNA

WARSAW

HAS SOMEONE BEEN TALKING ABOUT CENTRAL EUROPE AGAIN?

IGOR KOVAČEVIĆ
& YVETTE VAŠOURKOVÁ

–

The Urbanity Project is a several-year project initiated by MOBA platform and organised by the Centre for Central European Architecture. It is a research project which is rediscovering Central European urban values and seeks a new form for their integration into a broader European and world context. The tool for this process comes in various forms of inter-field cooperation where the topic of city and urbanity is interpreted, analysed, critically assessed and developed by a number of participants, ranging from non-government organisations and artists, architects and architecture students to city mayors, administrators and urban planners of Central European capital cities.

Despite the extensive number of players involved, the aim of the project is not to duplicate the work of urban planners, but to refine it in the long-term. By asking the question of how our city will look in twenty or fifty years we are opening a broader dialogue and trying to remove the ad hoc methods of the current governance of cities. By selecting capital cities in which the region's political and economic power is concentrated, we can follow cities which are easy to identify even outside the Central European space. The mechanisms which work in these cities are universal and can be monitored anywhere in the democratic world. Although the project is regional, "Urbanity - Twenty Years Later" is aiming to find answers for the future of our cities as such, regardless of their location.

Capital cities in the democratic world are not directly controlled, but are influenced by a concentration of diverse interests. Unlike other urban planners, Urbanity has the advantage that it is not something commissioned by someone and therefore does not follow any particular political or economic interest, but at a theoretical and practical level it attempts to communicate the idea of a better city. The principal communication channel of the project is architecture. We are not searching for new urbanism, but for a discipline which, in an architectural form, will assess the existing city and discover its further possibilities and visions.

Urbanism in Central Europe has been dormant for forty years, incessantly repeating the principles of Modernism. Paradoxically this dormancy protected the city centres and it would appear that after 1989 we will continue from where Modernism left off and will avoid the mistakes made by the more developed countries in urban planning. Today, when we begin to realise the potential which our cities had after the socialist conservation, we regret the mistakes

BERLIN

BRATISLAVA

BUDAPEST

007

LJUBLJANA

PRAGUE

VIENNA

WARSAW

of urbanism after revolution. Unfortunately, in the last twenty years urbanism has disengaged itself from visions and passed over its decision-making to the all-powerful market. The project is looking for the answer to the question of how to restore the aesthetic and moral quality to the discipline which designs space.

UNDERSTANDING

–
The publication we present here shows a path of the cooperation of seven universities from Central European capital cities. Thanks to the willingness of the students and tutors, these universities have become part of two-year research activities by which we are jointly defining and creating Central Europe twenty years after the fall of the Berlin Wall. The first question by many students asking why we are here and if we are really part of Central Europe opened up room to mutual recognition and understanding. The search of an answer to the question of what is Central European space aroused a series of discussions. A sincere understanding of their surroundings and stereotypes by which everyone from the environment lives became a starting point for future cooperation. Two workshops were jointly organised in Prague, further work took place in individual studios. An informal form of communication by email and facebook then became a real space where ideas appeared, visits were organised to other cities and discussions developed about the senselessness or essence of the project "Urbanity - Twenty Years Later".

The publication does not offer the range of procedures dealing with the problems of cities, but projects the thoughts of a generation of upcoming architects about the city and it's potential. At the same time it offers a comparison of various educational approaches which led to projects from paper architecture to the architecture of deeds.

BERLIN

BRATISLAVA

BUDAPEST

LJUBLJANA

PRAGUE

VIENNA

WARSAW

WORKSHOP

IGOR KOVAČEVIĆ
& YVETTE VAŠOURKOVÁ
-

The realisation that Central European cities repeated a number of mistakes in succession in the last twenty years is due, not least, to the absence of communication between professional circles in the region. Recurring mistakes such as excessive investments into the transport infrastructure or the belief that the market will resolve all urban problems moved in the 1990s from Vienna to Berlin, Prague and Bratislava without the experience of other cities being critically assessed. In this spirit the presented works are not attempting to resolve problems but to establish a scenario which the city can change without it having to be pronounced as doctrine.

The search for the responsibility by the architectural profession, as spoken of by Elia Zenghelis, is the important mission of schools of architecture. The feeling that schools, in view of their constant growth, are not coping with this dimension of education may be highly subjective, but also difficult to refute.

Despite all the pedagogical improvements made to the education system of which we have been witnesses in the 20th century, the moral education of architects has not changed from the level of direct instruction between the pupil and the teacher. Based on this we organised cooperation between seven teams where the optimum form of communication came through intensive daily work between students and tutors. The workshop, as a format for vivid discussion, became the initial and, at the same time, the control point for diverse criticism of the present situation. The ideas developed at the first workshop were further elaborated in two-semestral works carried out by individual studios.

Each group looked for a different way to a solution for their city. The free choice of each student to regard the city often led to the criticism of individual problems and a search for an opinion of a specific problem. But what makes this work different from the official methods of designing cities is the absence of a client and absolute freedom to take a design to the very extreme of a situation. Apocalypse, Privatisation of public space and Parkour are subjective answers to the condition of a city and a reaction to its daily absurdity.

Joint work, the renewal and newly built central European links and the awareness of mutual resemblances

BERLIN BRATISLAVA BUDAPEST

011

LJUBLJANA

PRAGUE

VIENNA

WARSAW

or differences are the basis for mastering the scale of a city. Abandoning urbanism as a discipline which is a political tool for controlling territory appears to be more and more unavoidable. How to disengage from colourful plans and coefficients, which are the manipulative tools for designing cities is a question that is being dealt today by a number of experts. This publication is only a helpful means for opening new fields of vision. The plan for creating a city in which we live and the clear formulation of its spatial qualities are topics which urbanism as a political tool can hardly resolve. We need to return to architecture which is the only discipline able to rediscover the city and its values.

URBANITY WORKSHOP I

when: April 24th - May 2nd 2009,
where: Veletržní palác, Prague

Work
Seven internationally mixed teams worked on seven themes:
History: How has the national capital been constructed?
Regional relationships: Is there a Central European identity?
Reading the city: Is there a true reading of the city using a professional method?
Representation: How is the identity of the city constructed?
Infrastructure: What are the political instruments for operating and regulating the city?

Lectures
The workshop was accompanied by a series of public lectures:

Tomáš Valena: The Place of the City. Between Image and Identity.
Mariusz Czepczynski: Urban Semiotics: Meaning and Form of Central European Cities.
Jiří Hrůza: Urbanistic Archetypes
Miroslav Marcelli: Towards Urban Anthropology
Christian Teckert: Curated Cities. On the Contradictions and Conflicting Realities of the City.
Elia Zenghelis: The Immeuble Cité.

URBANITY WORKSHOP II

when: December 3rd - 6th 2009,
where: Technical Library, Prague

Presentation
All seven city teams have presented their final work.
Berlin: Action Seed
Bratislava: City of Tests
Budapest: A_Void to Build
Ljubljana: Living in the City
Prague: Legible City
Vienna: Slow Capital
Warsaw: City Parkour

Events
The future of Central European cities - public debate with architect Elia Zenghelis, philosopher Lieven de Cauter and seven tutors.
Heterotopia revised - lecture by Lieven de Cauter

BERLIN BRATISLAVA BUDAPEST LJUBLJANA PRAGUE VIENNA WARSAW

INTERVIEW WITH ELIA ZENGHELIS

by IGOR KOVAČEVIĆ

CENTRAL EUROPE – ARCHITECTURE AND REGIME

—
In developing the idea of Central Europe with The Centre for Central European Architecture, we feel that a paradox exists for this region. A paradox in defining Cen-tral Europe: according to some thinkers Central Europe exists and to others it does not. We have a feeling, not during these days of the workshop, but through pure li-ving experience here, that something like the actual existence of a Central Europe can be formulated. Do you feel a difference, being here, from what you would call Western, or Eastern Europe?

I have always been conscious of the presence of "Central Europe", primarily in geographic rather than any other terms, in the same sense as one is instantly conscious of "the Balkans"

as distinct from what we are used to calling "Western Europe". While none of these are either clearly defined, distinct entities, or culturally homogeneous (in fact they are bestowed with a heterogeneous cultural richness) nevertheless they each call to mind a phantom 'character', partly induced by our imagination, partly by our literature and partly by their geographical, historical and (real or presupposed) cultural reality. Yet even this is hard to define and the definition (such as it is) is somewhat vacillating. Most of us think of Germany as "Western", yet it stretches from the West to the East. Slovenia was part of Yugoslavia; Yugoslavia was clearly part of the Balkans, hence the region that defines South-Eastern Europe. Yet we conceive Slovenia as decidedly part of "Central" Europe. And Romania? Is it Eastern Europe? Southern Europe? It embraces all categories, even the beginning of the North. In my consciousness it is also part of Central Europe. The way our imagination defines these regions, where they begin and whe-re they end, is more important than their geographic accuracy. It defines it by a motley assortment of inferences, like our relative knowledge of history and literature, our conception and/or experience of myths, geography, mountain ranges that we have read about or visited and finally the seas that surround the continent (from the Baltic to the Atlantic and the Mediterranean) which determine our vision of the interior continental regions. Central Europe is the "Interior" of the continent. The ancient Greeks saw Delphi as the "navel" of the world. Central Europe - and certainly the Czech Republic being more or less in the "Centre" of Central Europe - is the navel of Europe. As such it has, throughout its history and culture fulfilled this role. There are no national boundaries formulating central Europe, it is a kind of mentality: both our own mentality and the way we imagine it and the actual mentality of its inhabitants. Whether it is the combination of the Slavic element (traditionally thought of as North Eastern) and the proximity to its Teutonic and Magyar neighbours, it is a mixture that has produceda richness of intellectual and artistic resourcefulness that is unique to the region. Whether this comes from Western, Eastern, Northern or Southern influences, it is exclusive to this region - and this fact makes it the Centre and its difference: serious, intense and sincere.

—

At the same time, there is an experience of forty years here in Central Europe, which is now read in a certain way by contemporary observers..

These forty years are exceptionally important. The legacy they conferred on the collective unconscious of the nations behind the "Iron Curtain" is considerable and we can regard this as having had both positive and negative, but very important and ineradicable consequences: we cannot deny or forget this stirring part of History, as is the wish of certain German architects, politicians and planners (think of Berlin and the physical erasure of the Wall: such an important and poignant part of the city's History has been set to wilful oblivion - a tragic act of amnesia and loss of opportunity for Berliners). This forty-year period temporarily shifted our view of Central Europe as being part of the "Eastern Block": the "Iron Curtain" was the dividing line of a politically divided Europe: East and West, both conceptually and in fact; there was no "centre" of any kind in this.

—

These forty years were miserable for human rights, the law, ownership etc. But at the same time, during that period, architects realised fabulous buildings, some of which we visited.[1] Do you think that the regime took from something that already existed or is it basically something that it developed by itself?

I am sure that initially the regime took the principles of modernism that existed, since they were 'socialist' in nature. Even though Modernism was applied to the capitalist world it was essentially a socialist ideal: Socialism was part of the modernist dream. What is interesting (and this I attribute to the cultural sophistication of the Central Euro-pean countries) is that the Stali-nist maxim for a return to conservative principles in architecture (palaces for the people) did not get hold of in the built projects on the more sophisticated European countries to the same extend that it did in the USSR (for a similar reason you see so many successful Unités d'habitation built in Yugo-slavia at the time). The whole idea of collective living in the 'Unité d'habitation' was perfectly suited to a socialist dream. Le Corbusier had his own idiosyncratic view of socialism. So I believe that here it was definitely a question of continuing with something that had already been envisaged. Partly because of this, the Stalinist criticism of Modernism as corrupt and degenerately bourgeo-is, not only had a valid point, but in the case of the return to academicism did also produce magnificent urban contributions, as are the socalled 'quartalis' of Moscow: urban perimeter blocks on a very large scale, built for socialist apartments, palaces that have adorned the city and are amongst its most impressive Urbanist achievements, even as they recall fascist principles. Recently we saw the hotel Intercontinental in Prague[2]. It is easy to call it a 'fascist' building: but we must not forget the common principles between fascism and socialist realism and the fact that both ideo-logies produced striking architectural and 'urban' realizations. What was interesting is the fact that the modernists and the constructivists failed to contribute to the city: theirs were essentially anti-city projects, in that they rejected the legacy of the city as it had evolved during the autocratic principles of the Renaissance or the mercantile principles of the bourgeois revolution and sought to reconceive it on the ideological premise of a new relationship between the collective and the individual, a relationship that could only be accomplished by a "tabula rasa".

–
Let us focus on this relationship between the collective and the individual: perhaps seeing the relationship of city versus sprawl as a political issue makes a connection, which can help explain the sprawl as 'non-citiness'?

It should be a dialectical relationship; but it is not: it is a kind of escape from the city and the collective, which are seen as dangerous and corrupting. The city is the locus of 'protest' and escaping from its dangers is the outcome of the present form of 'liberalism', which engenders the cult of privatisation. Everything is now being privatised. It's the 'coup de grâce' of the public domain.

–
But this privatisation is actually also the process we have had here during the last twenty years - because we were in the collective - and now?

This is the point: it is a reactionary reflex, to do the opposite of what you did during forty years of oppressive collectivity. Imposed collectivity is repressive to the individual; and as such it cannot work; one of the prime flaws of Marxist socialism has been its disregard for the rising science of psychology: only a socialist ideology that embraced human psychology and could accommodate private desires would stand a chance to engender a successful collectivity. What is interesting is that after the Second World War, faced with what it saw as the communist the 'threat', capitalism absorbed socialist values and practices, on the one hand out of self-interest (in order to survive as such) but also out of some desire to improve social conditions; a shift towards a kind of capitalism with a socialist content: the 'welfare' state. It is noteworthy that such measures would have been inconceivable in the kind of capitalist democratic countries of the 1920s and 30s.

If we put the city as something common, the sprawl as something individual, where would be the na-ture in this very social hierachy?

BERLIN
BRATISLAVA
BUDAPEST
017
LJUBLJANA
PRAGUE
VIENNA
WARSAW

Let's face it; there hardly exists such a thing as 'nature' in our continent anymore. What we have in terms of nature is mostly artificial, agricultural, or inaccessible and hostile, as in the highest mountain peaks. If we look at this question in purely idealistic terms, nature should be collective, but in the present circumstances it is mostly in private hands, with exceptions that are comparable to the public parks that are set within the city (hence not 'natural'). The private gardens of the sprawl that spread around the cities are neither nature nor city: they are a cancerous erosion of the countryside by cities that have no limits. The only way we could safeguard the existence of any kind of 'nature' would be if cities had inviolable limits. By saying this I do not preclude the right of people to live outside the city. But I think that a careful and ecological balance of areas of habitation in the countryside should be designated outside the cities, with equally inviolable limits. They could form a dialectical relationship with the city - and the countryside as well. I should clarify that I also am not in principle against priva-te property, because I believe that this would be totally against human nature. One would only wish that there was a political system that would make this available to all in equitable terms - and I don't think this is a utopian wish: I am optimistic that one day our civilization will achieve it. In retrospect this is a reflection towards your earlier eloquent question "and now?" - It's the 64000-dollar question: no regime or religion has managed to implement the Christian notion of 'Equity'. While previous Socialist regimes failed, the appalling discrepancy between power and powerlessness, between "haves" and "have-nots" in our 'democracies'

remains in one piece. Is this the result of our collective negligence, or the product of the primordial nature of our species? Is it something that not even our civilization can discard?

EDUCATION

–

An idea of the workshop 'Urbanity Twenty Years Later' was to research and produce critical remarks on what happened in the last 20 years. There were moments when I felt that this period did not warrant such critical remarks.

On the contrary, I think the aims of the workshop were crucial and well conceived. If anything, I felt that there was an insuffici-ency of critical evaluation for the last 20 years; this, as a want for a critical comparison between 'before' and 'after', was perhaps the Achilles' heel of most presentations. I felt that there was too much of a celebration for what was won after the fall of communism, without any commentary on what was lost, which in fact is something that a large sector of the population in Russia (and even in Albania, the harshest of the communist regimes in Europe) is very much aware of and often reminisces about, with a degree of nostalgia: benefits that they used to have which they now don't, while life has become a struggle for survival of the fittest, in a perspective of capitalist exploitation.

–

You therefore had the feeling from these three days, that there is a need for this kind of criticism by the young generations?

Yes, in general I believe that criticism of our status and a critical mind is always essential if we are to have any hope of improving our lot. This goes back to education. Without being partisan this should encourage a sense of political awareness. And the problem with education, especially secondary education, is that political awareness is treated like a hot potato, in the name of impartiality (and 'fear' of encouraging mutiny). But as a result, students leave secondary school intellectually underprovided, a prey to extraneous trends and without the ability to discern or develop their own value system.

—

So basically we are some kind of 'criticising protagonist' here in Central Europe, but how can we avoid mistakes made before us in welfare countries?

Unfortunately, this is the question of a kind of farsightedness that we are short of: looking beyond our own lifetime and into that of future generations. It is not only a question of simply avoiding or repeating old mistakes, or even making new mistakes. It is another aspect of our negligent human nature. Even though our children are the most precious things we have, we are blind to the kind of future that we are building for them. It is a collective mentality. Think of the scientifically established fact of Global Warming: we cannot avoid a rise of 2 degrees. This means that Europe's Mediterranean will be like Egypt by 2050. We know that a rise of 5 degrees will mean the end of life for us on Earth. But we'll be dead by then: this is the kind of ephemeral thinking of today's politicians, who are totally impervious to what might be when they are already dead.

—

Yes, what happens after elections, today and in four years.

Politics in the real sense of the word is dead and we don't have a political future.

—

Speaking about society and architecture we always have politics as partners so how can we speak about a future in these circumstances? At the same time we have been trained to not forget the client, but thinking of the private client within the perspective of society is a puzzle. So the question is in which format our profession can communicate with the client?

We are facing a kind of schizophrenia about what is architecture. We have been trained to think that architecture has to be built, be 'rational' and comply with clients' requirements. But we are rarely reminded of the importance that unrealised architecture, (judgmentally called "paper architecture") and of the fundamental role it has played in the development of the discipline throughout the history of architecture. We only have to think of Boulée, Le Corbusier or the Russian constructivists among others, whose most important projects have been unrealisable within their social political and economic context: symbolic projects that demonstrated "possible" alternatives. I think that this is an imperative area of investigation. There should be a significant body of this kind of paper architecture being produced, published and being promoted by schools of architecture. It is not enough to train architects so that they know how to build, something that is too abstract in the classroom and that only can be learnt by experience.

**—
So is there some kind of misconception
about what schools should do then?**

I think so; in the main, schools
endeavour to train 'practitioners',
which is by far not a priority, nor
are schools the proper place in which
to learn practice: throughout history
architects learned the practice of
the architecture in the course of
apprenticeship. Schools of architecture
are a modern phenomenon and one would
think that their primary 'raison
d'être' would be theory. But
paradoxically, Schools of Architecture
are primarily empirical. Learning
from History (both architectural and
general) and matters of ideology and
generally principles (or the ability
to formulate theoretical speculations)
are either avoided - I believe for
political reasons - or (such as are
actually taught) are anachronistic and
result in an intellectual illiteracy
that deprives students of the necessary
authority to take a "position" in their
forthcoming career.

**—
Thank you very much**

----

1 National Assembly in Prague designed
by Karel Prager realization: 1966-72

2 Hotel Intercontinental a socialist
realism building constructed in Prague
during the dominance of Stalinist
dictatorship by size incomparably
smaller than the Warsaw Palace of
Culture and in Prague designed by
architect František Jeřábek, 1951-59

INTERVIEW WITH LIEVEN DE CAUTER

by IGOR KOVAČEVIĆ
—

I would like to begin by focusing on your reading of the Central European region. Could you formulate your vision of Central Europe with regard to the western world?

That is very difficult for me, because the idea of Central Europe is strange to me. For me there is only one Europe. When I came to Prague for the first time, what charmed me most about the city was how European it felt. I suddenly discovered one of my capitals! I suddenly discovered I was at home. This idea that somebody from the sea, raised in Flanders, in Belgium, which is some thousand kilometres from here, could immediately feel at home in Prague, was wonderful. I am deeply panEuropean, not so much by ideology, but by sentiment. If somebody would have asked me when I was 13 years old, what are you? I would have responded: a European. And I still believe it in the sense that I am Flemish a Belgian, a Catholic and

an atheist, and I'm many things, but I am first of all European. And of course I can say: I am Greek, because as you could see yesterday, I'm very much inspired by Greeks. And I am also a bit Jewish, because I'm inspired by European Jewish thought. So for me the only identity, which I would go for, is European, for the time being. So you could say it's ignorance, but I would never say I'm a Western European. No. So I never would say Belgium is Western Europe, it's Europe. Maybe I'm completely wrong, but I would say: forget about Eastern Europe, Central Europe, Western Europe. Because if you for instance think of the Palais Stoclet in Brussels built by the Viennese architect Hofmann, and Art Nouveau in general, it was not localized. The same could be said about Baroque. Prague and Brussels are both very Baroque, and are both capitals of Art Nouveau. It was everywhere, I mean it's one movement, isn't it? Maybe that might be just one example. I know, but this complete mixing of influences is what makes Art Nouveau European. Of course, one can say: this is more Austrian Art Nouveau, this is more French, Belgian, Scottish Art Nouveau,

but the most important thing is
the exchange. So for me it's one world,
one Europe.
–

**This experience you're describing
is the very goal of our activities, but
there are national movements, which
have developed very late. You speak
about the XIX century, but basically
the last independent countries have
been realized within neoliberal
society. What is important for
the understanding of a Central European
region, as you pointed out yesterday
in your lecture, is the raw capitalism
which was rampant here for the last
twenty years. The raw capitalism as
the first stage of capitalism, happened
much earlier in the Western world, in
the 19th century. Do you see some kind
of correlation with what happened here
after the fall of communism?**

Well, that's a big question. Let's
start with a short history of
capitalism. You had the industrial
revolution, which gave lot of impulses,
first to England, then to Belgium and
then this industrialization spread
all over Europe. Of course this
industrialization produced lots of
money, but also a lot of misery. To be
more specific let's look at one of
the most important, maybe iconic
industries: the coal mines. Together
with the train, the coal mine was like
the core of steam energy and steam
energy was the core of all
industrialization. It was grim, it was
awful, and it was exploitation. Think
of the scenes of Zola, he described
in his novel "Germinal", as nobody
before him, the horrendous and hellish
circumstances of people working in
the coal mines. Then came, as
described in the novel, a sort of
self-consciousness of the workers. So,
the second phase of this industrial
capitalism was dominated by a gigantic
social battle: the collision between

socialism and raw capitalism. This
collision produced the welfare state as
a sort of synthesis between capitalism
and socialism. The synthesis between
freedom and equality, via the third
term of the French revolution
'brotherhood', what we now call
solidarity.

So, this is a very quick history of
course. We are already in
the postsecond world war period, and
of course there were many battles
etc. Marxism rejected this synthesis,
because, as a good Marxist you can see
that the welfare state is maybe too
good, there will be no revolution once
you have the welfare state. And I think
it's a big mistake of Marxism rejecting
the welfare state. I don't reject it,
because I think it's the best form of
society world history has produced.
I think we beat the Greeks, we beat
the Romans and we beat everybody. If
you look at world history and you ask
yourself: what moment in history was
the best for the population in general,
it is definitely the welfare state.
I think there is no comparison,
the only thing you can say of course
against the welfare state is that we
were still exploiting Congo and we have
to mention it.

Then came Thatcher, Reagan and
the whole wave of neoliberalism, with
globalization in its trail. They said:
this is the moment, we don't like this
redistribution of wealth. The welfare
state is a bad idea, so let's get rid
of it. Thatcher tried to get rid of
it, by breaking the trade unions, by
deregulating and privatizing as much as
possible. She didn't manage completely.
The battle Obama is now facing in
America, is exactly the battle to
rebuild the welfare state. Of course,
his opponents say Obama is a socialist
and they are completely wrong, but in
America the word 'socialism' has evil

connotations, just like communism.
So it is the devil, but in a sense
it's right too, because the welfare
state was and is a synthesis between
socialism and capitalism.

I think my short history of capitalism
has nothing to do with Western Europe,
Eastern Europe, Central Europe; it
has to do with raw capitalism. When
communism fell, everything was kicked
out instead of making the same
synthesis the welfare state had made.
They should have said: we take the best
of communism and keep it within
a democratic, capitalist frame:
health care, social security for the
unemployed free education, free public
transport, free museums, etc., all
the wonderful things of communism. I am
aware that saying this here, in Prague,
that there are wonderful things about
communism, could sound shocking. But,
by making the synthesis between
capitalism and socialism, you get rid
of the whole totalitaian aspect of
communism, you get the heavily
corrected capitalism, which is the
welfare state. That is, in my opinion,
what you should try to do here. It's
a task for the whole of Europe
(Eastern, Central and Western), because
of course we in Belgium have to fight
for the welfare state too, because of
globalization. For instance, think
of the socalled delocalization of
industries: industries say: ok, we have
to keep growing, keep having high
profits, so how can we do that? How
did they do that in the 19th century?
Easy: very low wages, Marx according
to the letter. So they go to the real
proletariat, the sweatshops of
the second and third world. Maybe it is
important to make a point on
the concept of proletariat here. In
the 80s, people said: haha, Marx was
wrong, where is the proletariat? In the
welfare state the proletariat seemed to
have disappea-red, which of course was

the idea itself of the welfare state:
redistribution of wealth. But,
the proletariat has never been as big
as today. The 'reserve army' of
the unemployed, as Marx called it, has
never been bigger. I mean there is
a huge 'reserve army' in Africa, there
is a 'reserve army' in Asia, millions,
they're almost billions of people, that
you can exploit for no wages. Not low
wages, no wages. So that's what they're
doing, that's raw capitalism. Another
form of raw capitalism is Dubai, which
is incredible. I hope Dubai will
collapse; it is collapsing in a sense.
I mean it could be dangerous also; so
much money could be dangerous maybe it
should collapse in a gentle way.

So for me that is very important,
that's important for Central Europe.
Like we were discussing Havel, he
might be pro-American, because
totalitarianism was so awful. I cannot
myself say many good words about
communism, my friends know it, I have
many communist friends and I've said:
people wake up! Bye, bye to
the dictatorship of the proletariat,
no dictatorship, not even of
the proletariat. Totalitarianism is
the most dangerous political form.
But the idea of social redistribution
of wealth, is good, even in the most
strict economic terms. I mean if I'm
employed and I can keep consuming, it's
good for the economy. Because if I'm
unemployed and I'm completely poor, I'm
a danger to the society, I'm a danger
for the economy, I'm wasted. And this
is raw capitalism, you have people who
make money, a lot of money, and you
have people who just fall out of
the boat. And that's dangerous, it's
bad for your economy, it's dangerous
for your social cohesion. This is
something like basic lessons in welfare
statehood, but I think it's crucial.

What happened here after the revolution is that basically the communist elite became the owners, they are in the position of these first capitalists. So they took the same private logic as for public values. I have the feeling that this is happening in a lot of countries, that world politics means just maintaining the money, producing capital, not developing society?

These are difficult questions and they need specific historical answers, no? I think the battle as I see it is also a political one, for instance from an urban, urbanistic point of view. This idea that politics is about preserving the economy and is like the grease that has to oil the privatization of everything, is of course wrong. Think of the example of the pavilion of the EXPO[1] that is now privatized and all the examples you gave in the workshops on Budapest, Ljubljana and elsewhere. This idea that private is better then public is almost theological ideology. Think of the privatization of British rail; it proved disastrous. Why? Because if you say the company doing it has to make money, it doesn't work, you cannot make money with trains to Scotland, you do it as a public service. So the idea of public service, public goods, and public heritage is crucial and neoliberalism in its most raw phase has no eye for this.

–
I think it's important that these topics are not even formulated by architects. I think that is important for the young generation to see and understand things what happened here. It is as if nobody had time in this last twenty years to look back.

Indeed, I think it is very important work, what you do as CCEA: to really look at these capitals of Central Europe and to try to get a process going with architec-tural schools,

but also in the youngsters and in the audience, that, the architecture of the city is in fact a crucial way to defend, and preserve the city, but also as a sort of example of what has gone wrong in the last twenty years. For instance Prague is such a wonderful city, because under communism it was frozen, the building mania of capitalism was not there. So learn and learn quickly, because otherwise things will go wrong. I think that's a very urgent project, a very relevant project, and a very beautiful project. Yes, it needs all the support it can get, in both intellectual and financial ways. Also important is to go to Western Europe and get Western Europe over here, as you do already. A next step is to bring you experience back to Western Europe. Because of course all these capitals are now hot, Prague is hot, Vienna is hot. I mean the youth goes to Central Europe, Eastern Europe. I mean even the real Eastern Europe.

–
Too much congratulations.

My last advice would be to redefine the whole analysis of the publicprivate opposition. You know it's one of my themes: the third sphere. I think it is important to start to think about this third sphere, the heterotopias or the cultural sphere, which is neither political nor economic. I think people need to understand this. The task is to open up this theme and to tell these old Marxists that it's not true that culture comes after eating. It is just as important as food. Culture is not only "superstructure", but it is a crucial, anthropological activity. Whether it is sports, art, religion, philosophy, schooling, it's all one sphere in itself, which should be supported, protected, and defended - critically of course. Museums and universities are not economic enterprises. On the other hand,

we don't have to turn everything into
a museum, which is another risk.
Heterotopias should not eat everything.
What I call the equilibrium of
the three spheres (the economic,
the political and the cultural) is
crucial. And I think this is something
that neither totalitarianism nor
neoliberal capitalism have understood.
In totalitarianism the spheres of
culture and economy are eating away,
absorbed, swallowed by the political
sphere. That is the totalitarian
utopia, which of course is a total
failure, a dystopia. There is no
independent art and there is no real
private sphere, nor a real private
sector. There is only generalized
suspicion and fear. In the neoliberal
utopia economy eats everything, there
is nothing else left beside economics.
People now say to me everything is
economy. I hate it! Not everything is
economy. To make the picture complete,
there is a third utopia. That is when
heterotopia eats everything, which is
the universal theme park on the one
hand and fundamentalism on the other.
Thisutopia is very strong today:
the temple, the mosque, the church
absorbs the whole social life, it eats
everything. So I think these analyses
should be made clear to people and to
architects. There are many architect
students who logically, all of us in
fact, are imbedded by management,
marketing, and capitalism. We breathe
it. We sweat it. All of us more and
more become capitali-sts and capitalist
ideologists without knowing it. Without
being too ideological, this project
could be a sort of seed, an action
seed, spreading critical thoughts.

–
Thank you very much.

----
1 The Expo pavilion of Czechoslovakia
   presented in Brussels in 1958 was moved
   to Prague. After the revolution it was
   privatized as headquarters of a PR
   company

Only such forms of settlements which know contrast, polarity of the public and privacy, and in which this contrast is combined with the appropriate contrasting forms of human behaviour, can be described as urban.

Albrecht Göschel on Berlin

BERLIN

BRATISLAVA

BUDAPEST

029

LJUBLJANA

PRAGUE

VIENNA

WARSAW

At the background of "battle" for territory and lucrative lands, developers are carrying out an intensive construction, exploiting the absence of mandatory territorial documents, dissolving Office of Main Architect and for a long time also the function of Main Architect.

Ľubomír Falťan on Bratislava

BERLIN

BRATISLAVA

BUDAPEST

031

LJUBLJANA

PRAGUE

VIENNA

WARSAW

Budapest is so fragmented competence-wise that an efficient
housing and welfare policy is practically beyond reach.

Janos Ladanyi on Budapest

BERLIN

BRATISLAVA

BUDAPEST

033

LJUBLJANA

PRAGUE

VIENNA

WARSAW

Ljubljana is namely one of the youngest and also the smallest capital cities in Europe, with no historic record of being a capital.

Blaž Križnik and Matjaž Uršič on Ljubljana

BERLIN

BRATISLAVA

BUDAPEST

035

LJUBLJANA

PRAGUE

VIENNA

WARSAW

The Prague's authority lacks comprehensive vision of spatial
development and regulation for particular zones in the city.
The development is strongly dependent on activity of supply
side and the public demand and interests are adjusted to
the needs of developers.

Martin Ouředníček and Jana Temelová on Prague

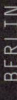

BERLIN

BRATISLAVA

BUDAPEST

037

LJUBLJANA

PRAGUE

VIENNA

WARSAW

The urban development policy in the 80s had been characterised by sustainable quality and circumspection - and it has changed radically into some kind of "urban management" of often isolated projects that mainly achieve private economic and party political interests.

Reinhard Seiss on Vienna

BERLIN

BRATISLAVA

BUDAPEST

039

LJUBLJANA

PRAGUE

VIENNA

WARSAW

Warsaw is first of all a space of symbolic gestures rather than a real city built from flesh and stone.

Krzysztof Nawratek on Warsaw

BERLIN

BRATISLAVA

BUDAPEST

LJUBLJANA

PRAGUE

VIENNA

WARSAW

BERLIN
ACTION SEED

Students: Isabella Dolmanska | Florentine Dreier | Matthias Frimberger
Agnieszka Gaczkowska | Suoyi Ma | Anja Neupert | Ania Pas | Haris Piplas
Moritz Stork | Jyri Tartia | Linda Wortmann

Tutors: Thomas Arnold | Birgit Klauck

BERLIN STUDIO

BIRGIT KLAUCK & THOMAS ARNOLD
–
Since 1989 Berlin has transformed
itself in an unprecedented scale
and speed. Whole city quarters were
rebuild, transportation networks
were redesigned, a lost centre was
reconstructed. Some is still in
the making, like the quarter north
of the new central station, however
the master plan for the entire
Berlin is already drawn.

What remains still open? There are
some prestigious building projects
of high priority, like for example
the reconstruction of the former
palace or the extension of
the federal state library. Also,
the area of the former airport
Tempelhof still waits for
conversion. And for sure Berlin has
some socalled problematic districts,
like North Neukölln, where urgently
action is needed. Despite all that
the future-oriented decisions for
Berlin were made in the late 90s and
today, 21 years after
the reunification, there are no more
visions but facts.

In the past there were different
master plans for Berlin, many were
contradictory. Every plan left some
traces in the city fabric. However
hardly any of the preceding plans
led to such a comprehensive
restructuring of the city, as
the present valid master plan did.
Given this fact plus the emerging
criticism on the current situation,
we asked ourself the question, what
could be an alternative planning
strategy for Berlin's future?

Berlin 1940

Berlin after World War II 1953

Berlin today 2010

BERLIN AS FOUND

–
Before World War II the city
structure was extremely dense as
a result of the rapid developments
in the second half of the 19th
century. Many buildings were
bombed in WW II or got demolished
afterwards and left plenty of voids
which were not filled because
of Berlin's specific situation
– a divided city kept alive
artificially. Hence after 1989
Berlin experienced an unprecedented
push for revitalisation. The main
protagonists Josef Paul Kleihues and
Hans Stimmann, the Senate
building director of the time,
introduced the socalled "critical

reconstruction" which implemented the reconstruction of a 19th century city layout. Both pushed the idea of a "Berlin-Prussian" style which led to a homogenous perimeter block development and to the erasing of unloved buildings. Applied as a universal principle all over Berlin the results are uniform exchangeable buildings with repetitive, mostly meaningless stone facades. These developments were fostered through the restructuring of the real estate market and the emergence of global players who are interested in figures not buildings. Based on the guidelines of the "critical reconstruction" and the aesthetic values of the "Berlin - Prussian" style, right now Berlin is working with an applicable urban model plus territorial master plans for specific sections.

BERLIN

BRATISLAVA

BUDAPEST

047

LJUBLJANA

PRAGUE

VIENNA

WARSAW

hope that by adapting its central position Berlin could become the turntable between East and West but that was not accomplished.

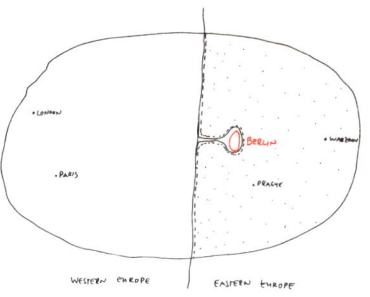

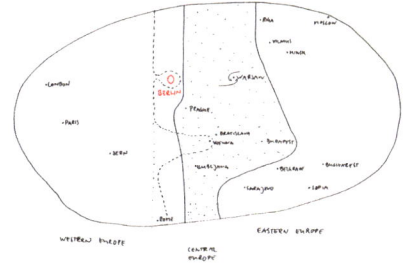

Mental maps showing the relative position of Berlin in the context of Central Europe - before and after unification, Thomas Arnold

Nevertheless Prague, Bratislava, Budapest, Ljubljana and possibly Vienna managed to renew a collective spirit of which Berlin is not part of.

BERLIN IN THE CONTEXT OF CENTRAL EUROPE

IS THERE A CENTRAL EUROPEAN IDENTITY?

—
Caused by its partially interlinked history collective characteristics of Central Europe existed in the past. These were neglected by the socialist republics and disappeared almost entirely. So, too, in Germany the idea of a Central Europe, Mitteleuropa, vanished and Berlin, previously in a central geographical position in Europe, became the "last outpost" of the West. In the euphoria of the unification there was a strong

WHAT MAKES THE IMAGE OF THE CITY?

—
In order to capture the "identity" of our city and to grasp the potentials within the given urban model of Berlin, we started the studio work by looking both

at groundbreaking theoretical and methodical works, surveys and design studies of Berlin. In 1960 Kevin Lynch introduced a vital method for the evaluation of city form. According to his findings city dwellers understand their city creating mental maps. Now Lynch formulated a new criterion - imageability - which was consequently based on certain memorable characteristics and on qualities of distinct neighbourhoods.

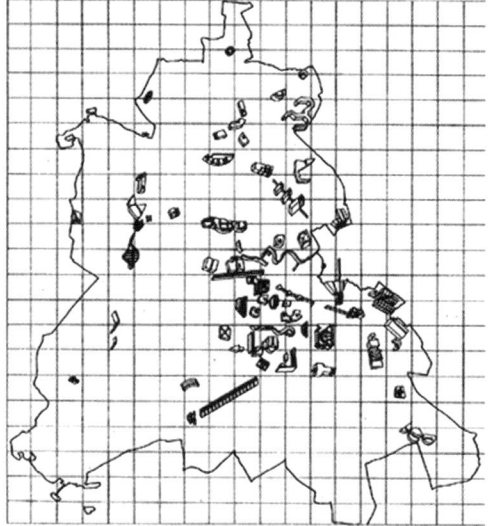

Drawing showing „ The city within the city" - Berlin, 1977 by O.M.Ungers, Rem Koolhaas, Peter Riemann, Hans Kollhoff, Artur Ovaska

Likewise most prominent in the study on Berlin called "city within the city" was the exposure of distinctive elements, here unique architecture. In their view as a collection these architectural elements determine the future development of Berlin.Looking at both studies it became apparent that cities are not conceived as a totality by its dwellers or visitors. People have a selective

view on the city in which distinctive architectural and atmospheric qualities and characteristics play a vital role. Based on the existing map of Paris, Guy Debord drew a psychogeographical map showing nineteen fragments.

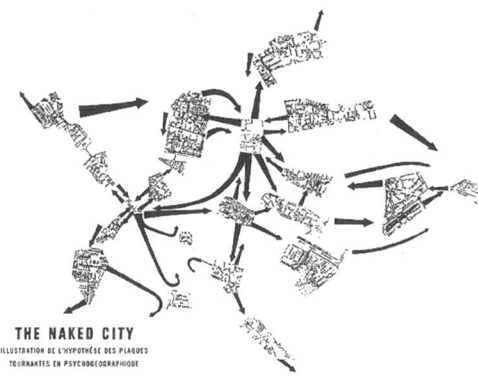

THE NAKED CITY
ILLUSTRATION DE L'HYPOTHÈSE DES PLAQUES TOURNANTES EN PSYCHOGEOGRAPHIQUE

Map of „The Naked City" 1954 by Guy Debord

This map was meant to be a critique on established city representations, offering a different model of Paris relating to actions, the dérives of the situationists. These psychogeographic hubs were based on narratives and thus again had distinct qualities. For our purpose within the studio we decided to adapt a similarly "selective view" on our city and focused in an initial research, which will be described later, on unique qualities - qualities of which we believe that city-dwellers identify themselves with.

Since the current urban model is a purely formal approach which denies the anthropological basis of urban developments, we asked: how do we create a more vivid urban landscape, concentrating on the found uniqueness of certain areas? Berlin established strong aesthetic guidelines, but at

BERLIN

BRATISLAVA

BUDAPEST

049

LJUBLJANA

PRAGUE

VIENNA

WARSAW

the same time a solid tradition of alternative planning strategies developed, various microplanning tactics, bottom up initiatives, such as „Zwischennutzung" or urban pioneers formed the urban landscape in the past 20 years. One of the first and most famous protagonists of this tradition is Hardt-Waltherr Hämer who in 1984 developed 12 principles for how urban renewal should take place. His call for cautiousness became a standard for urban renewal in Berlin and lay the foundation for various user strategies of participative architecture and spatial appropriation as well as community designs. These initiatives vary between more aesthetic interventions of resistance like Köbberlings and Kaltwassers urban actions and other examples of self authorisation where users test the range and success of different spatial appropriations. All of them have in common that they consider personal preferences and dreams of users. At the same time their actions stimulate to imitate and multiply and thus offer answers how to deal with the uncertainty of urban processes. As it turned out in a small scale they are gaining legitimacy. All Berlin studio projects called on this tradition.

Now the Social Media, that what is popularly known as web 2.0,

The problem is that the Bewag (Electricity Company) is not responsible for the electricity.

44%

Film-stills: of Gropiusstadt-Gecekondu, 2004 by Folke Köbberling & Martin Kaltwasser. An improvised structure built overnight and activated communally. This structure was illegaly erected in a field opposite the Gropiusstadt development. It playfully confronted its high-rise neighbours and became an ad-hoc meeting place for area residents.

facilitates city-dwellers to involve themselves far more easily and to become part of what is happening in the neighbourhood. Community designs and participative planning processes benefit by various ways of interactive information sharing and collaboration. Accordingly the students of the Berlin studio tested various interactive applications in addition to the "actions" or interventions which they realised in February 2010.

In the context of the Urbanity Berlin Project the students focused on distinct qualities and characteristics of public spaces. Our first challenge was to detect these qualities and characteristics. And then to find ways to enhance hidden characteristics, to make qualities more visible and memorable...
The studio followed an anthropological approach. The aim was to intensify existing identities, to involve Berliners and to get them to imitate what we

METHODS

–

For the initial research we focused on Berlin's place within Central Europe and used two approaches, the „Dérive" and the idea of the „Action Seed".

As a start we devised the notion „Falling from the sky". What makes the identity of a place if we only have our vision, smell, sound and touch to experience it? By eliminating the sense of history and narrative, we thought preconceptions are minimised and an open mind is assured.

The studio used the overview map of the Berlin Ordnance Survey Map System to choose pages or single 1:5000 maps of Berlin. Everyone had three different maps. The research area was chosen by placing a 2€ coin on the map and circling it. Then everyone went to their chosen location to spend some time to observe and document surfaces. In that way very rapidly a catalogue of the surface types of the different parts of Berlin evolved. The result

was edited and presented in the form of photo panels.

Our approach is a variation of a Dérive (english „drift"), an attempt of an analysis of the totality of everyday life, through the passive movement through space. The french writer and Situationist Guy Debord first theorized this concept. Originally it was the exploration of a built environment without preconceptions, to refuse to limit legitimate discussion to architectural styles or residential percentages, but to discuss the reality of actually inhabiting the environment. But it also draws on the possibilities chance offers in design. Our approach is linked to the work of John Cage, Merce Cunningham, Yves Klein and Robert Rauschenberg, to name a few which used chance deliberately. Following is part of a conversation between Merce Cunningham and Elizabeth Farnsworth to illustrate the point:
Elizabeth Farnsworth
As you well know, there's been lots of writing about the fact that you design a dance sometimes by chance. You've even thrown dice, and depending on the roll of the dice, decided important elements of the dance. Tell us about that and why you do it.

Merce Cunningham
Because on the simplest possible level, it opens up things I wouldn't have thought of. It opens up. And chance does this for anybody. You can toss the coin about something in your daily life. And you do what it says, and you find out something you hadn't thought of before. Well, in the larger sense with this, I have done it in all of the dances, used

it in various ways, all of
the dances since... 20 or more
years, more than that, 30 years
probably… ,because it is such
a large way of working. It can be so
complex that it's almost impossible
to decipher it. What it does do
for me is if something comes up
even that is, you might say it's
physically impossible for humans,
okay. But you look at what it is,
and you see something else that you
can do, which you had not thought of
before.

During the Dérive the students found
themes or topics of interest, which
they followed. The found topics are
ranging from cataloguing traces to
abstracting the colours using
the computer or discovering
the corner pubs of Neukölln.
In order to find out which surfaces
are important for the identity of
Berlin, we conducted a questionnaire
in each area, asking for the place
people would take their visitors to
and places they would not recommend.
This resulted in a map of Berlin,
showing the places people from all
over the city identify with.

To further test our research methods
we went to Warsaw for three days.
Without concern to the culture and
history we undertook walks in five
parts of the city we choose from
the map.

BERLIN

BRATISLAVA

BUDAPEST

051

LJUBLJANA

PRAGUE

VIENNA

WARSAW

Photo panels showing an examples of selected topics
of observation for the initial research by Birgit
Klauck and Jyri Tartia.

Each member of the group had another
topic to observe; facades, windows,
street surface, lamps, baskets,
graffiti, street art and others.
This was pre-agreed and let to
a catalogue of surfaces of Warsaw to
act as a reference to our research
in Berlin. During the walks each of
the group also concentrated on their
themes or topics of interest. That
helped testing the ideas for
possible Action Seeds in Berlin.

theory

a Dérive is an attempt at analysis of the totality of everyday life, through the passive movement through space. It is translated as drift.

French writer and Situationist Guy Debord first theorized this concept[1] in his studies of architecture. The original concept was the exploration of a built environment without preconceptions, to refuse to limit legitimate discussion to architectural styles or residential percentages, but to discuss the reality of actually inhabiting the environment.

dérive Berlin

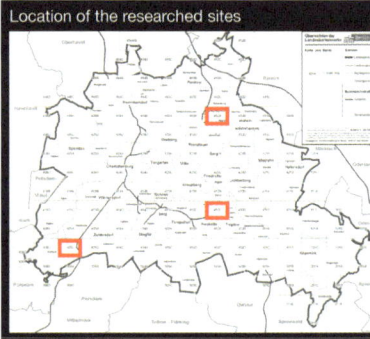

Location of the researched sites

Chance dérive Berlin. *Ordenance Survey Map, overview*. Each student choose three detail maps, one in the center, the edge and in the middle between the two.

use of chance

ELIZABETH FARNSWORTH: As you well know, there's been lots of writing about the fact that you design a dance sometimes by chance. You've even thrown dice, and depending on the roll of the dice, decided important elements of the dance. Tell us about that and why you do it.

MERCE CUNNINGHAM: Because on the simplest possible level, it opens up things I wouldn't have thought of. It opens up. And chance does this for anybody. You can toss the coin about something in your daily life. And you do what it says, and you find out something you hadn't thought of before. Well, in the larger sense with this, I have done it in all of the dances, used it in various ways, all of the dances since... 20 or more years, more than that, 30 years probably ... in various ways, because it is such a large way of working. It can be so complex that it's almost impossible to decipher it. What it does do for me is if something comes up even that is, you might say it's physically impossible for humans, okay. But you look at what it is, and you see something else that you can do, which you had not thought of before.

Still from „Beeing John Malkovitch". The notion *falling out of the sky* minimises pre-conceptions and helps to keep an open mind.

Heinersdorf (432A)_Research Area

Chance dérive Berlin. *Ordenance Survey Map, overview*. Within the detail map, the student choose a point od interest and marked a circle around it using a 2 Euro coin. Thus the survey area was decided.

tool:test

Color Code. To eliminate the figurative elements within the photopanels, all the pixels are sorted by value. Mathematical comparisment is possible.

tool:panel

Photopanel. During the dérive photographs have been taken to document tactle elements of the urban fabric.

tool:m

Mental maps s...
within Europe

action seed: scale 1:1

The authors of the project *Ostverkauf* reflecting about the disappearance of historic city scape. The projection on the facade of *das Haus der Statistik* acts as eye catcher for the web 2.0 blog, to gather peoples voices.

Illustration of methodical approach by Thomas Arnold and Birgit Klauck

BERLIN

BRATISLAVA

BUDAPEST

053

LJUBLJANA

PRAGUE

VIENNA

WARSAW

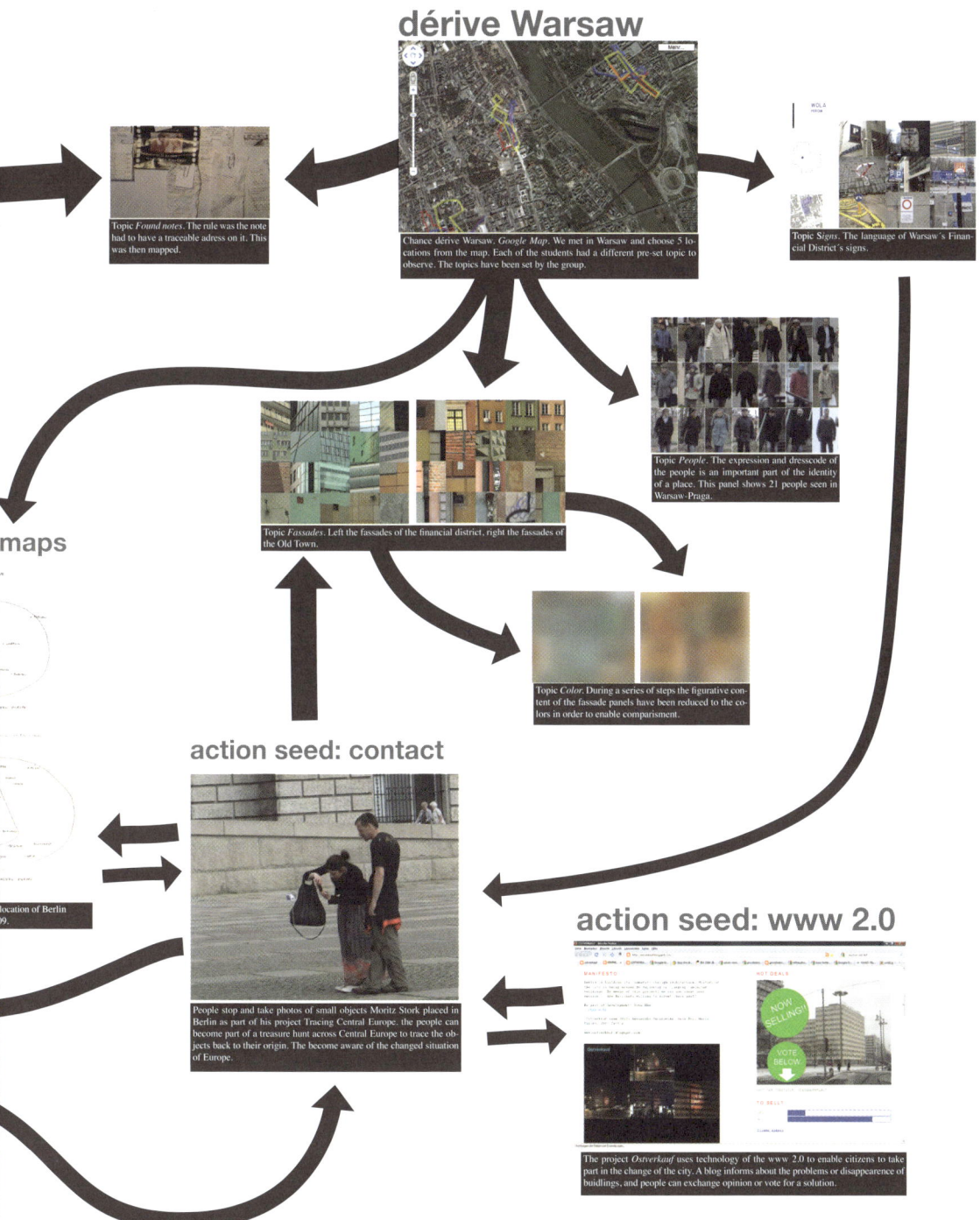

dérive Warsaw

Topic *Found notes*. The rule was the note had to have a traceable adress on it. This was then mapped.

Chance dérive Warsaw. *Google Map*. We met in Warsaw and choose 5 locations from the map. Each of the students had a different pre-set topic to observe. The topics have been set by the group.

Topic *Signs*. The language of Warsaw´s Financial District´s signs.

Topic *People*. The expression and dresscode of the people is an important part of the identity of a place. This panel shows 21 people seen in Warsaw-Praga.

Topic *Fassades*. Left the fassades of the financial district, right the fassades of the Old Town.

Topic *Color*. During a series of steps the figurative content of the fassade panels have been reduced to the colors in order to enable comparisment.

maps

location of Berlin
09.

action seed: contact

People stop and take photos of small objects Moritz Stork placed in Berlin as part of his project Tracing Central Europe. the people can become part of a treasure hunt across Central Europe to trace the objects back to their origin. The become aware of the changed situation of Europe.

action seed: www 2.0

The project *Ostverkauf* uses technology of the www 2.0 to enable citizens to take part in the change of the city. A blog informs about the problems or disappearence of buidlings, and people can exchange opinion or vote for a solution.

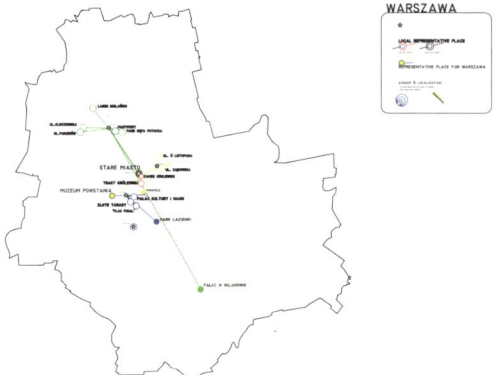

Map illustrating the results of the Warsaw
questionnaire by Mathias Frimberger

ACTION SEED

—

The term „Action Seed" was coined by
Titus Spree, an architect and artist
working in Japan. It describes a way
of changing urban situations by
creating small actions within
the urban fabric to get the citizens
to think about their environment in
a new way. Like planting a seed in
the heads.
Ones people start to see their
environment in a different way or
at least become interested in it,
then they start to act and become
involved with the politics of it.
Thus change in their own interest
can take place.

Action Seeds have to be 1:1 in scale
and can be implemented by
a small group. The students twisted
the meaning of 1:1 scale and used
their generations main means of
communication; the web 2.0. Most of
the action seeds had, apart from
their real world occurrence
an counterpart in the internet.
Using face book, blogs and chat

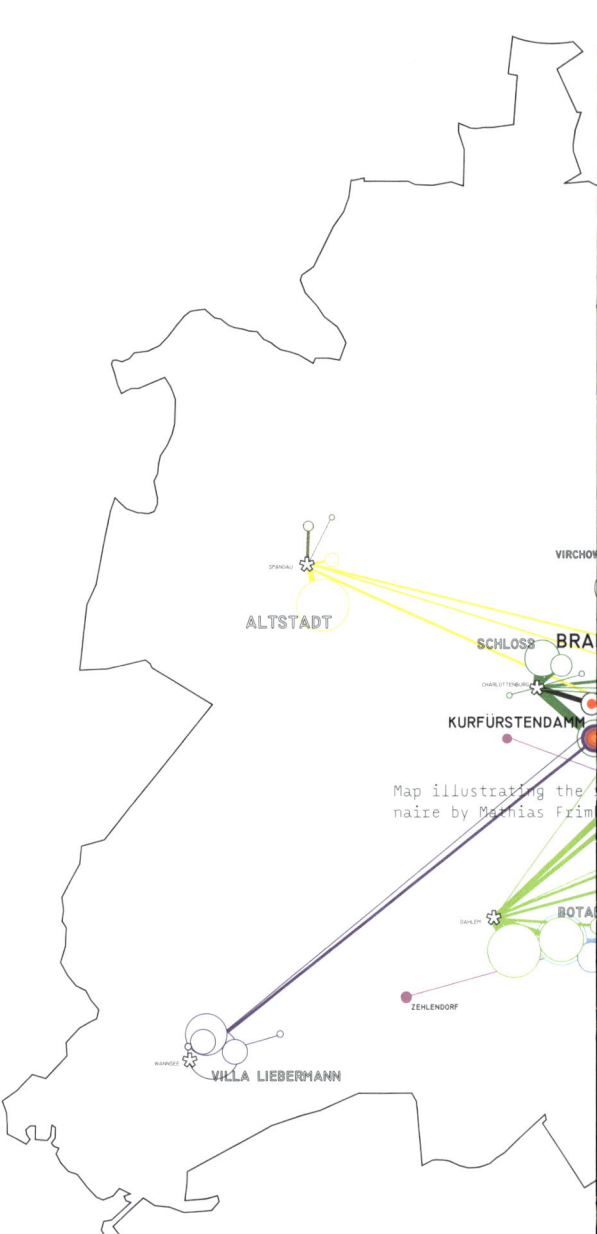

Map illustrating the
naire by Mathias Frim

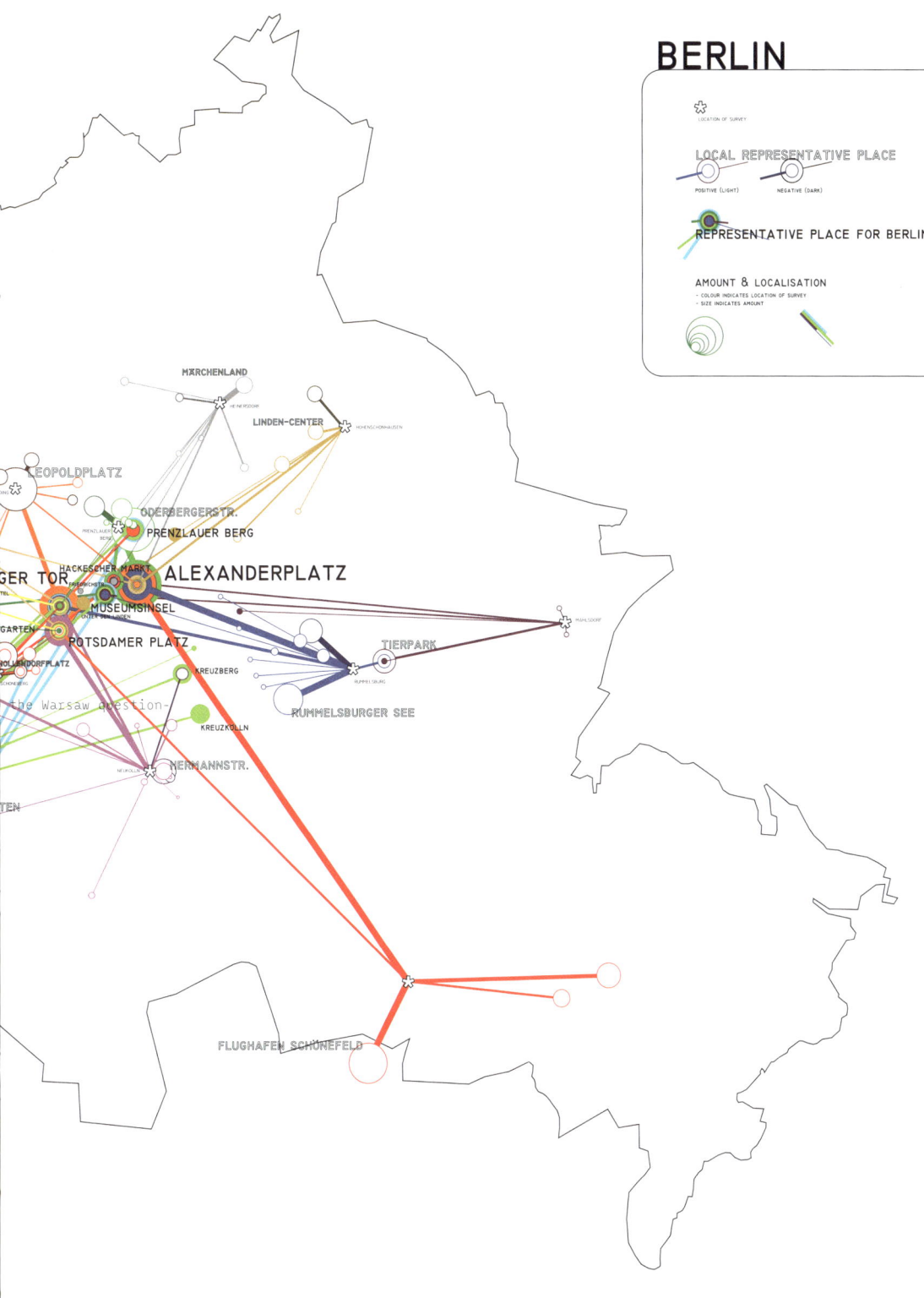

BERLIN

LOCATION OF SURVEY

LOCAL REPRESENTATIVE PLACE

POSITIVE (LIGHT)   NEGATIVE (DARK)

REPRESENTATIVE PLACE FOR BERLIN

AMOUNT & LOCALISATION
· COLOUR INDICATES LOCATION OF SURVEY
· SIZE INDICATES AMOUNT

MÄRCHENLAND

HEINE RODGAP

LINDEN-CENTER

HOHENSCHÖNHAUSEN

LEOPOLDPLATZ

ODERBERGERSTR.

PRENZLAUER BERG

PRENZLAUER BERG

HACKESCHER MARKT

GER TOR   ALEXANDERPLATZ

MUSEUMSINSEL

UNTER DEN LINDEN

GARTEN

POTSDAMER PLATZ

KREUZBERG

MAHLSDORF

TIERPARK

RUMMELSBURG

ROLLENDORFPLATZ

SCHÖNEBERG

the Warsaw question-

KREUZKÖLLN

RUMMELSBURGER SEE

HERMANNSTR.

NEUKÖLLN

TEN

FLUGHAFEN SCHÖNEFELD

BERLIN

BRATISLAVA

BUDAPEST

055

LJUBLJANA

PRAGUE

VIENNA

WARSAW

Map illustrating the results of the Berlin questionnaire by Mathias Frimberger

rooms to promote the actions and to get people to interact was essential for them. Location based services and existing specialised user groups like treasure hunt groups were employed to develop the action seed. The research group was directed in an non-ideologic way, trying to enhance the particular interests of the students. This resulted in very different projects.

THE GREAT NEUKÖLLN KNEIPENTOUR

-

This project draws on the German culture of the „Eckkneipe", the pub on the corner. The „Eckkneipe" is an extended living room of the working class and can be found in every German city. Most have a small main room for drinking and snacks and a back room for card games, fan clubs and other group activities. Each pub is very individual and the owner client relationship is very strong, since the clients come everyday for drinking and socialising.

The project focused on North Neukölln a traditional working class area with a large immigrant population. The area around Donaustrasse is close to Kreuzberg and the process of gentrification is already visible. The corner pubs and their clientele are about to disappear from the area.
Since Berlin became a major tourist hot spot more and more tourist come frequently. Especially these frequent tourists try to experience the true local Berlin and because of that the students saw a chance to

protect a significant tradition. The authors of the project selected eight pubs along Donaustrasse which they proposed to be part of the Great Neukölln Kneipentour, a scenic theme route. They approached the owners of the pubs and got them to participate in the route. Eight pubs have been drawn in isometric line drawing and photographed. The route was marketed by a flyer with two special made beer felts as cover, the same beer felts that have been used in the participating pubs. These flyers could be stamped to get one free beer for each four consumed. The route was also marked in the street using a similar sign system as bicycle routes. The idea to make this everyday culture of Berlin visible to tourists and to help the pub owners to survive the gentrification of the area found a wide interest and is awaiting further development.

OSTVERKAUF

-

Thinking about the identity of Berlin represented in architecture, the group realise, Berlin's identity is changing very fast. What once was a specific Berlin architectural mix, turns into the always identical blend modernism and globalisation provides us with. The group focused on Alexanderplatz, which was the showcase of East Berlin and, as we found out during the research, became one of the most important places city dwellers identify with. Next to Alexanderplatz right now one of the East German office complexes, the „Haus der Statistik" is about to be demolished and replaced by a faceless commercial development of a local architectural practice. The „Haus der Statistik" was part of the idea to represent the important parts of the socialist society in architecture. Originally there have been „Haus der Ministerien", „Haus der Presse", „Haus des Lehrers", „Haus der Gesundheit" and „Haus des Reisens". These buildings are still important in the consciousness of the city" and their demolition is widely unknown even though every master plan is available on the Berlin Senats website. The group decided to make this process visible and invented the notion of „Sold"- the selling out of the identity of Berlin to who ever bids more. Using the „Haus der Statistik" as example, the group started a blog http://ostverkauf.blogspot.com/ explaining the idea and asking people to vote about the demolition. Signposts on Alexanderplatz pointed to the building and named the blog and a huge red dot with the word „sold" was projected on to the building.

TRACING CENTRAL EUROPE

—

The project was clearly developed following a very specific inter-est from the start of our research. The author is concerned with trac-es which are connecting different places of Central Europe, especially paper slips with data on them, like receipts, bills, tickets or sale slips. By making the place of origin visible and highlighting the found objects in situ he hopes to make people aware of the place of Berlin in Central Europe.

The action seed has two parts. One is the replacement of the found object on site, so people are aware of it and get pointed to the online platform www.tracingcentraleurope.org where the traces are documented. The interest is gradually extended by integrating the idea into an existing network the online community of geo caching www.geocaching.com. This is a modern form of treaure hunt using GPS and other geo loction services. By tagging a facsimile of the found object and hiding it in a geo cache it can travel back to its origin. While doing so people paticipate in the process of tracing and discovery and become playfully aware of the re-established close links of Berlin with the other capitals of Central Europe.

BERLIN

BRATISLAVA

BUDAPEST

057

LJUBLJANA

PRAGUE

VIENNA

WARSAW

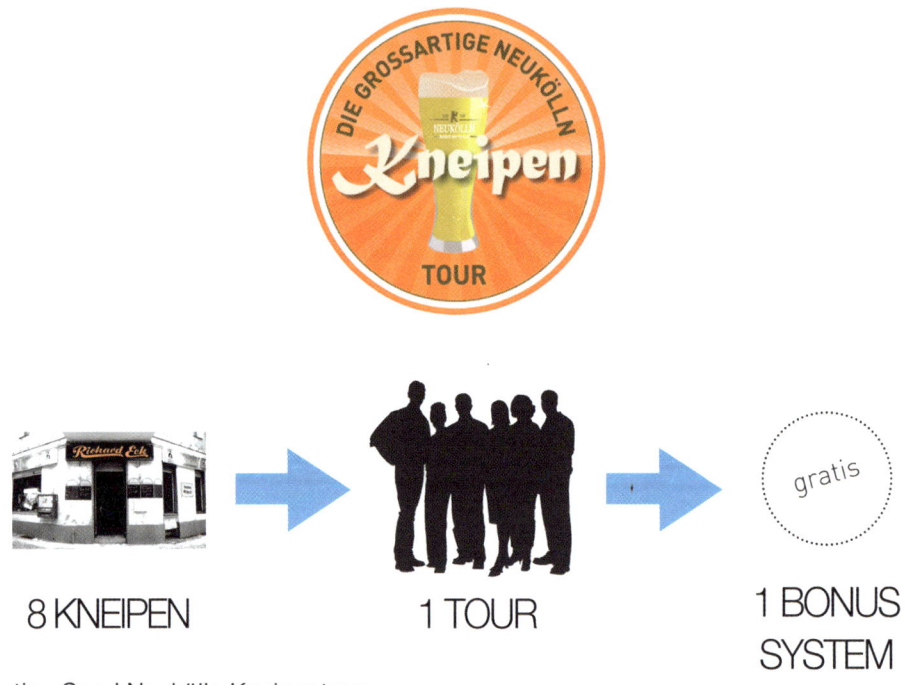

8 KNEIPEN   **1 TOUR**   **1 BONUS SYSTEM**

Action Seed Neukölln Kneipentour

In order to introduce one characteristic of Neukölln, the Eckkneipe, to the tourists and the new Berliners, we organized the Great Neukölln Kneipentour. The Kneipentour works in a simple way: In every attended pub, where you drink a certain amount, you receive a unified bonus-stamp in the Kneipen-Pass during the tour. If you drink more than three beers, you get another for free.

The guide for your tour is a Kneipen-flyer. It contains the introduction of eight Kneipen in Neukölln, some basic knowledge of Kneipen in Berlin and the rules of etiquette. The flyer is available in the above mentioned eight Kneipen, in tourist information centers and in souvenir shops. The flyer also works as a Kneipen-Pass in which one collects stamps. The beer cap, Bierdeckel, that we designed serves as collection item, advertisement and giveaway.

BERLIN

BRATISLAVA

BUDAPEST

059

LJUBLJANA

PRAGUE

VIENNA

WARSAW

Kneipen in Neukölln

The district Berlin-Neukölln is more than a problem borough – Neukölln is the real, the traditional working class Berlin, a borough that is charming especially with all its long-established pubs, the Eckkneipe. These originated in the second half of the 19th century. The population increased rapidly, therefore living space became rare. For many people the corner pubs became a compensation for the missing living-room.

ALTE RATSKLAUSE

1 column

2 bar counter

3 beer cap

4 cupboard

5 window ledge

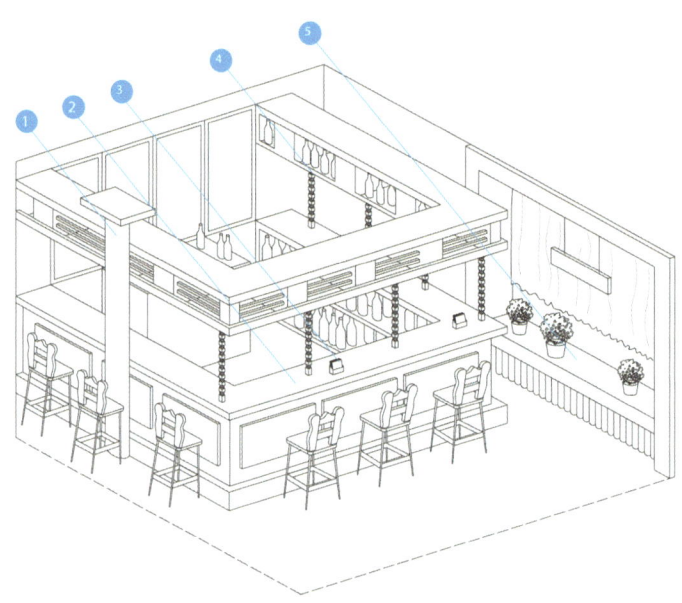

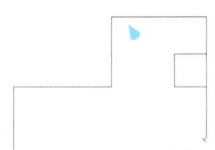

Students: Isabella Dolmanska | Suoyi Ma | Linda Wortmann

KINDL KLAUSE

1 decorating disk

2 dart

3 game facility

4 awarding cup

5 painting

6 window ledge

7 window

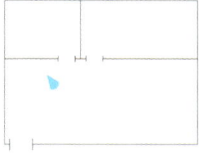

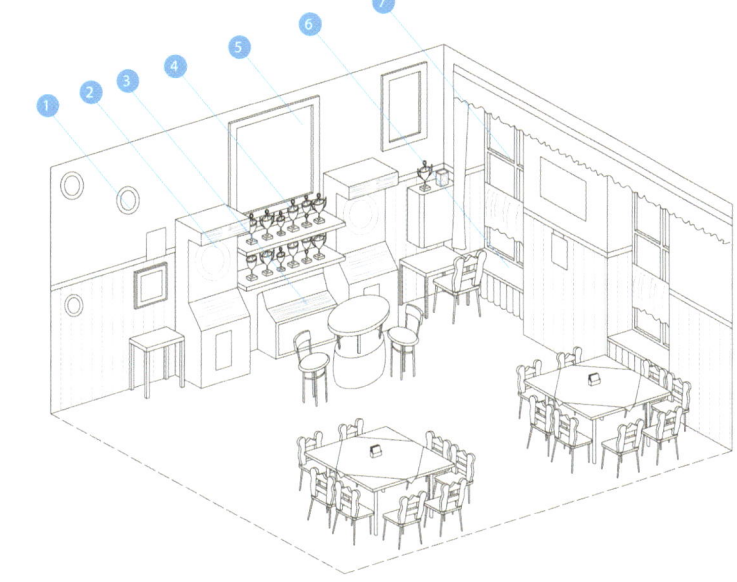

THE SALE PROJECT OF THE BERLIN URBANITY GROUP

The image of Berlin is reflected in the design of its urban space and the city builds up its identity through architecture. The cityscape definitely changed in the last 20 years. Many urban modifications were made with the aim to delete East-Berlin's socialist history. On the example of "Alexanderplatz" we point out a one-way development of urban space, meaning that nowadays a "sale out" of urban identity is taking place. Our red-dot marks what has already been or is close to be "sold" and shows where those changes in the city-image are happening.

Photo by Silke Sohler, Germany

Photo by Stelb, Germany

Example: the facade of Berlin's department store "Galeria Kaufhof, a formerly modernist building was completely modified and lost its architectural identity.

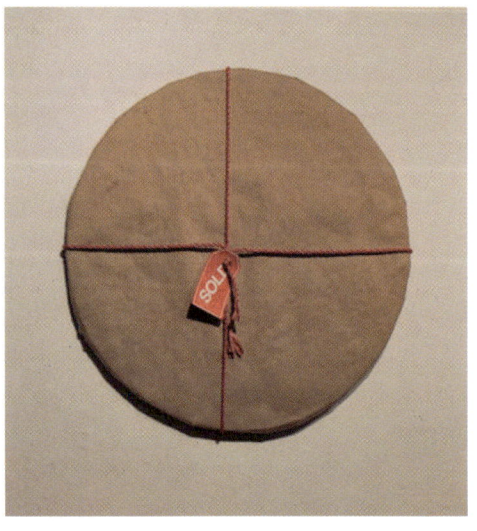

Symbolism for Action Seed - the red dot symbolized sold items and in this case the "sold" urban identity of post-socialist East-Berlin.

The "Haus der Statistik" is a recent example of the erasure of Berlin's urban symbols. The building will be demolished in 2011 making place for a mixed-use complex. Not valuing the architectural or urban quality of the new development, we focused on the fact that many popular buildings, especially in East Berlin, are being destroyed or completely modified in order to erase the socialist and modernist history.

Left: "Haus der Statistik" - already abandoned.

BERLIN

BRATISLAVA

BUDAPEST

063

LJUBLJANA

PRAGUE

VIENNA

WARSAW

Left: Fan products of the "Haus der Statistik" with the specific detail of the facade which is beloved by the Berliners.
Right: the proposed future development of the "Haus der Statistik", a mixed-use neighbourhood.

Alexanderplatz's historical development - "Haus der Statistik" marked with a red dot.

the
proposal

LICHTINSTALATION

CAD tests and visualisations of different proposals for the intervention on the building - including light, poster installations on the building and the surrounding fence.

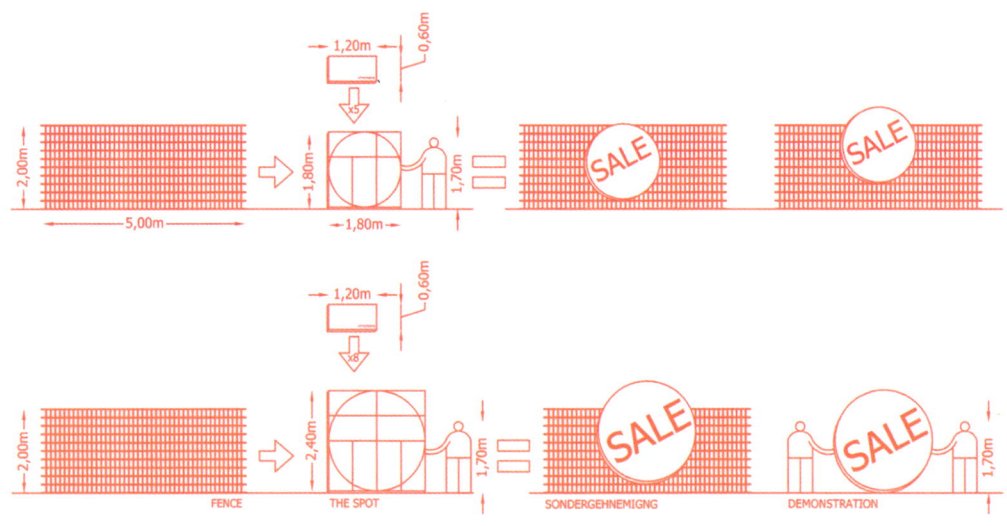

Students: Agnieszka Gaczkowska | Ania Pas | Haris Piplas | Jyri Tartia

BERLIN

BRATISLAVA

BUDAPEST

065

LJUBLJANA

PRAGUE

VIENNA

WARSAW

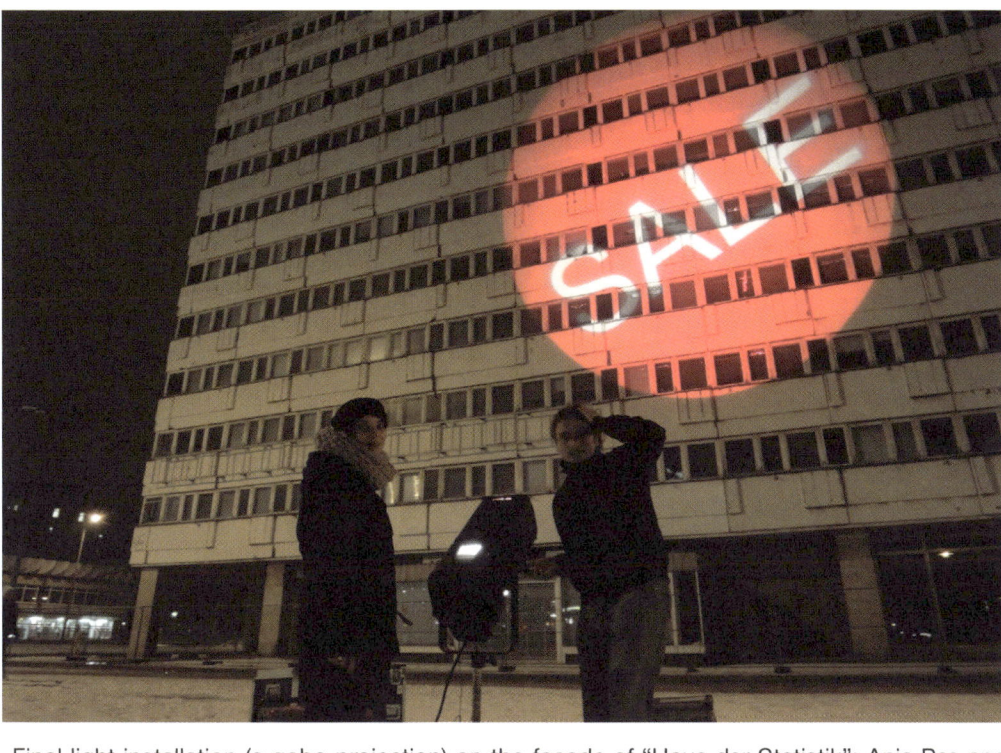

Final light installation (a gobo projection) on the facade of "Haus der Statistik": Ania Pas and Haris Piplas making the projection, Jyri Tartia and Aga Gaczowska were filming the action.

Arrows on the wider Alexanderplatz were pointing on the "Haus der Statistik" and promoting the blog. The blog ostverkauf. blogspot.com was an important communication tool to get in touch with Berliners. We were asking them to participate in a voting if "Berlin´s identity should be sold piece by piece".

Screenshot of the blog http://ostverkauf. blogspot.com including the movie "Ostverkauf" of the projection and a voting.

"Tracing Central Europe" is designed to make traces visible, which connect the various places in Central Europe. By exposing found traces (e.g. bills, tickets, receipts from any Central European country) to the public, documenting those within an online platform (tracingcentraleurope.org) and extending the audience gradually beyond passers-by and tourists by integrating an existing network and its community (geocaching.com), this project is creating a network between countries, cities and people. Through the playful approach of "caching", a modern, GPS-based treasure hunt, people are encouraged to take part in the process, discover, document and experience the connections and take a replica of the trace back to its origin. Meanwhile the task of the director, who planted the action seeds, merely is to take care of the online platform and install new showcases for traces added by the community.

RESEARCH

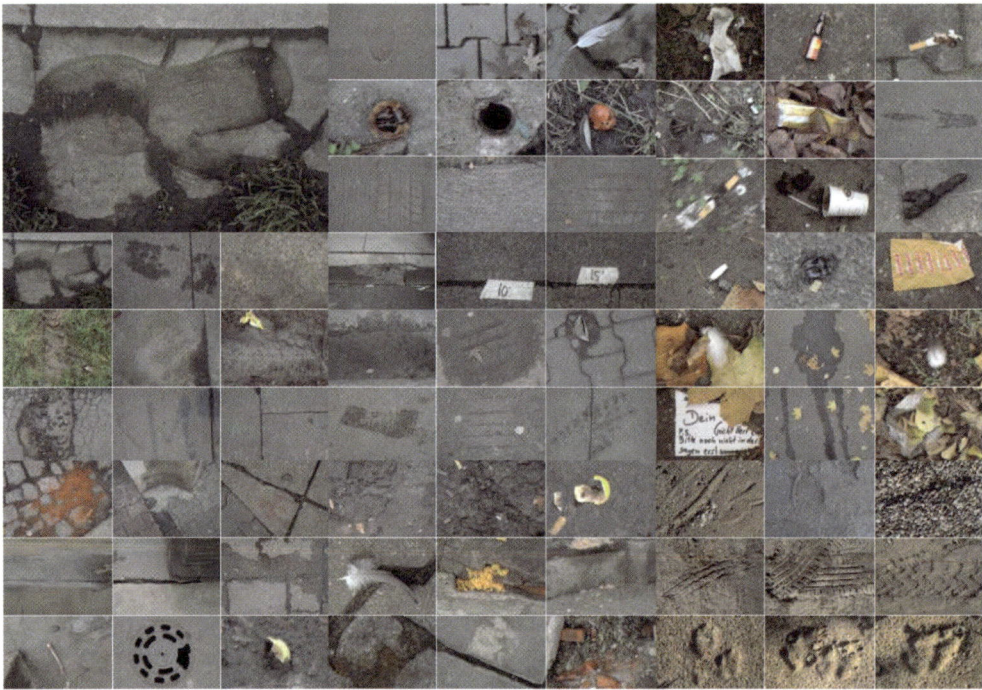

catalogue of traces (warsaw/berlin)

first storytelling-traces, mapping of find place and trace origin (warsaw)

Student: Moritz Stork

INTERVENTION

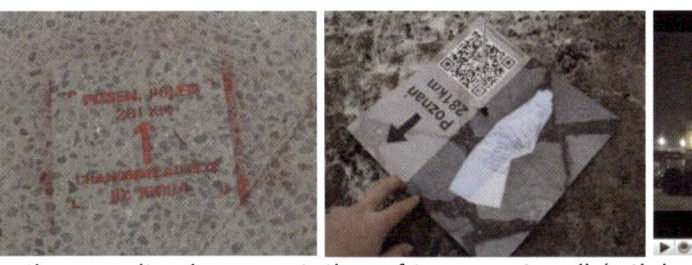

testing on-site-documentation of traces, stencil / sticker / projection

showcase installed at "Reichstag" where trace (train ticket from praha hl.n.)
was found, displays trace, short project info, link to tracingcentraleurope.org

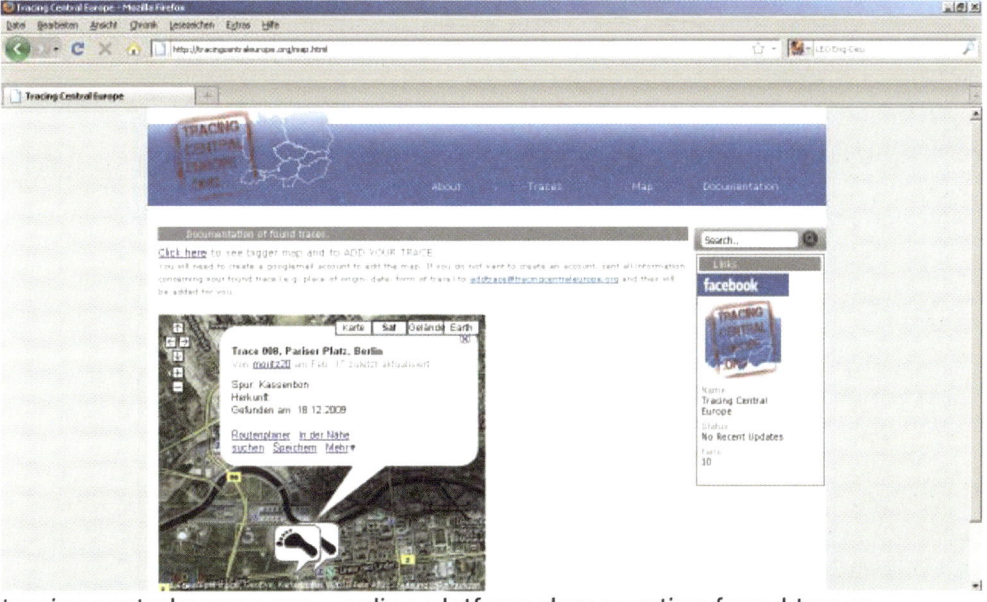

tracingcentraleurope.org - online platform documenting found traces

PROJECT

action plan

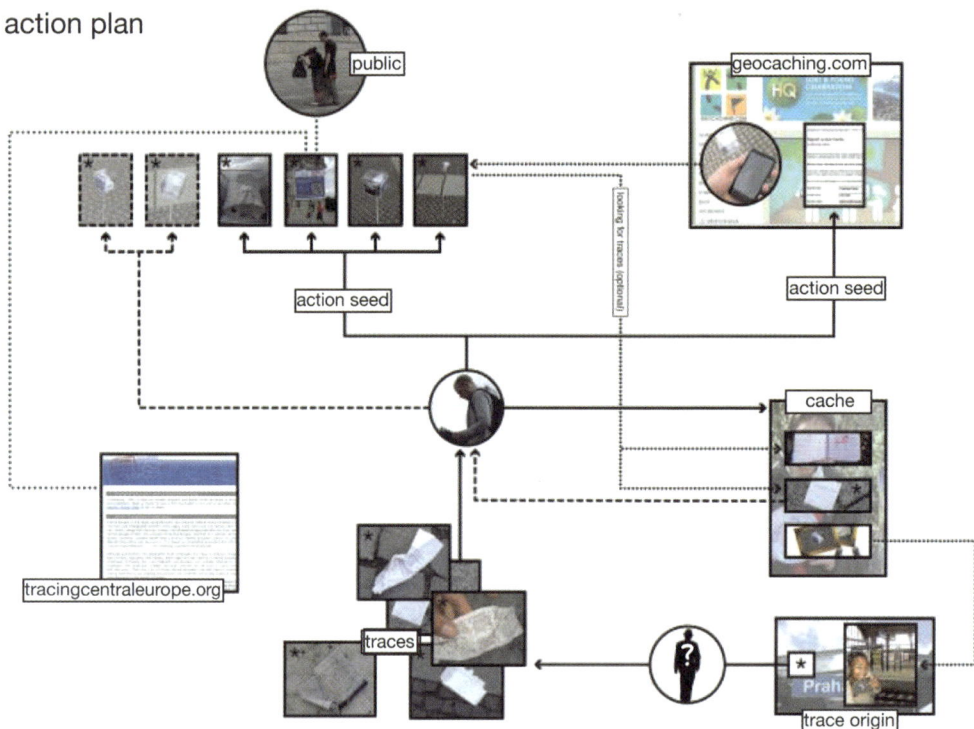

actors

DIRECTOR - collects initial >>traces, builds and installs >>showcases, (adds showcases for traces collected by cachers)

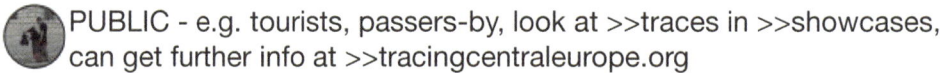
PUBLIC - e.g. tourists, passers-by, look at >>traces in >>showcases, can get further info at >>tracingcentraleurope.org

CACHER - user of >>geocaching.org, reads task planted by director, finds certain >>showcase and >>cache, (adds traces)

websites

TRACINGCENTRALEUROPE.ORG - online platform, documenting found traces and >>showcases, project info, run by director

GEOCACHING.COM - network for geocaching (GPS-based treasure hunt), currently caches in 100 countries, community with over 1.100.000 active cachers, action seed: report new >>cache including >>travelbug

items

BERLIN

BRATISLAVA

BUDAPEST

069

LJUBLJANA

PRAGUE

VIENNA

WARSAW

TRACE - e.g. train ticket/bill/receipt from central european country, found by >>director or >>cacher, displayed in >>showcase,

SHOWCASE - displays >>trace at find place, shows internet adress for further info, leads >>cachers to cache

CACHE - hidden treasure, contains logbook to document finds, >>travelbug, (traces can be added to the cycle by cacher here)

TRAVELBUG - replica of trace, gets picked up at cache and gets dropped of at different cache (closer to destination), each item has its own webspace, where cachers log the path, current status and place, goal: replica gets taken back to origin of trace

BRATISLAVA
CITY OF TESTS

BERLIN

BRATISLAVA

BUDAPEST

071

LJUBLJANA

PRAGUE

VIENNA

WARSAW

Students: Peter Buday | Anna Cséfalvay | Adriana Debnárová
Eliška Gálová | Valéria Gašparová | Terézia Grešková | Filip Hodulík
Richard Kilo | Júlia Kolláthová | Kristína Králová | Tomáš Kučera
Tomáš Letenay | Marek Lüley | Katarína Mačková | Daniela Majzlanová
Katarína Martonová | Peter Mihaľák | Veronika Partelová | Daniel Silva
Adrián Švec | Veronika Trnovská | Martin Václavík | Martin Varga
Martin Zaiček | Janka Zatlukajová

Tutors: Imro Vaško | Martin Gsandtner

BRATISLAVA CITY OF TESTS

IMRO VAŠKO
-

The author thesis of tutors of academic-architectural research at the Laboratory of Architecture of the Academy of Fine Arts and Design (VŠVU) BRATISLAVA CITY OF TESTS is a conviction about the phenomenon of the city of Bratislava which, in historical or typological terms, is not a prototype of any typical Central European city. Bratislava is not part of the history of the emergence of big cities, industrial or capital cities in the late 19th and early 20th century. Bratislava may have been an important coronation city of the Austria-Hungarian rulers however without further political attributes. Its identity was equally divided among Hungary (Poszonyi), Germany (Pressburg) and Czechoslovakia. Apart from the trilingual Hungarian-German -Slovak population, Bratislava (especially in the first half of the 20th century) also consisted of Jews, Bulgarians, Croats and other nationalities which to this day provide the characteristics not only of the past, but also of the present of Bratislava as a mixed city without a clear determining identity. So by this nationally unclear identification of the relatively short history of modern Bratislava, a precondition is created for perceiving this city as territory interesting for the study of processes which emerged by a random and spontaneous mixture of cultures. So the geographic and topographic quality of the city on the dividing line between the Alpine-Carpathian Massif, in the bend of the large river Danube, on the edge of the Carpathian basin and Czech-Moravian Highlands, and on the boundary of the Mediterranean climate provides Bratislava with foundations for a complex reference study. Just as the indistinct influences and multisource generation of the image of the city at the turn of the 20th century, is complicating our direct identification of the city, so the architectural and building impulses during the entire 20th century confirm the difficult to identify gene code of the city. Hence, the hypothesis of the research of the Laboratory of Architecture at the VŠVU is that the gene code of Bratislava is tests. The mega structure of the city arises from its own "Bratislava" subsystems which cover the universe of uncontrolled cohesion. An ideal example of the visualisation theory of Rem Koolhas is "junk space". "Junk city", "cheap city", "large village" may by terms characterising the systems of "a spoiled city" where it is possible to test – study the amount of acupuncture points existing – emerging from a complicated amount of connections and networks of identified particles. By confirming this thesis – the city of tests is a heterogeneous building image of a city. The non-contextual leftwing ideals of Modernism were of fundamental importance for Bratislava in the last century. From the functionalist interwar interventions in the city's historical nuclei, the radical concepts of a university and governing city in the 1940s to the magnificent and monumental architectural intervention of the new authentic generation of Slovak architecture after the Second World War during the communist era of Czechoslovakia – Slovakia. Lastly, the final and current twenty-year history of Bratislava after 1989 confirms the development of the city by a system of "tests" – uncoordinated acupuncture points of radical and extreme speculative plans. The resulting hypothesis authorised the Laboratory of Architecture to the method of testing the urban scale of Bratislava from the position of the "spontaneously" resolved projects. The Laboratory of Architecture was engaged in the problems of the "urbanity" of Bratislava during two academic terms of 2009.

At the incentive of the international project of the Centre for Central European Architecture in Prague (CCEA) whose ambitious goal was to map out the capital cities of the Central European region by academic teams from these cities, the Laboratory of Architecture was engaged in work on Bratislava in two phases. In the first – analytical part of the programme of research students drew up diagrams of Bratislava on its topography, boundaries, history, transport, shopping, confessions, vegetation, settlements, migrations, monuments and visionary architectural projects. In view of the late industrialisation and identification of Bratislava in comparison with the neighbouring cities, the thesis of the tutors of the project for Bratislava was an attempt at an analysis of the historical-political structure of Bratislava divided into four periods marked as years 1918

(self-identification of Slavonic Bratislava after the break-up of Austria-Hungary), 1948/49 (workers' city / proletarian Bratislava) 1968/69 (communism / normalisation / parallel Modernism), 1988/89 (fall of the iron curtain, fall of communism and entire social collapse) up to 2008/09 (global economic and financial crisis / recession). This initiatory system of a testing attempt at formulating the time axis of the development of Bratislava in the last ninety years aimed to create an animated picture of the short and turbulent history "of the century of the late birth of a metropolitan city".

The architectural planning process continued from this analytical phase which generated academic projects directed at the "speculative tests of Bratislava's urban environment". The political thematisation of the last one hundred years of Bratislava and its diagramming has created a precondition for the independent and experimental objectivisation of the city. It has given rise to a series of independent testing strategies reacting to various, often contrasting theses and starting-points. The aim of these "Bratislava tests" was not only to create perspective proposals for the city of Bratislava, or propose general valid schemes for architectural-urban environments also generally applicable for another contemporary Central European or global urbanity, but mainly find the specific acupuncture points of the city of Bratislava which, by its uniqueness, controversy or exceptionality could be the initiators of new specific as well as general solutions or procedures. Besides generally known and frequent architectural urban

BERLIN

BRATISLAVA

BUDAPEST

073

LJUBLJANA

PRAGUE

VIENNA

WARSAW

departing points such as "infrastructure", density", "chaos", "alternative culture" or "apocalyptic vision", the Laboratory of Architecture's attention was also drawn to the non-architectural thesis of "climbing", "aura", "sin" or "Avatar", speculation directly tied to the specific Bratislava situation, stories, events or scandals. The most controversial example of the "test of the laboratory of architecture" is the combination of "gambling or sin" and the architecture of the "department" in the SIN CITY - CASINO CITY Project (Katarína Mačková, Adriana Debnárová and Veronika Partelová). The mapping of the problematical theme of the sins of the city and study of the "seven sins" in the urbanity of Bratislava, for example, helped to react to the current Bratislava developer project of a suburban casino, populist one-sidedly rejected by Christian politicians and a manipulated public. This project, despite the generally rejected attitude to "the dirty layers of the city", attempts to return to architecture unpleasant themes known from the past such as "industrialisation", sociology", "function" or Venturi's "strip". Martin Václavík's project, which generated the theory of building up the density of "sparse" Bratislava by new urban block structures based on computerised voronoi geometry from analysis of the transformation of suburban Bratislava to a city of Shopping Centres and increasing dense car traffic. The Laboratory's other tests were the team projects "Chaos" (Eliška Gálová and Danka Majzlanová) or "Avatar" (Marek Lüley and Martin Zaiček) presented in more detail in this book, as well as inspiring and amusing attempts at thinking about disaster scenarios of the city "Apocalypse" (Kristína

Králová and Martin Varga) or the implication of sport and "climbing" to a generative urbanism of the "Climbing City" (Adrián Švec and Janka Zatlukajová).

"BUTTERFLY EFFECT" IN THE CITY

balance 1:1 in city entropy system consists of six strategies
in every urban structure are the strategies the same
system of fuelling and exhausting energy

mapping places in Bratislava-
acupuncture points for each rationalisation strategy

TYPE:

ABANDON
KEEP
RUIN
RECONSTRUCT
FOUND
SUPERSTRUCTURE

ENTROPY DIRECTION:

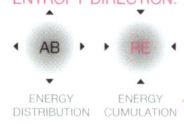

ENERGY   ENERGY
DISTRIBUTION   CUMULATION

ENERGY OF BRATISLAVA

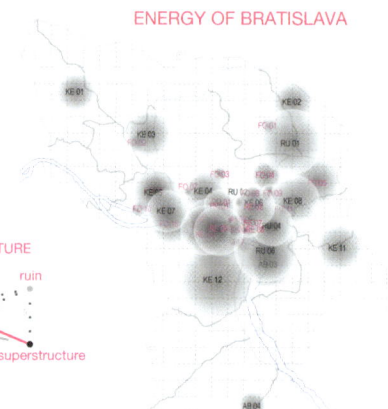

EXTEND SIZE:

0,25 km 0,5 km 1 km   2 km   3 km   > 3 km radius
   1   2   3   4   5   6

SOCIALISM WITHOUT SUPERSTRUCTURE

abandon   keep   ruin

reconstruct   found   superstructure

Local entropy diagram-Karlova Ves

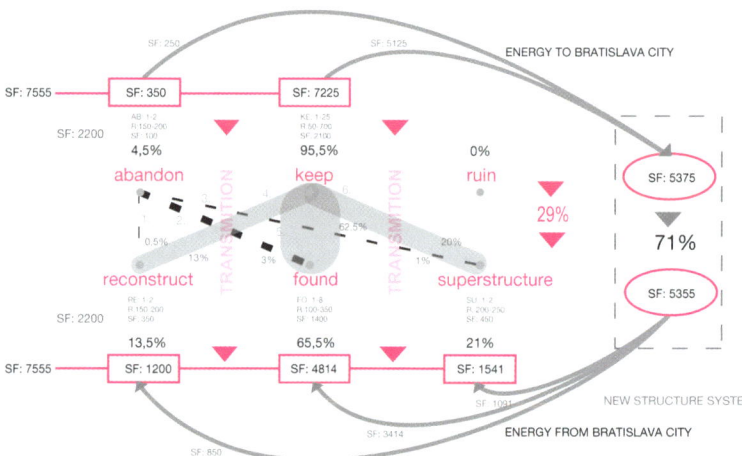

ENERGY TO BRATISLAVA CITY

Every special ratio characterise
special city occasion

PHENOMENON

1. Centralization
2. Flow
3. Change to Posh
4. Political Interest
5. Shopping
6. Socialism without Superstructure
8. Unappropriate finantial redistribution
8. Generation gap
9. Inappropriate cultural redistribution

NEW STRUCTURE SYSTEM

ENERGY FROM BRATISLAVA CITY

Bratislava>Karlova Ves_system zoom in

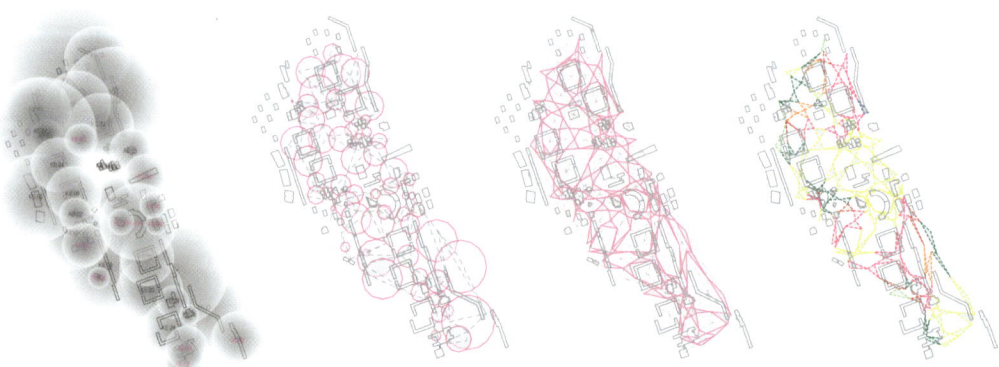

Radiuses from Karlova Ves | Centers of Border spaces A are centers for B radiuses - 70% from BA | Grid B forms Border spaces B | Border spaces B divided in 7 groups

Students: Eliška Gálová | Daniela Majzlanová

Bratislava>Karlova Ves_system zoom in

BERLIN

BRATISLAVA

BUDAPEST

077

LJUBLJANA

PRAGUE

VIENNA

WARSAW

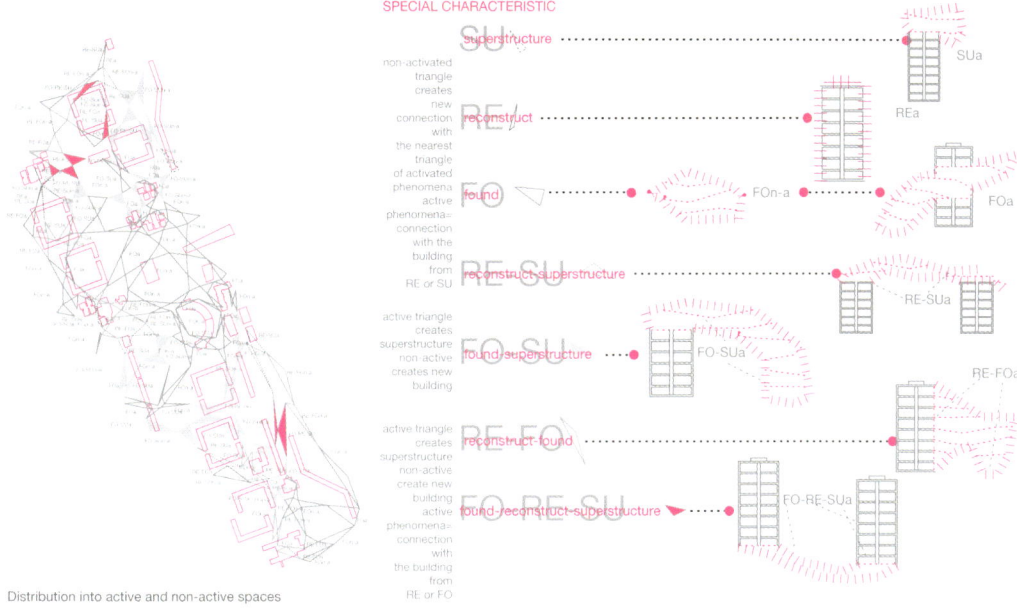

SPECIAL CHARACTERISTIC

SU — superstructure .... SUa

non-activated triangle creates new connection with the nearest triangle of activated phenomena

RE — reconstruct .... REa

active phenomena= connection with the building from RE or SU

FO — found .... FOn-a .... FOa

RE-SU — reconstruct-superstructure .... RE-SUa

active triangle creates superstructure non-active creates new building

FO-SU — found-superstructure .... FO-SUa

active triangle creates superstructure non-active create new building active phenomena= connection with the building from RE or FO

RE-FO — reconstruct-found .... RE-FOa

FO-RE-SU — found-reconstruct-superstructure .... FO-RE-SUa

Distribution into active and non-active spaces

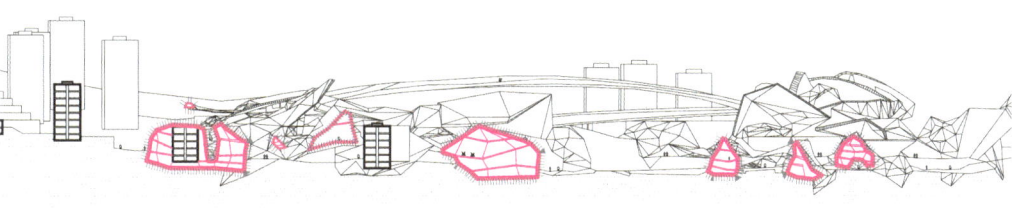

APOCALYPSE

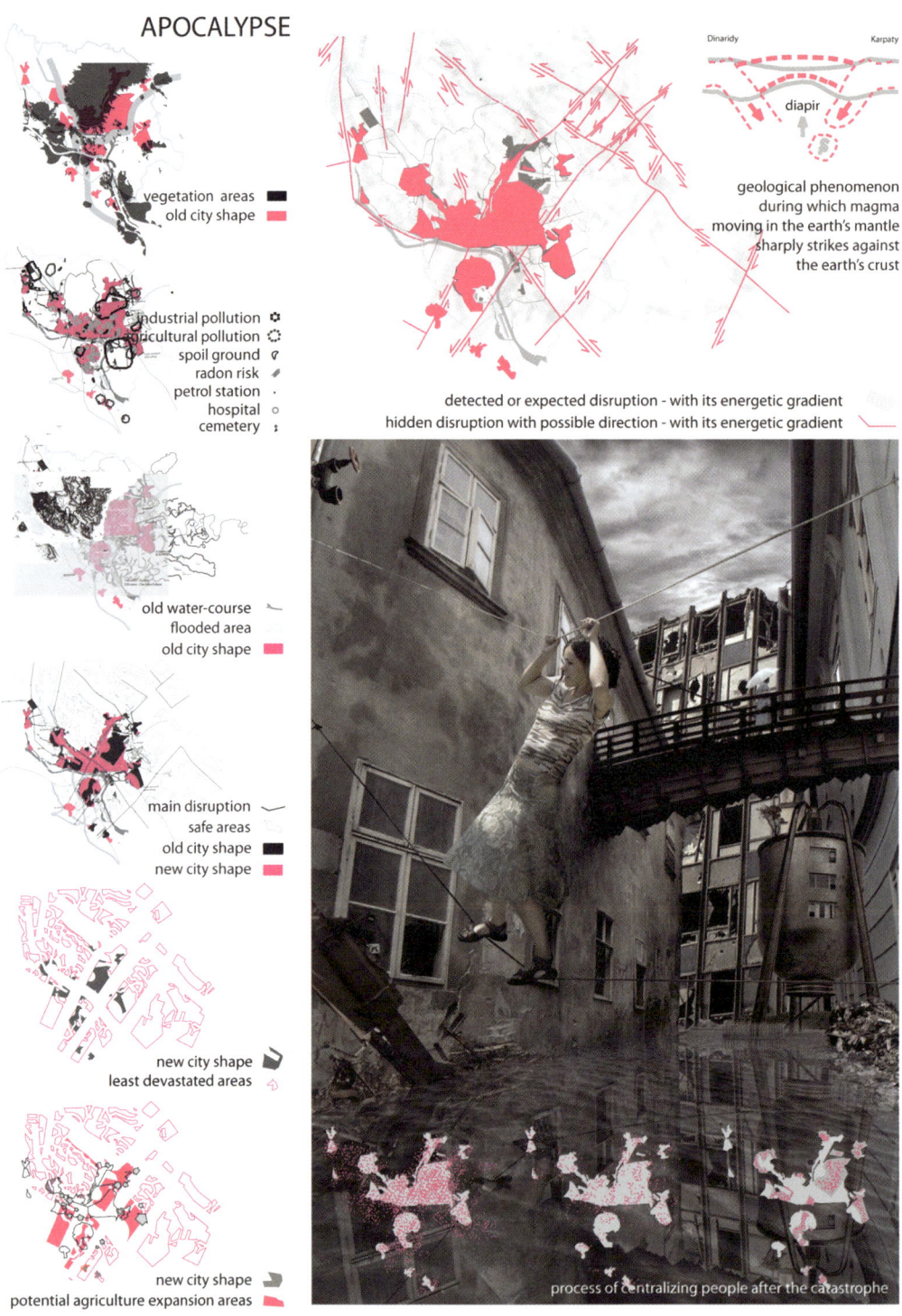

vegetation areas ■
old city shape ■

industrial pollution ✿
agricultural pollution ✿
spoil ground ℘
radon risk ✦
petrol station ·
hospital ○
cemetery ⁑

old water-course ～
flooded area
old city shape ■

main disruption ⌒
safe areas
old city shape ■
new city shape ■

new city shape ◣
least devastated areas △

new city shape ◥
potential agriculture expansion areas ▰

Dinaridy   Karpaty

diapir

geological phenomenon
during which magma
moving in the earth's mantle
sharply strikes against
the earth's crust

detected or expected disruption - with its energetic gradient
hidden disruption with possible direction - with its energetic gradient ⌒

process of centralizing people after the catastrophe

In this project the source of the disaster is a diapir. It causes an earthquake which destroys the infrastructure. The industrial centres and petrol stations will be swallowed up in chain explosions, damage to hospitals, cemeteries and city dumps will contaminate the soil. The destruction of the dam will create a flood wave and part of the city will end up under water.

Students: Kristína Králová | Martin Varga

APOCALYPSE

BERLIN

BRATISLAVA

BUDAPEST

079

LJUBLJANA

PRAGUE

VIENNA

WARSAW

A prediction arose from a study showing the new layout of Bratislava. In it urbanism is depicted as a parasitic fungus planting its centres in the remnants of urban structures. The ruins are a refuge while the contaminated territory provides building material, natural uncontaminated areas are used to cultivate crops and the dams on extensive water areas provide a source of energy. A functional urban unit emerges from the post-apocalyptic chaos.

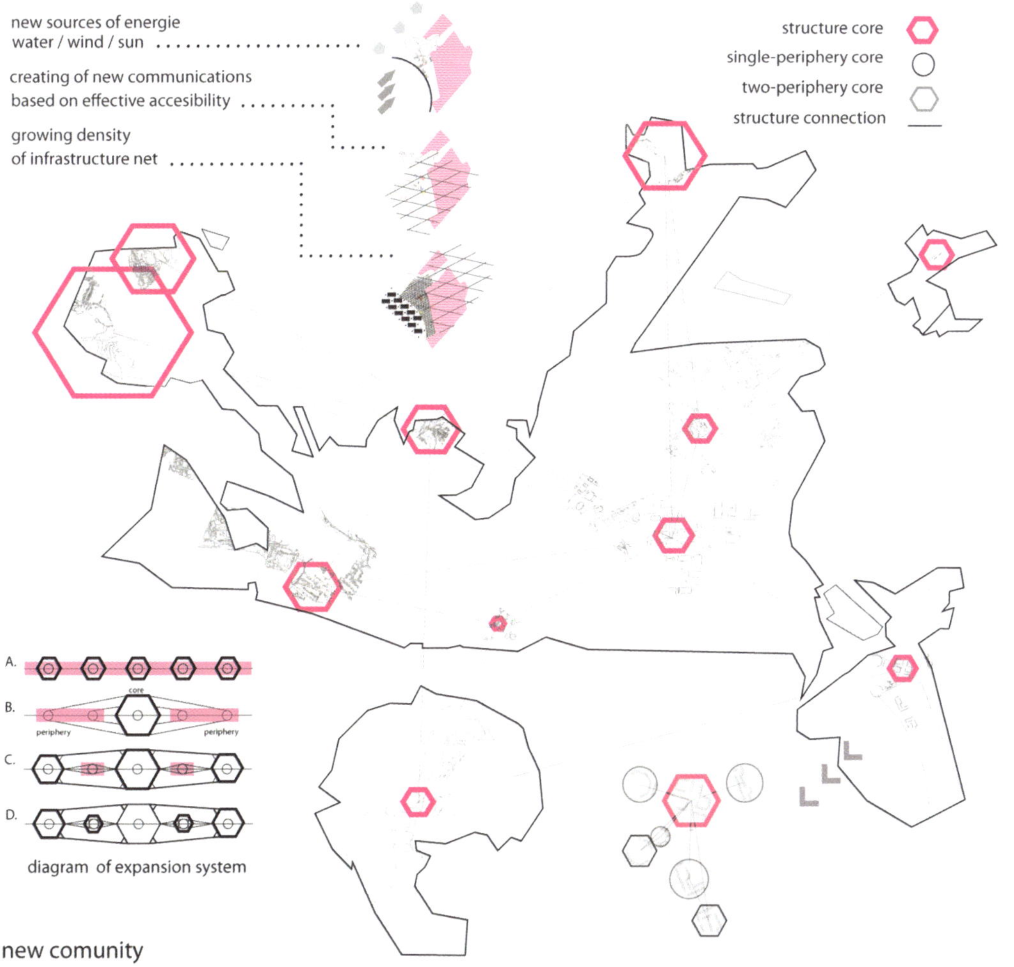

new sources of energie
water / wind / sun . . . .

creating of new communications
based on effective accesibility . . . .

growing density
of infrastructure net . . . .

structure core
single-periphery core
two-periphery core
structure connection

A.
B. core / periphery / periphery
C.
D.

diagram of expansion system

new comunity

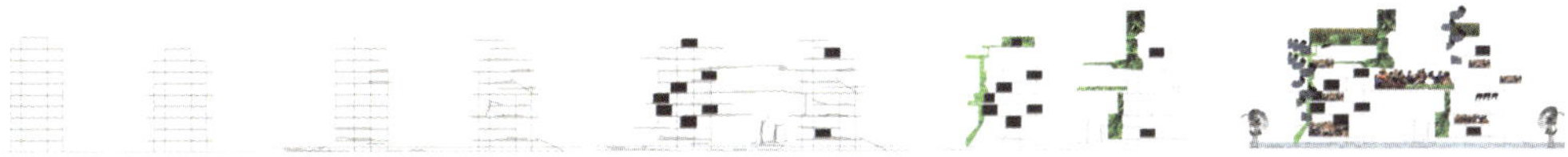

initial situation / apocalypse / begining of regeneration / new vegetation / new source of energy / building of new comunity

City Avatar

This abstract machine explore Bratislava through generation growth from first enter anonymous entity through associated entities back to start one. The whole process has rules how the generation growth works. There three types of connection, Active, Passive and Activated. According to this, the system generates from group of equal anonymous entities renew reference points which has different qualities.In this point we can start to talk about our new city topography as the swarm system of reference entities recovering the information flow over the Bratislava.The goal of this project is to create new interactivity of Bratislava to itself and to over regional information knots.

City map

All generations/Petrzalka-active connections

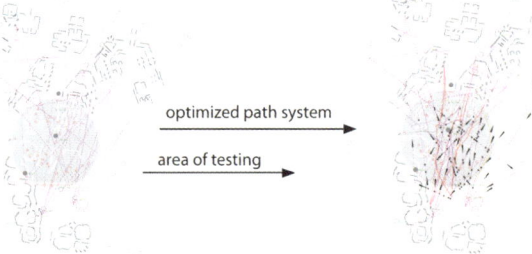

optimized path system

area of testing

Every reference entity has a field o influence, acording to it. Avatar generate Interaction points/information knots which define spatial use of the next structure.

All generations/Petrzalka-passive connections

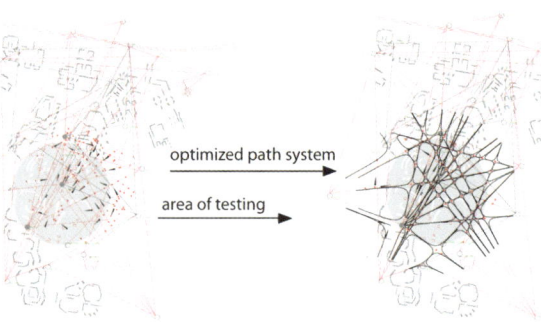

optimized path system

area of testing

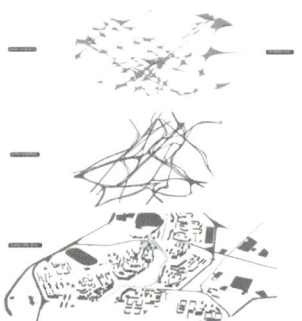

Generation relation diagram for Petržalka

Generation growth of reference entities recorded to linear diagram
for better orientation/ Extract for Petržalka.

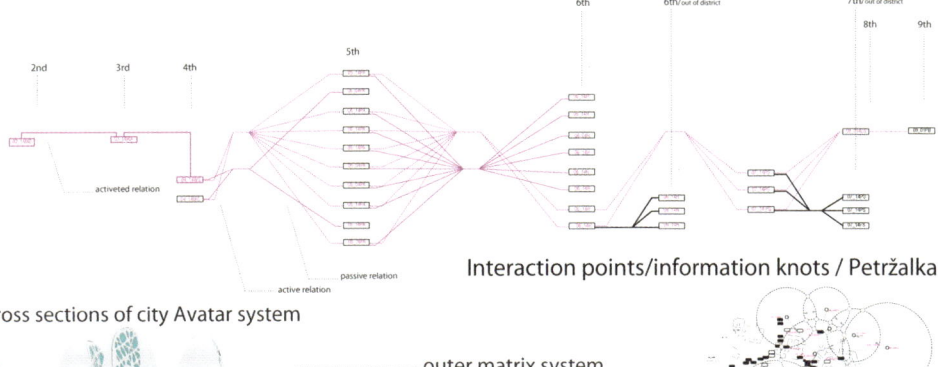

Cross sections of city Avatar system

BERLIN

BRATISLAVA

BUDAPEST

081

LJUBLJANA

PRAGUE · VIENNA ·

WARSAW

Interaction points/information knots / Petržalka

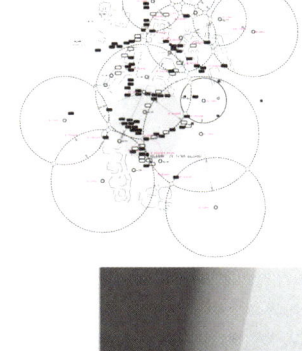

outer matrix system

information modul

modul perforation
multistorey modul

public space

outer matrix system

existing structure

garden modul

water tube
hydro plans farm
watering system

water reservoir

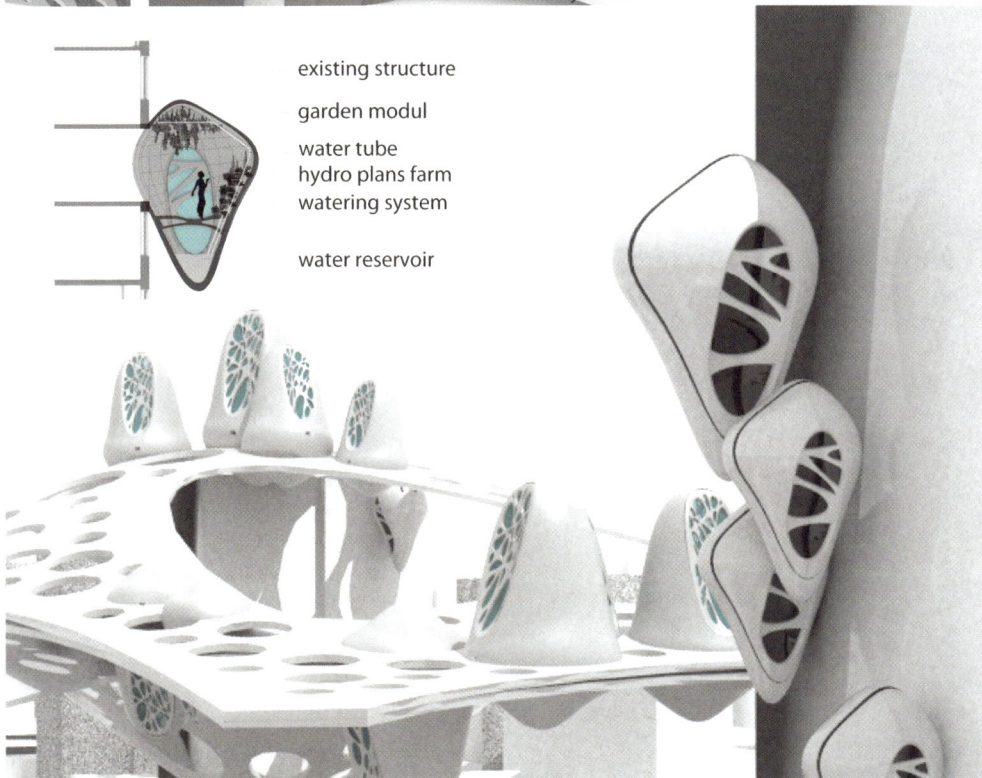

Despite its size and big city status, paradoxically Bratislava offers little adequate space for untypical sports activities. One of these is climbing.
Currently there is one climbig bouldering centre in Bratislava. In the summer there is also one outdoor climbing wall. The limiting factors of these official spaces are either that they are overcrowded or have inconvenient hours and prices.
The Climbing City Project provides the opportunity for creating activities virtually at every step, not just for climbers, but for the ordinary resident wanting to practise some form of activity.
The new urban slopes are seen as virtual possibilities for new activity. It is in constant motion, constantly responding to current needs. It affects the residents in the existing buildings only to a minimum and only for a short time without disturbing the privacy. This way the resident also has a new possibility of moving around the city. The need is removed of solely using the ground, the use of the third dimension of free space through diagonal and vertical directions is appearing. Man is free from the city as he moves. He establishes a basic relationship between space and body which flows with life and energy.

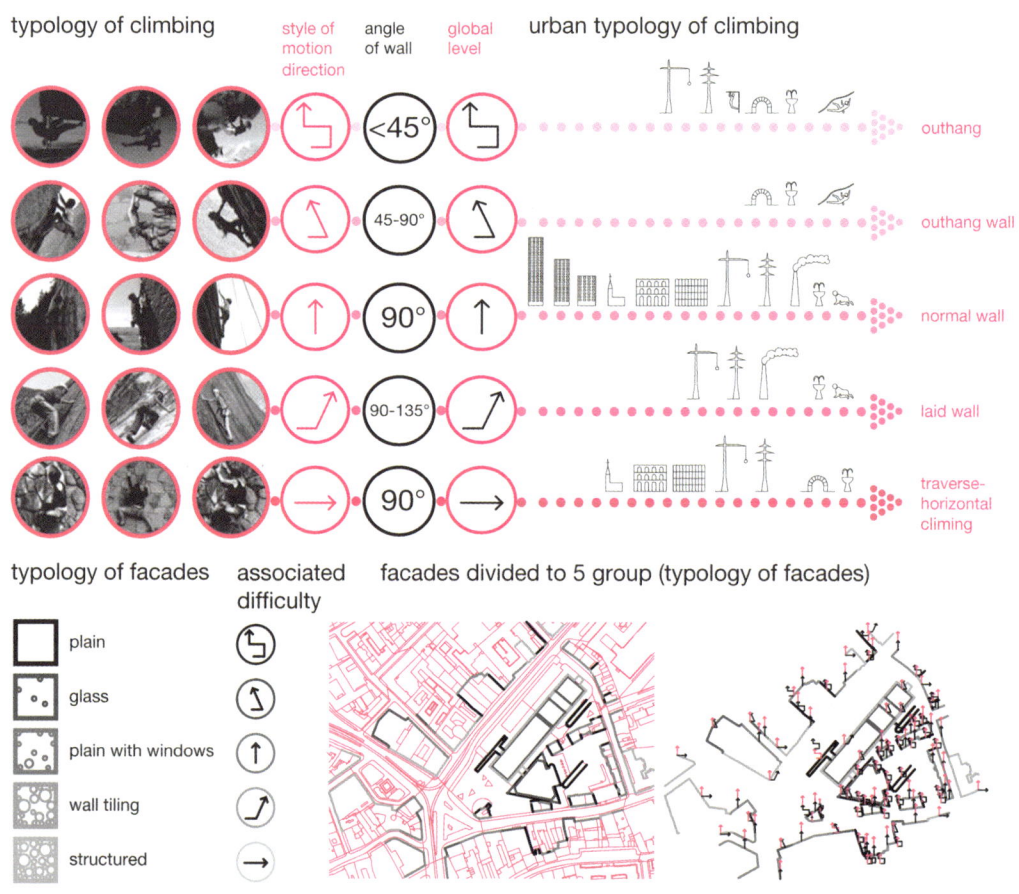

typology of climbing

style of motion direction / angle of wall / global level

urban typology of climbing

<45°	outhang
45-90°	outhang wall
90°	normal wall
90-135°	laid wall
90°	traverse-horizontal climing

typology of facades

- plain
- glass
- plain with windows
- wall tiling
- structured

associated difficulty

facades divided to 5 group (typology of facades)

IMPACT ON FACADES BY CLIMBING OPPORTUNITIES IN CITY
- symbol representing real shape of the wall
- symbol of common level

- impact of every opportunities
- impact of minority opportunities
- impact of majority opportunities

components of new structures created from influence of climbing opportunities

line follows vector from middle point of KAMENNE NAMESTIE at an specific angle to the first affecting opportunities belonging to group of facade

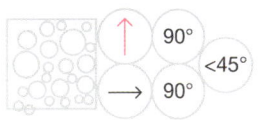

90°
<45°
90°

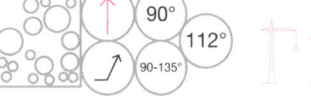

90°
112°
90-135°

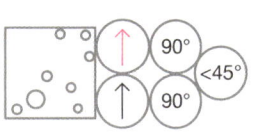

90°
<45°
90°

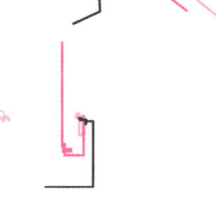

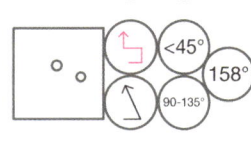

90°
68°
90-135°

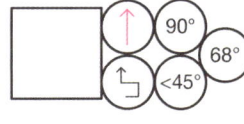

<45°
158°
90-135°

90°
68°
<45°

083

Climbing facilities in Bratislava according to the typology of climbing

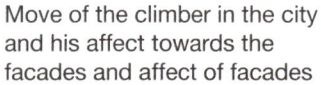

Move of the facade towards the climber

Move of the climber in the city and his affect towards the facades and affect of facades

BERLIN

BRATISLAVA

BUDAPEST

LJUBLJANA

PRAGUE

VIENNA

WARSAW

CAsinO CITY

The 7 levels lines are metaphorical meaning- Gille Delleuze´s phylosophy: 1000 platures, there are planes with no beginning, no ending, they only have the middle point, they are not one and not many, each platform can be re-decode, it´s a plane, level, it has a centre and consists of rhyzoms. By this way comes into pleatures and they are graduated by intensity of the sin in Bratislava.

level lines   points of fastest change

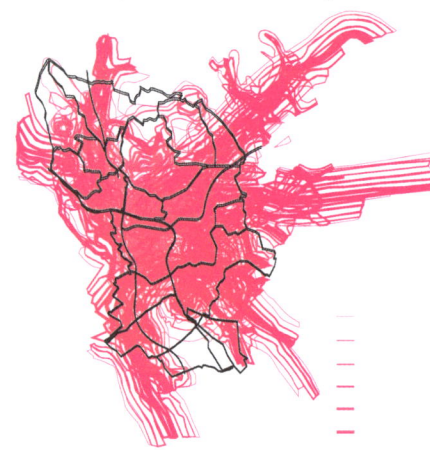

covering of layers   points of intensity

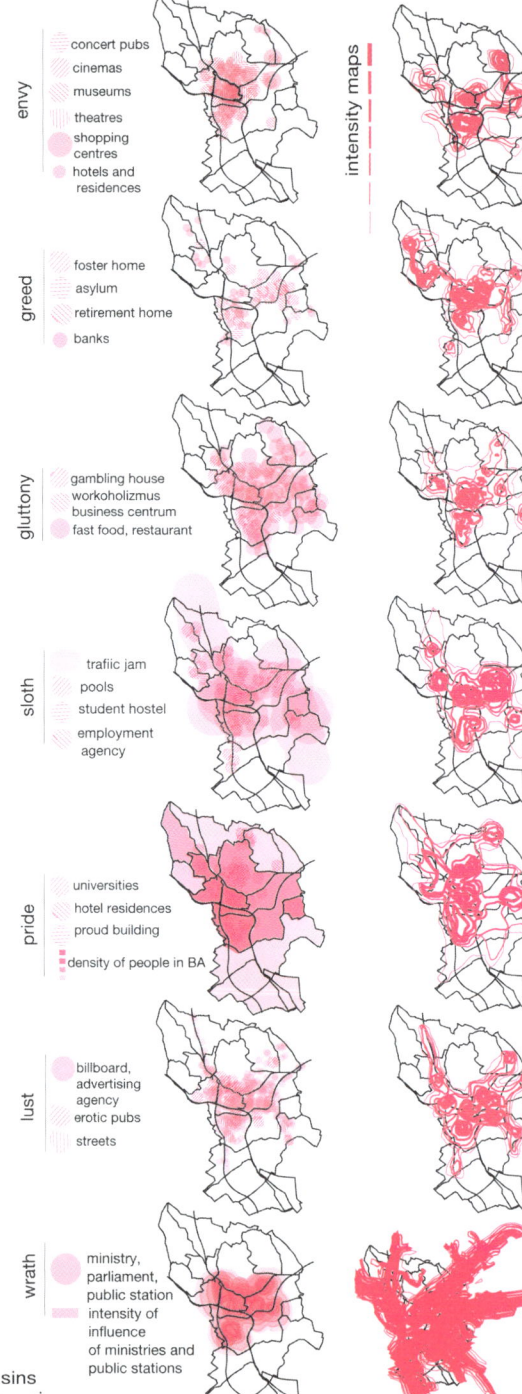

intensity maps

envy
- concert pubs
- cinemas
- museums
- theatres
- shopping centres
- hotels and residences

greed
- foster home
- asylum
- retirement home
- banks

gluttony
- gambling house
- workoholizmus
- business centrum
- fast food, restaurant

sloth
- trafiic jam
- pools
- student hostel
- employment agency

pride
- universities
- hotel residences
- proud building
- density of people in BA

lust
- billboard, advertising agency
- erotic pubs
- streets

wrath
- ministry, parliament, public station
- intensity of influence of ministries and public stations

primary sins
secondary sins

 >  >

level lines deformed by common intensity of sin

surfaces created by intersection of each other level lines. there are a spaces between two platforms- slots

surfaces without level lines. selection is based on suitable typology.

 >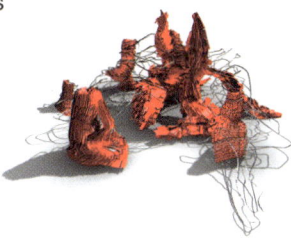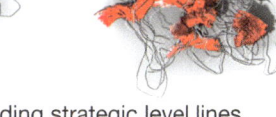

surfaces influented by tools. they are depended on characteristic of sins and their high levels.

perspective and top view including strategic level lines. they create a infrastructure of sin city.

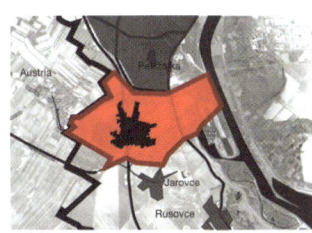

location of casino city between petržalka and jarovce. it is very strategic and special position. there is a good acces from three countries. traffic with high quality.
this location gives the best rise for the biggest casino in central europe.
this casino lives like an independent city with own structure focused on all possible sins and pleasures.

BERLIN

BRATISLAVA

BUDAPEST

085

LJUBLJANA

PRAGUE

VIENNA

WARSAW

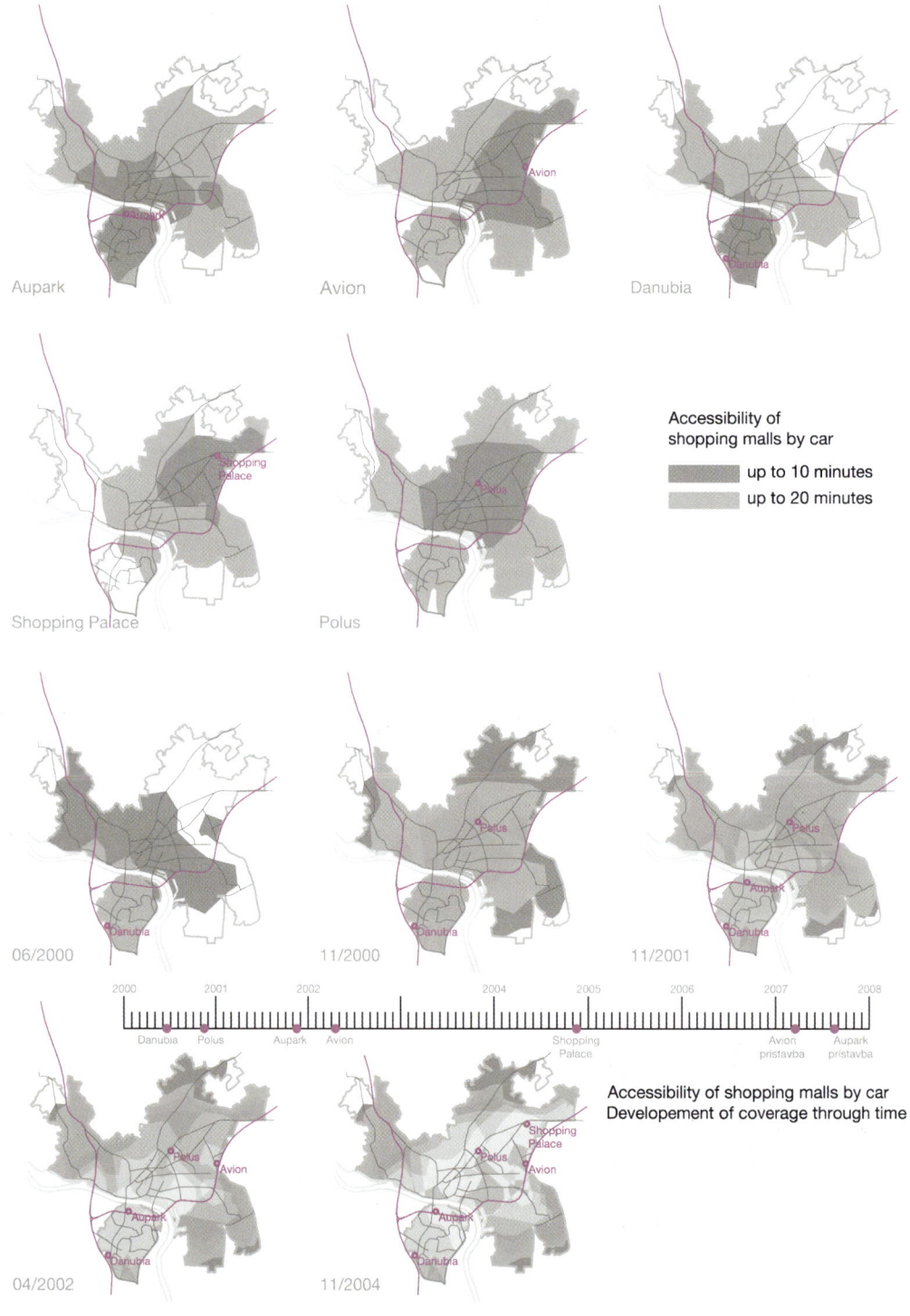

DEVELOPEMENT OF SHOPPING MALLS IN BRATISLAVA

Aupark

Avion

Danubia

Shopping Palace

Polus

Accessibility of
shopping malls by car

up to 10 minutes
up to 20 minutes

06/2000

11/2000

11/2001

2000 2001 2002 2004 2005 2006 2007 2008

Danubia Polus Aupark Avion Shopping Avion Aupark
Palace pristavba pristavba

Accessibility of shopping malls by car
Developement of coverage through time

04/2002

11/2004

BERLIN

BRATISLAVA

BUDAPEST

087

LJUBLJANA

PRAGUE

VIENNA

WARSAW

CITY ZONES - ACTIVE SPACES / DEAD SPACES

residental zones & scales

compact blocks
housing estates
villages
greenery

dead spaces
present or potentional brownfields

industrial area
gardening colony area
empty area
abandoned area

BARRIERS IN THE CITY

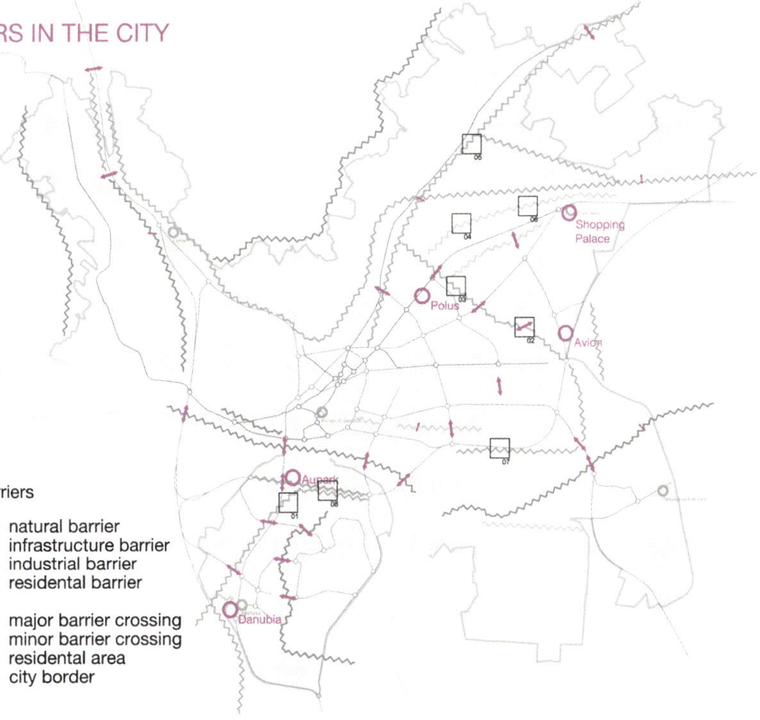

City barriers

natural barrier
infrastructure barrier
industrial barrier
residental barrier

major barrier crossing
minor barrier crossing
residental area
city border

CITY AS A SECTION GRAPHS

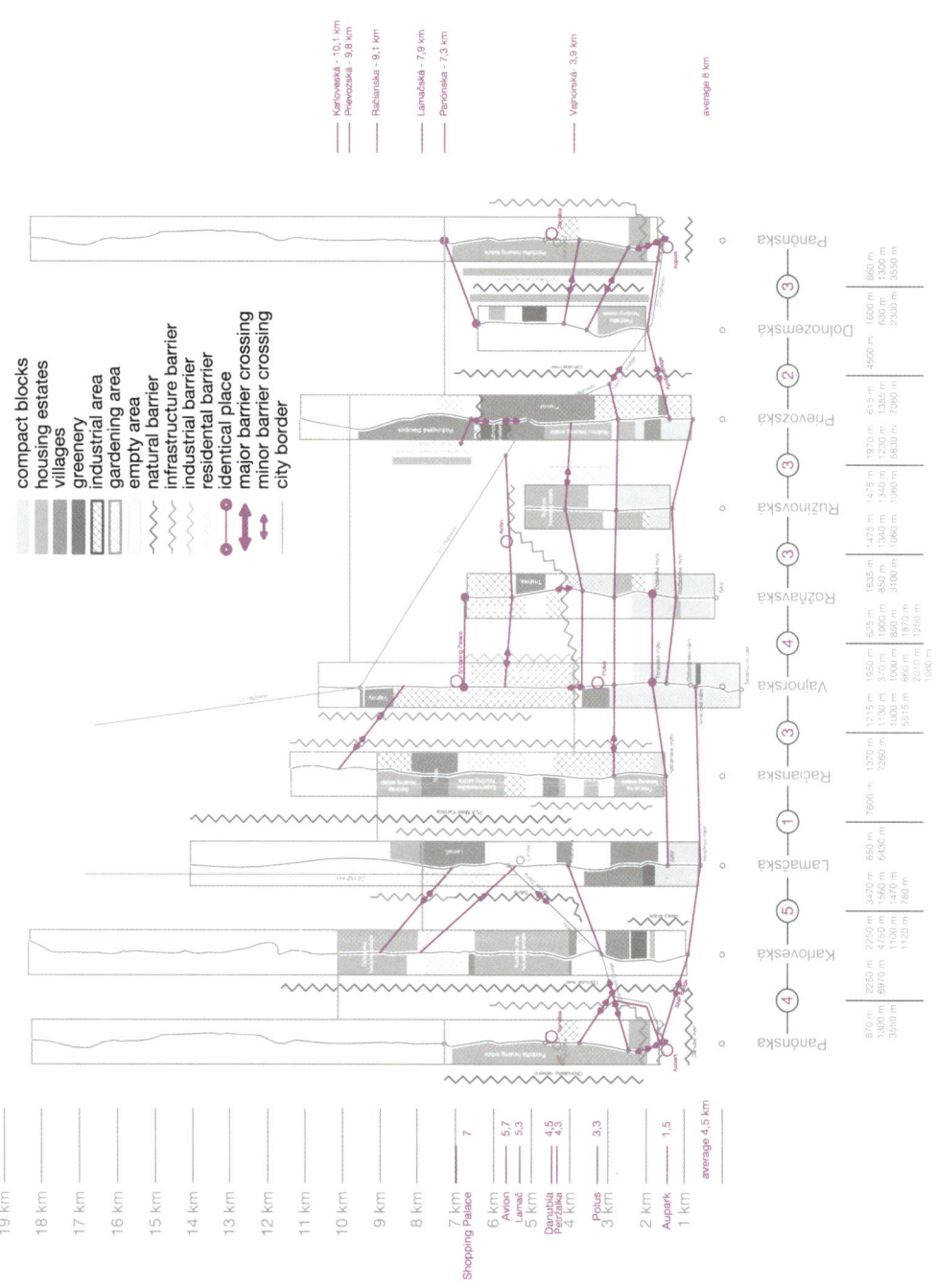

BERLIN

BRATISLAVA

BUDAPEST

089

LJUBLJANA

PRAGUE

VIENNA

WARSAW

CITY DISTRICTS ANALYSIS

 **downtown**
radius - 0,45 km
area - 137 432 m2 - 55%
overall area - 550 000 m2 - 220 %

 **horsky park**
radius - 1,7 km
area - 35 585 m2 - 14 %
overall area - 71 000 m2 - 28 %

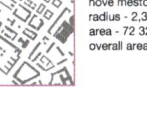 **februarka**
radius - 2,1 km
area - 39 542 m2 - 16 %
overall area - 277 000 m2 - 112 %

nove mesto
radius - 2,3 km
area - 72 322 m2 - 29 %
overall area - 362 000 m2 - 145 %

 **petrzalka**
radius - 2,4 km
area - 39 065 m2 - 16 %
overall area - 273 000 m2 - 112 %

 **koliba**
radius - 2,5 km
area - 42 619 m2 - 17%
overall area - 85 000 m2 - 34 %

 **ruzinov**
radius - 3,5 km
area -36 339 m2 - 15 %
overall area - 254 000 m2 - 105 %

 prievoz
radius - 4,3 km
area - 30 768 m2 - 12 %
overall area - 62 000 m2 - 24%

 **trnavka**
radius - 4,7 km
area - 37 129 m2 - 15 %
overall area - 74 000 m2 - 30 %

 **experimentalka**
radius - 6,4 km
area - 29 566 m2 - 12 %
overall area - 207 000 m2 - 84 %

 **dubravka**
radius - 6,8 km
area - 37 552 m2 - 15 %
overall area - 263 000 m2 - 105 %

 **dolne hony**
radius - 7,3 km
area - 30 202 m2 - 12 %
overall area - 211 000 m2 - 84 %

 **raca**
radius - 7,5 km
area - 31 730 m2 - 13 %
overall area - 63 000 m2 - 26 %

 vajnory
radius - 9,2 km
area - 23 021 m2 - 9 %
overall area - 46 000 m2 - 18 %

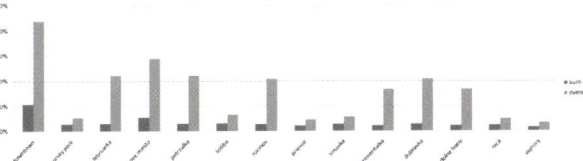

REBUILDING THE CITY

Two steps of
Voronoi subdivision

buildings original
buildings new
main roads and highways
tramway
main roads - new

BERLIN

BRATISLAVA

BUDAPEST

091

LJUBLJANA

PRAGUE

VIENNA

WARSAW

BUDAPEST
A_VOID TO BUILD

BERLIN

BRATISLAVA

BUDAPEST

093

LJUBLJANA

PRAGUE

VIENNA

WARSAW

Students: András Beke | Attila Fábri | Zsolt Szendrei | Szilvia Tóth
Katalin Wéber

Tutors: Bálint Kádár | György Alföldi

A_VOID TO BUILD

BÁLINT KÁDÁR

—

Many things have changed in the last 20 years, but Budapest is not among them. The city is quite the same as it was at the end of the communist era. Without conceptual development strategies the few isolated large-scale developments had no good effect on the city as a whole. In fact all of the few positive changes were small ones: new pedestrian streets, empty buildings occupied by bars or cultural centers. In fact these really made Budapest more livable – without building anything.

Can we make a competitive urban strategy out of the failures of the past 20 years? Can we change our city without large building developments? Can the existing built environment host a completely new structure of usage? Can we treat our newest building developments as rehabilitation areas? Can voids in a city's development form the future of it?

Three works tried to answer these questions, seeking for a new future for the classical European cities, making an advantage out of their incapacity to renew their spatial structures.
The Urbanity project of Budapest avoids to build new structures in Budapest, instead it searches for the voids of the urban system where the new future of the city can be built.
None of the projects involve new building proposals, only soft interventions. All projects examine the failures of post-socialist urban scenarios, and work with the voids remaining in the city structure. In a physical way, voids are the empty spaces left for development, but in a more metaphorical way, we work with processes leading to underused spaces in the past 20 years: the voids of a city's possibilities.

VACANT LOTS

—

Works in the dense and problematic neighborhood of Józsefváros. It is focusing on empty plots and the developments made on these. The war generated many empty lots in Budapest, now days only in this district a relevant number of them remained unused: all were built in by commercial architecture or bad quality housing. In Józsefváros the permanent temporary usage of these can make an uprising neighborhood out of the most problematic one. In the dense eclectic fabric, these voids bring hope for a sustainable development, social renewal and some fresh ideas for better public spaces.
The project develops a sensible strategy for soft rehabilitation, using vacant lots and goods containers to create new possibilities for a poor population. Flexible development, that makes the history of the city's voids remain intact.

UNFINISHED MILLENIUM

—

Is a rehabilitation project with a brave statement: big building projects of the past 10 years (!) need urgent rehabilitation to make them properly used parts of the city. The project focuses on the so called "Millenium city center", a new urban development placed by the Danube in an outstanding location. It was developed with a cultural focus, that of the new National Theater and the Palace of the Arts. The housing, offices and cultural buildings float rootless and without real connections with each other nor other parts of the city, while this supposed to be a real central node in the city life. Even if the empty plot left from an old railway station was built in, this is a real void in the city structure, as it has no connections, no traces of history, and no real function. Culture floats here in a vacuum space, nothing really lives. Traffic problems, lack of services and public spaces are the main problems. Changing the structure of these spaces, making modifications on the buildings themselves, increasing density, rethinking transportation infrastructures and redesigning the river bank can be the solution. As the plot is one of the most worthy in the city, rehabilitation must start now.

PRIVATIZING PUBLIC SPACES

-
Experiments with the re-distribution of ownership and usages in public spaces. In Budapest more than 90% of the apartments are privately owned now - this is a result of the privatization of all housing in Budapest during the changes of 89-90. Freedom from the unifying ideology of the communist era bought egoism: everyone has it's own little property, so the common spaces lost their values. Public money for maintenance is limited, such as public interest for common property. Dirty, degraded public spaces are real voids in the urban system, and such are the underused private spaces. Ownership of these problematic places should be rethought. Our statement: post-socialist affection to the private property can lead to a better public life.

Three proposals were born for three different urban situations.

-
1
In the dense city center locals are alienated from the streets and squares they live in. Tourists from other parts of the city or from abroad also use these spaces: they are used by everyone, therefore owned by no one. Costs and benefits are all on the municipality, a suspicious entity for the post-socialist citizen. If the inhabitants could have the ownership of the streets, the duties and benefits would be all theirs, and they could decide how to use the spaces. This project shows how the anarchy of this system would quickly turn into an ideal land usage and public spaces - without a municipal organization. The result would be the same as in a well functioning democratic city - but who knows when Budapest will turn into such a place without playing with the ownership of public spaces.

-
2
The prefabricated building of huge socialist housing estates have a sad feeling of boredom even if all the flats inside are owned by someone else. People living here can

BERLIN

BRATISLAVA

BUDAPEST

095

LJUBLJANA

PRAGUE

VIENNA

WARSAW

hardly change their houses,
but could easily change the immense
public spaces between them.
The greenery is nice, but underused
- these are mostly publicly owned
green deserts. If condominiums could
decide what to do with the land
surrounding them, a variety of
uses could complement the small
apartments, making the environment
of the prefabs colorful,
distinguishable, competitive with
other urban forms. This project
experiments with temporary ownership
and usage inside the communal
property. Locals could own a piece
of land for a limited time for one
function. They could use public
spaces around them according to
their needs or moods. Around
the uniformity of prefabs the
variety of urban lifeforms could
flourish.

–
3
Egoism of today's post-socialist
society is imprinted into
the suburban neighborhoods. Detached
family houses in the middle of their
small gardens are little kingdoms
each. As the small gardens surround
on all sides the houses, rarely
the small strips of land between
fences and buildings are intensively
used. New developments of gated
communities with condominiums have
better services - such as sport
fields, pools and barbecue fields
- because the land use is more
compact. Can the suburban streets
of small villas learn from these
condos? By giving the full control
of a street to the owners of
the plots, these could form
communities and act together. This
project shows the process of making
public places with the tools of
privatization. The closed street
makes fences obsolete, people living
in a newly formed street
-community could decide how to use

their land in a better way, opening
together once divided gardens,
creating facilities that only bigger
communities could afford before.

BERLIN

BRATISLAVA

BUDAPEST

097

LJUBLJANA

PRAGUE

VIENNA

WARSAW

LOCAL PROBLEMS

After the research I zoomed in to a problematic neighbourhood on the edge of the historical city-centrer. In these blocks there are people living in **deep-destitution**. The rate of the **violence** is extremely high, people have an opportunity for **no work**, they live from social aids. Very big families are living in **tiny flats**. There are some bigger flats in the area, flat-owners don't rent them for local families, however they could pay for it. There is a **lack of public buildings** and places, there are no kindergardens enough, no libraries, no communiy- and education-centers. So who don't work, mostly spend their days in cheep **wine-pubs and casinos**. Wealthy people already moved away from this area, and many local people stopped beliving in the renewal of the neighbourhood. As a solution I picture a social rehabilitation, so in this project there was designed the architectural and urban background of this process. The project is based on the principle, that local problems can be solved by local resources. Using this precept local people can be led back to the sociaty, giving them skills and motivation for work, through making their environment more comfortable. Paralelly the rehabilitation of the Teleki-sqare-market would be also realised in the neighbourhood. This two pilons would make the area more attractive for the outsiders, and a gentrification could be started, without loosing the present residents of the neighbourhood.

LOCAL SOLUTIONS - using containers for civil purposes

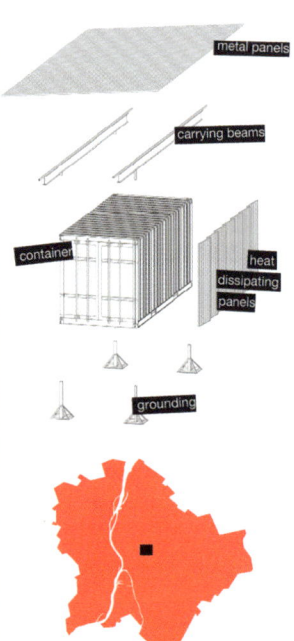

ACTORS
outsiders

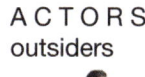

- entertainment
- services
- safity
- quality shopping
- nice environment

local government and organisations

- proper stately funds
- better environment
- happy inhabitants
- control

inhabitians

- chance to learn
- own home
- chance to work
- chance to entertainment
- better environment

shop-owners

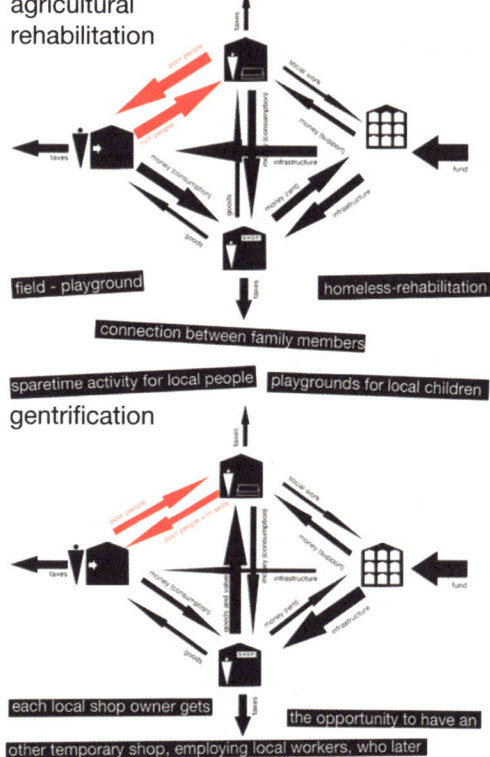

- making money
- cheep rents
- safity
- solvent customers

SCENARIOS
craft and work

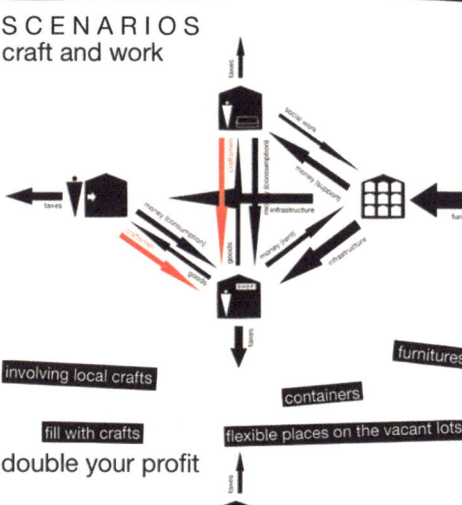

- involving local crafts
- furnitures
- containers
- fill with crafts
- flexible places on the vacant lots

agricultural rehabilitation

- field - playground
- homeless-rehabilitation
- connection between family members
- sparetime activity for local people
- playgrounds for local children

double your profit

- change of the population
- new shops
- building in the vacant lots increases density
- new facilities

gentrification

- each local shop owner gets
- the opportunity to have an
- other temporary shop, employing local workers, who later
- can get the right for running the shops
- government can control crime easyer

BERLIN

BRATISLAVA

BUDAPEST

LJUBLJANA

PRAGUE

VIENNA

WARSAW

REALIZATION

social housing
surveying
demolishing existing ruins
preparing the first container-house
finishing the house by the inhabitans
do the house-building cycle,
until the last house is completely finished
merge small containers to each other
taking ownership of the houses to the inhabitians

agricultural rehabilitation
surveying
preparing the first field
planting the first flowers and vegetables
preparing the other fields
start to build a glass house and agricultural school
working small gardens
local vegetable market/shop

double your profit
forum for inhabitians
writing agreements with local shop-owners
opening the first shops employing local labour
attract locals/outsiders to the shops
educate worker to run the shops theirselves
open new shops without supervision
moving shops to 'normal' marts

craft and work
finding craftsmen who are interested
preparing the first workshops
preparing products for the houses
education of the workers
involve different type of workshops
improving new products
workshops selling new products

sparetime and education
surveying
preparing the first playground
start to build a nursery
start to bulid a kindergarden
establish a sport-field
start to build an education center
for grown ups

gentrification
(regulated by the market)
renovation of empty flats
rehabilitation of public places
the first outsiders show up
the district is attractiv for outsiders

1st phase — preparing time (2 years)

2nd phase — experimenting time (2 years)

3rd phase — construction time (6 years)

4th phase — finishing time (2 years)

Student: Attila Fábri

BERLIN

BRATISLAVA

BUDAPEST

101

LJUBLJANA

PRAGUE

VIENNA

WARSAW

social housing

private terrace

glass-house on the roof

wine-pub

kindergarten

social housing

social housing

small gardens

double your profit

social housing

playground

workshop

workshop

social housing

cafe

vertical garden

nursary

semi-private terrace

library tower

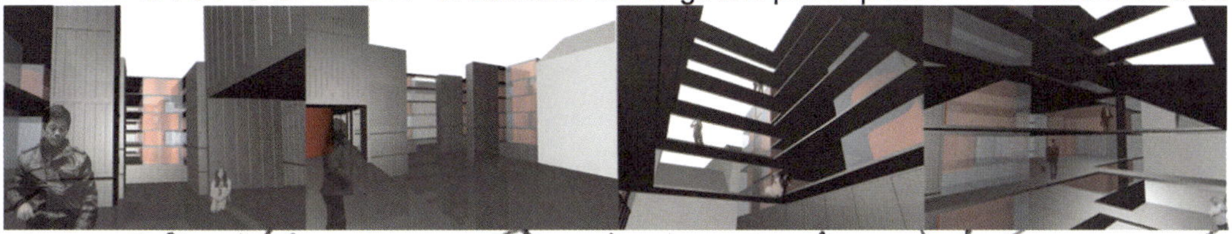

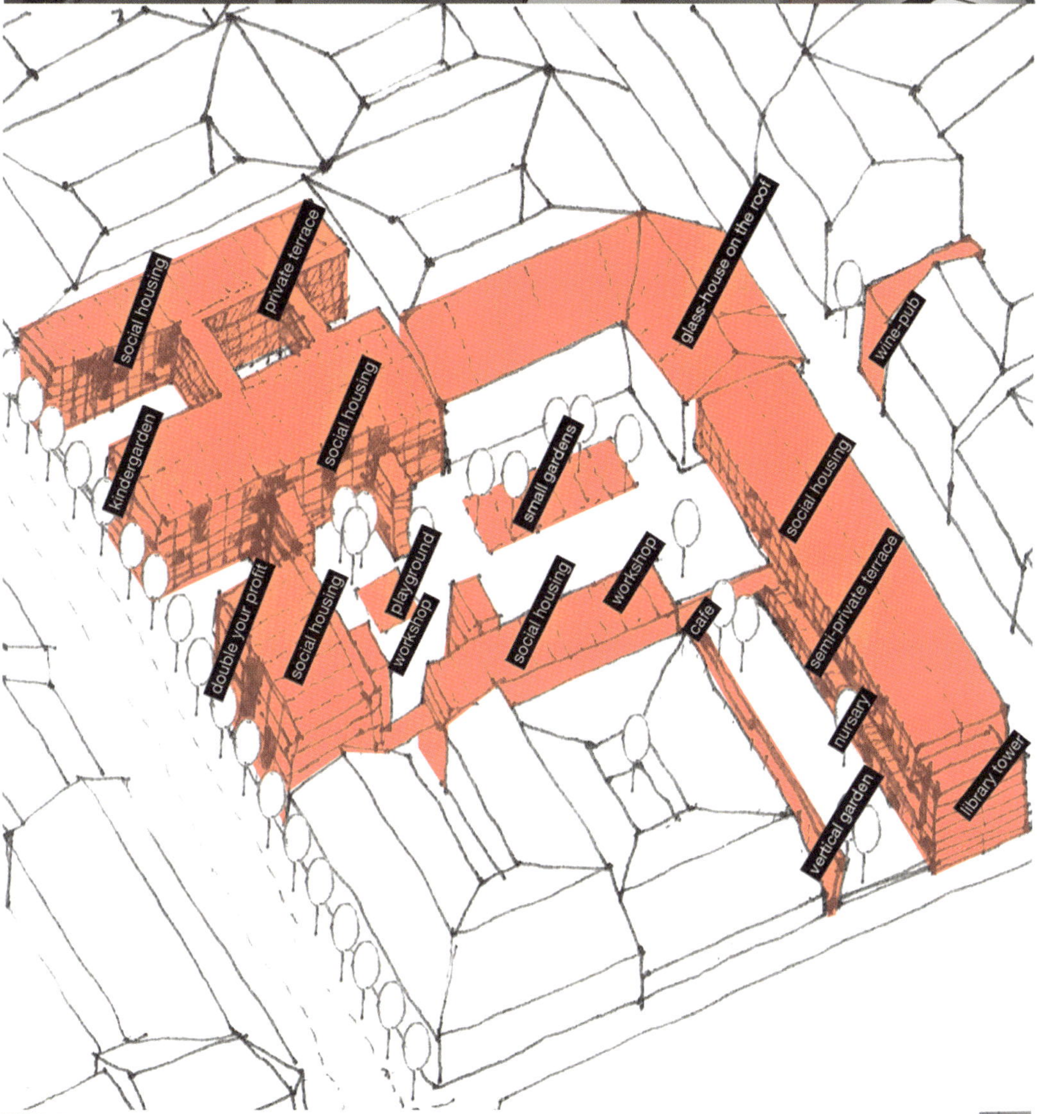

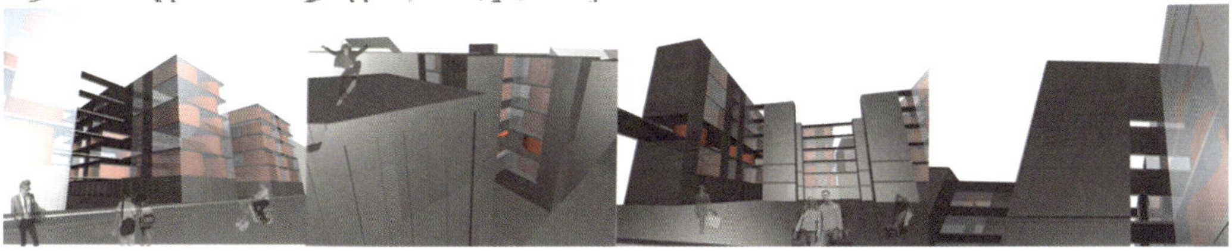

Problems

The Millenium City Centre is one of the best situated areas in Budapest. Before 1996 the area served as a goods station. Because of the increased value of this land, the station was wound up and this field was designated as the 1996 World Expo area. Hungary backed out of the Expo in 1995 – few years after Vienna did the same. The field was sold , and a contract between the investor and the state defined part of the building works as a PPP project. This area of the city has good potentials, but now – almost completely built up - it is underused. Among the reasons of its failure area bad master plan, investor's too strong proposals, bad architectural design.

On the east side of the Millenium City Centre there is the wide and busy Soroksári road, which isolates the area from other parts of the city. It is a really important road for the city, connecting the center with the outskirts and the motorway. The most important transport way of Csepel island is also connected to this road, taking more than half of the whole traffic of Csepel. The road is 6 lanes wide and it is completed with a two lanes wide service road and a tramline. Crossing over the street is so complicated, as there are just 3 traffic lights where it is possible.

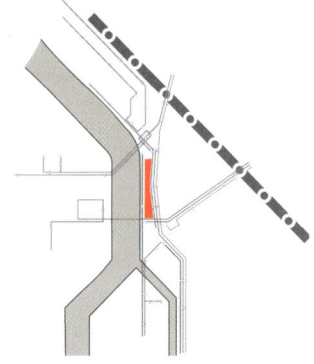

public transport approach of the National Theatre

public transport system of tht environs of the field

Huge disadvantage of this area is the bad public transport connection. The approach to this area is so complicated that it's influence can be seen on the number of visitors. The local railway is a small help to this problem, but it breaks off the area from the Danube. The stop's dimension is far under-designed for it's public functions.

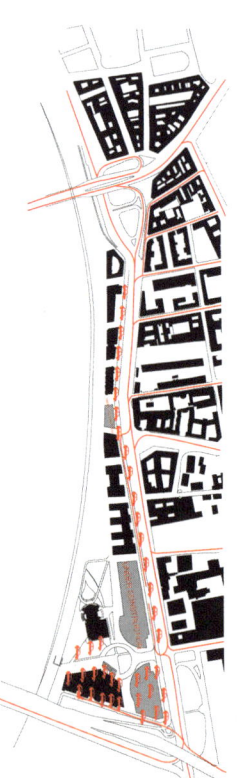

The riverbank promenade is cut into two by the suburban railway, isolating the buildings and the public from the Danube. Just a narrow path lays between the office buildings and the fence of the railway. The shops in the groundfloor of the buildings are absolutely unusable and empty.

In the middle of the field there is a playground. The only problem is that it is unused. This fact show, that the use of the all „City Centre".For example in this case the main reason is that too hard to go there with a child.
There are some possibilities in the using of Danube, but until this time the river has been unused.

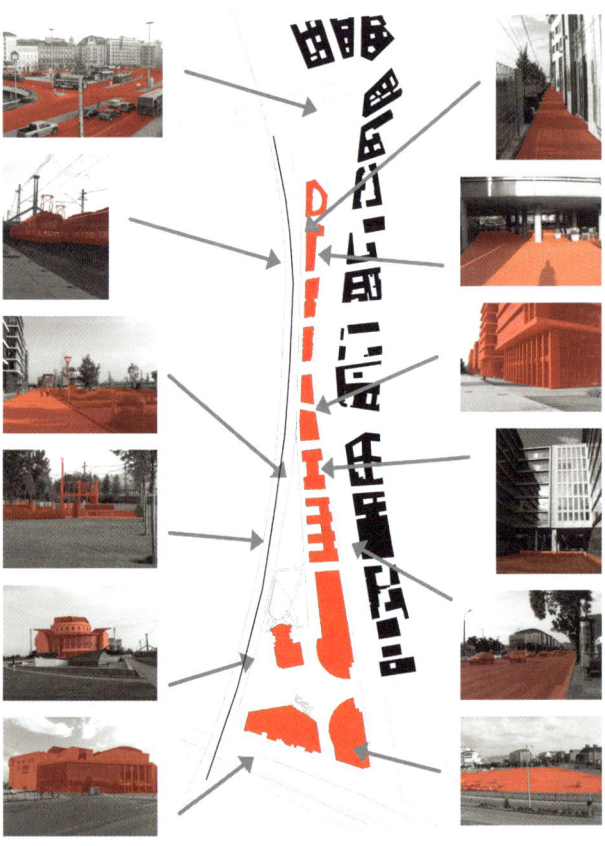

parking places around the fields

parking places around the fields

Concept

One of the main point of the Integrated Strategy of City Devepopment of Budapest (IVS, 2009) is to make a stronger connection with the Danube. This is one of the best places for this.

The connection is solved by a landing-stage, which provides possibilities for walking and for the docking of ships. There is possibility for water connected events like Uszálystrand (floating pool) to be here, and docks for watertaxi or regular sailings can be accomodated.

At present the land of the ex-slaughterhouse is used as the headquarter of small indusrtial companies. In the future these spaces will become the target of new cultural investigation, and become the continuation of the new city centre. The city centre therefore can develop in two directionS (the Kvassay sluice and ex-staughterhouse), and it will become continously improvable.

The existing public building zone of the Millenium city centre is already filled up, so there aren't any space to develop it further. New public functions could be placed into the brownfields of the old industries across the Soroksári road, connecting the now isolated Millenium zone to the existing city fabric.

The signed pathches in the existing city structure mark empty spaces which can complete the riverside area. These fields can create well usable public spaces in junction with the crowded city.

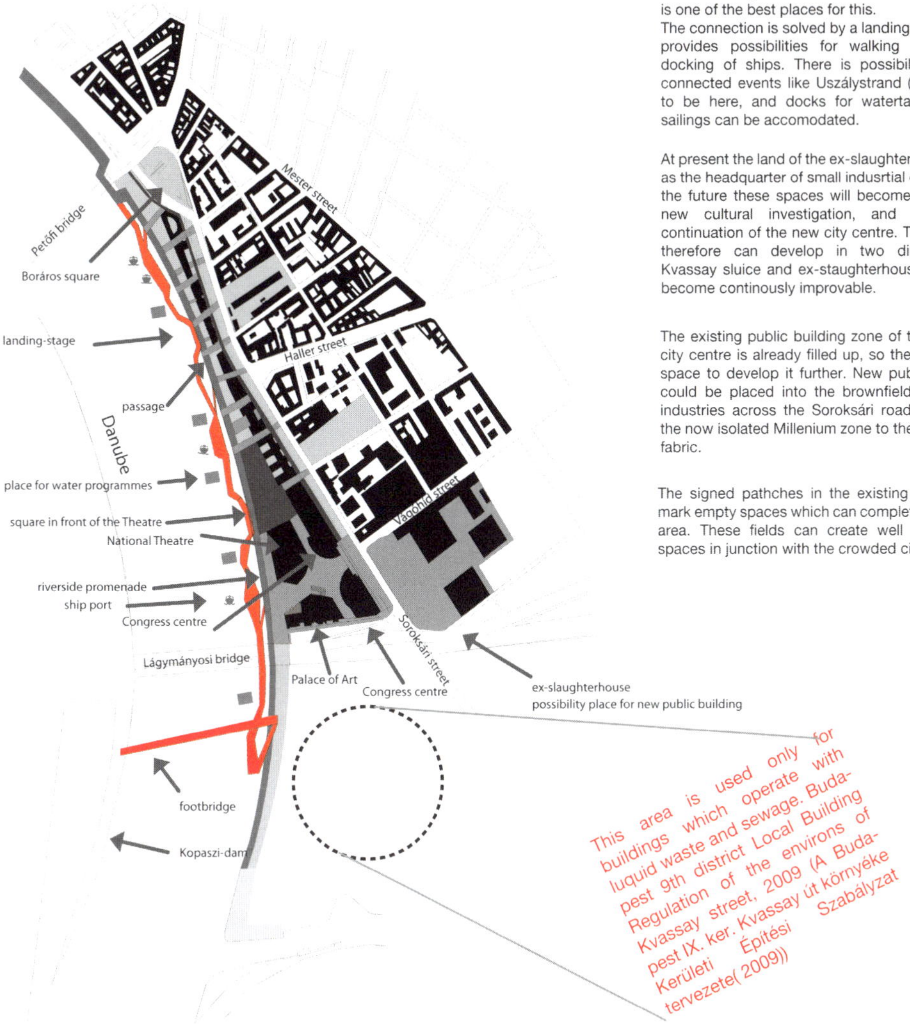

Mester street
Petőfi bridge
Boráros square
landing-stage
Haller street
passage
Danube
place for water programmes
square in front of the Theatre
National Theatre
Vágóhíd street
riverside promenade
ship port
Congress centre
Soroksári street
Lágymányosi bridge
Palace of Art
Congress centre
ex-slaughterhouse
possibility place for new public building
footbridge
Kopaszi-dam

This area is used only for buildings which operate with luquid waste and sewage. Budapest 9th district Local Building Regulation of the environs of Kvassay street, 2009 (A Budapest IX. ker. Kvassay út környéke Kerületi Építési Szabályzat tervezete(2009))

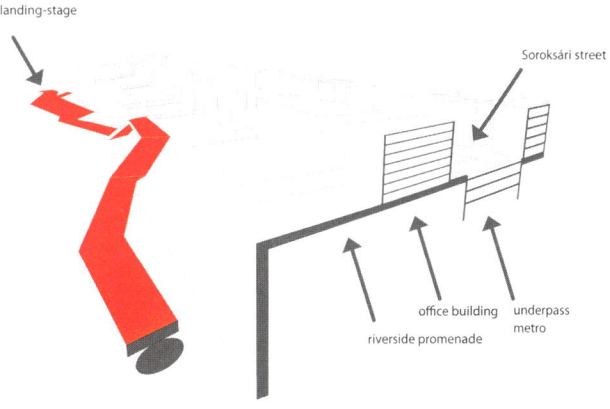

landing-stage

Soroksári street

office building   underpass
riverside promenade   metro

The problem to solve is the approach of the land. After the suburban railway is moved out, the field can become passable from the beginning to end. The developement of the public transport system including the 5th metro will result in stronger connections to the city structure. The integrated strategy of city devepopment of Budapest (IVS, 2009) aims to make stronger the connection between the city and the Danube. The new landing-stage gives an opportunity for approaching the water here. The closing of the landing-stage is a foot bridge which leads to the newly finished but still hardly approachable Kopaszi dam, connecting two important public spaces on the bank of the Danube.

Between the Boráros square and The National Theatre small funcions are placed like benches, coffee bars, restaurants, and also the groundfloor shops of the office buildings can be used.

This promenade, pressed between two bridges, have very strong end points. The continuation of the bank promenade is a solution to it.

Approach of the Theatre

pedestrian traffic around the theatre at present

At the south part of the plot there are some public buildings as the National Theatre, Palace of Art, Conference Centers. The square between the buildings doesn't function well because of the mistakes of the master plan. Also the National Theatre doesn't work good enough, because some important functions are missing, as the entrance hall, garage and service funcions for the riverside promenade while the theatres technological equipment is quite advanced.

Solution of these problems could be the completion of the Theatre with new functions around the present building, like a proper entrance hall. In this new skin of the building there could be also service funcions for the promenade which could help to bring life to the area. The Theatre should become accessible from the south part, which is important, because after the metro line 5 will open, the main arrival direction will be from this side.

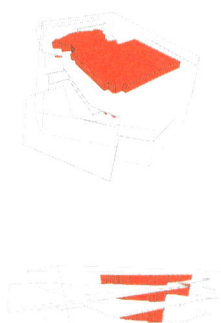

reshaping of the National Theatre

The actual layout of the buildings is not concieved according to the true transport directions. The National Theatre and it's surroundings (garden and public space design) look north, but the visitors arrive from the south part. It is not possible to walk over the area, there are only 2 possibilies to cross the suburban railway line. The nearest public transport junction is from the south part of the Theatre.

The bad orientation of the National Theatre made worse the square between the public buildings. The main aim of the proposed modification is to open the square towards the ex-slaughterhouse, where important developments will take place, and to make accessible every building from this square

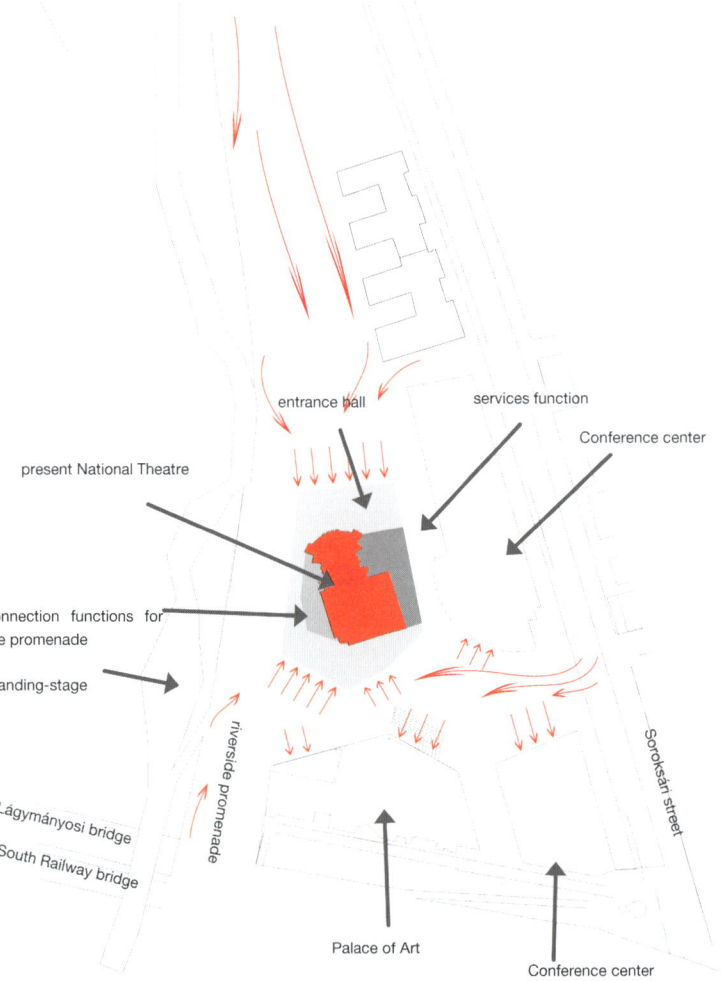

new functions of the theatre

Crossing the street

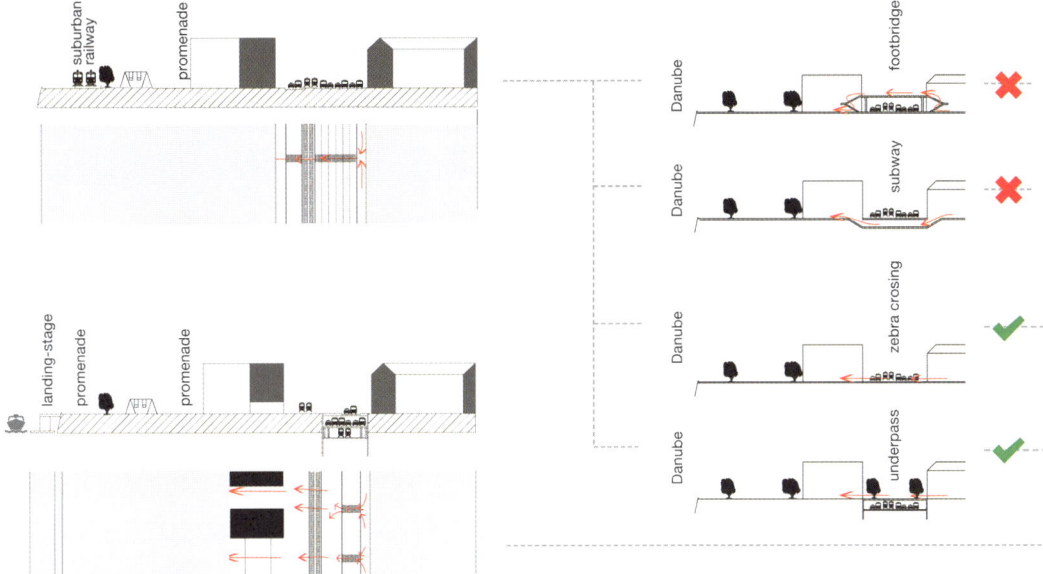

Development of the field

The suburban railway is the last memory in sight of the times of the goods station. The field has transformed around this linear infrastructure, and now its position is disturbing, cutting the Danube bank from the city.

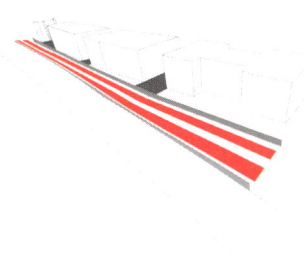

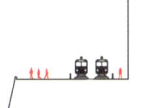

First step to do to help solving this problem is to pull down the fence and take the rails permeable. It could function like a tramway wih grassy railbeds. The walking passages and the rails can be connected in the same level.

The long time period plan is to move the suburban railway. This idea can be connected to the 5th metro concept, which will link the northern and the southern suburban railways. At the same time a decrease of the traffic on the Soroksári road can be achieved.

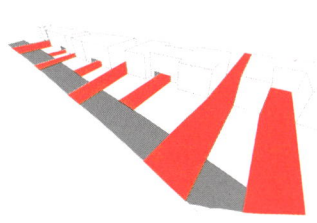

Today some international company headquarters - like Vodafone, Nestlé, Morgan-Stanley and K&H bank – seattled here. Because of the good situation of the land the number of the huge companies could increase, but there aren't enought place to build new buildings, but it could be possible to enlarge the available buildings.

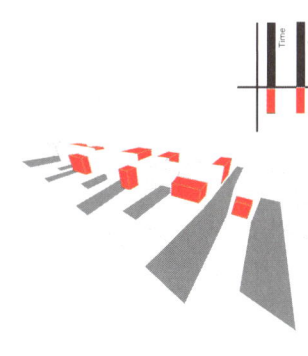

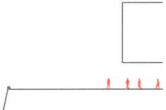

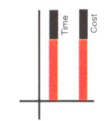

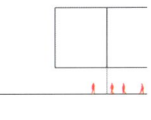

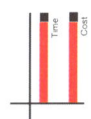

Models of "user-owner system"

light gray - hasn't got the right to use/go there

dark gray - has the right to use/go there

black - owner

Residental functions

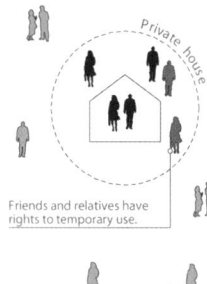

Private house

Friends and relatives have rights to temporary use.

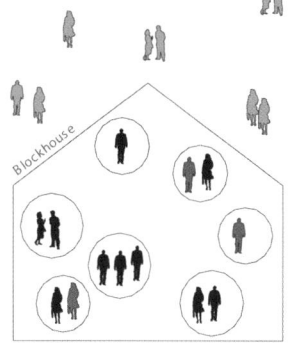

Blockhouse

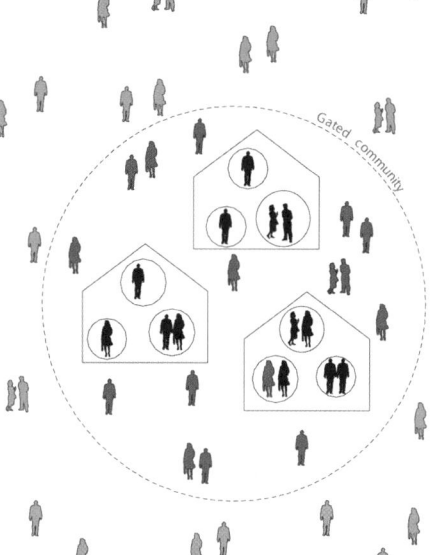

Gated community

Public functions

Shopping mall

The right to enter is depending on your dress and behaviour

Church

Hotel

Visitors buy owner-ship limited in time

Public spaces

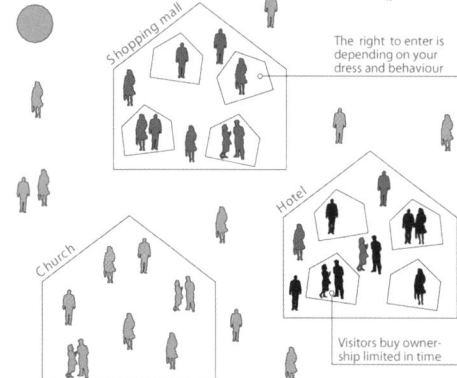

Street

Privatised, when...

demonstration
construction period
parade
coffee terrace
closed by the inhabitants
embassy

Square

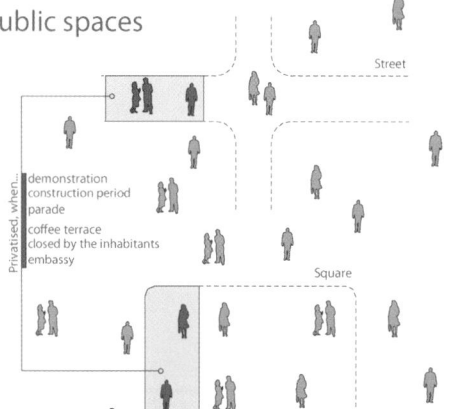

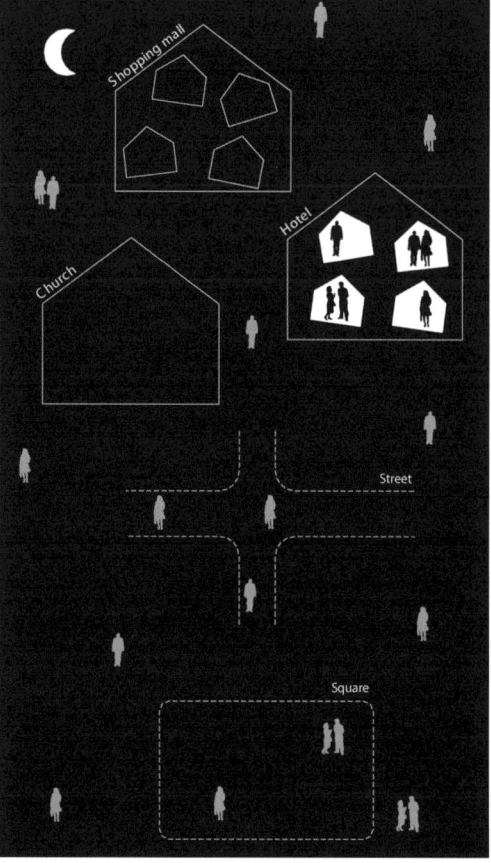

Shopping mall

Church

Hotel

Street

Square

Dividing methods

To indicate the behaviour of the three dividing method we've made a model of two different part of the common place:

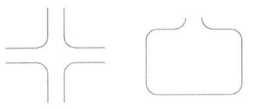

The street and the square.

The area

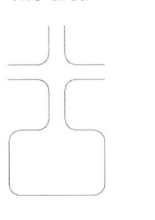

Dividing the area

Method 1:
Subdivision of common spaces to micro-ownership.

Method 2:
Using public spaces as private parcels - leaving the connections public.

Method 3:
Selling whole areas.

True models

We have chosen three different places in Budapest to try these methods.

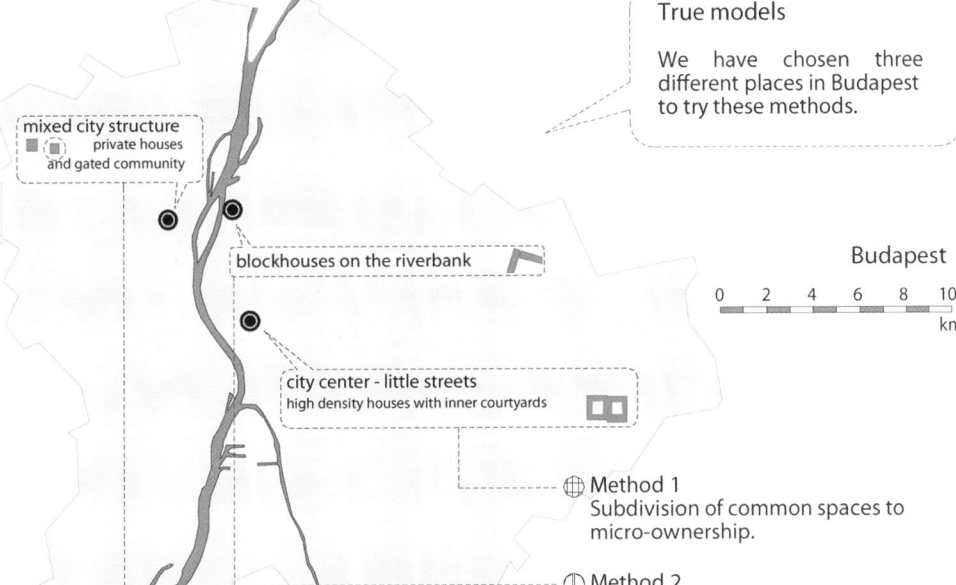

mixed city structure
private houses and gated community

blockhouses on the riverbank

city center - little streets
high density houses with inner courtyards

Budapest

0 2 4 6 8 10
km

Method 1
Subdivision of common spaces to micro-ownership.

Method 2
Using public spaces as private parcels - leaving the connections public.

Method 3
Selling whole areas

METHOD 1 - DIVIDING COMMON PLACES - LOTS OF OWNERS - MIKSZÁTH KÁLMÁN SQUARE

This area is in the very center of Budapest. Streets are narrow, houses are tall (about four floors). This area is good to indicate, what would happen, if we gave the common areas to the inhabitants, and they could do anything they want.

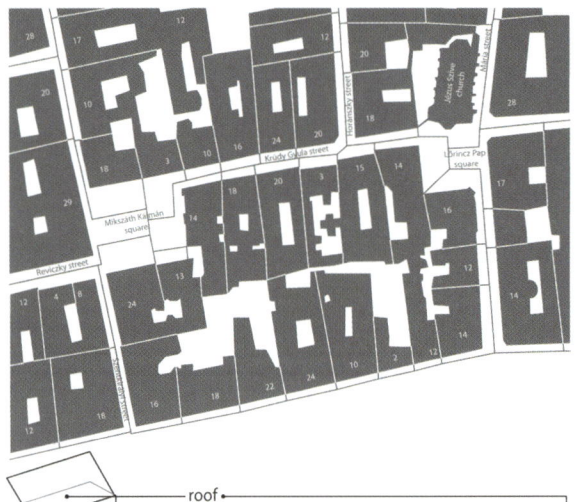
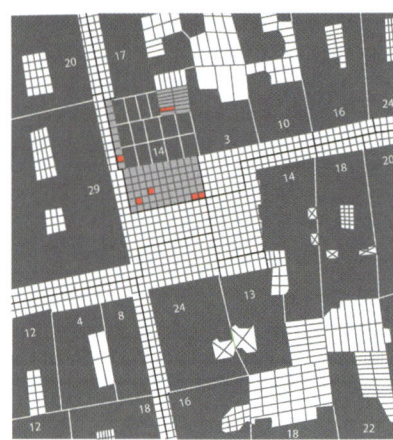

roof →
facade →
inner courtyard →
street →

→ divided by the number of the habitation
and each area will belong to an onwer

THE PROCESS

STEP 1 - everyboby has his own parcel
People doing their own

STEP 2 - collaborate
People get connected

STEP 3 - ask for help
People ask an architect

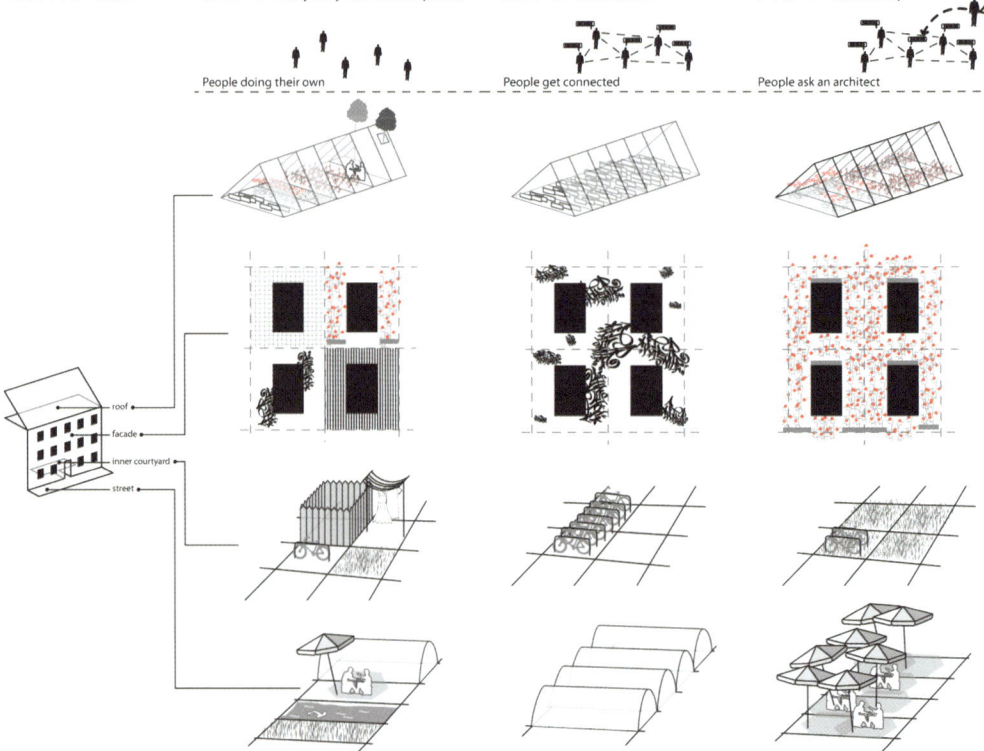

roof
facade
inner courtyard
street

Unusable spaces...

Usable, but ugly spaces...

Usable and well-designed spaces...

CONCLUSION:

BERLIN

BRATISLAVA

BUDAPEST

109

LJUBLJANA

PRAGUE

VIENNA

WARSAW

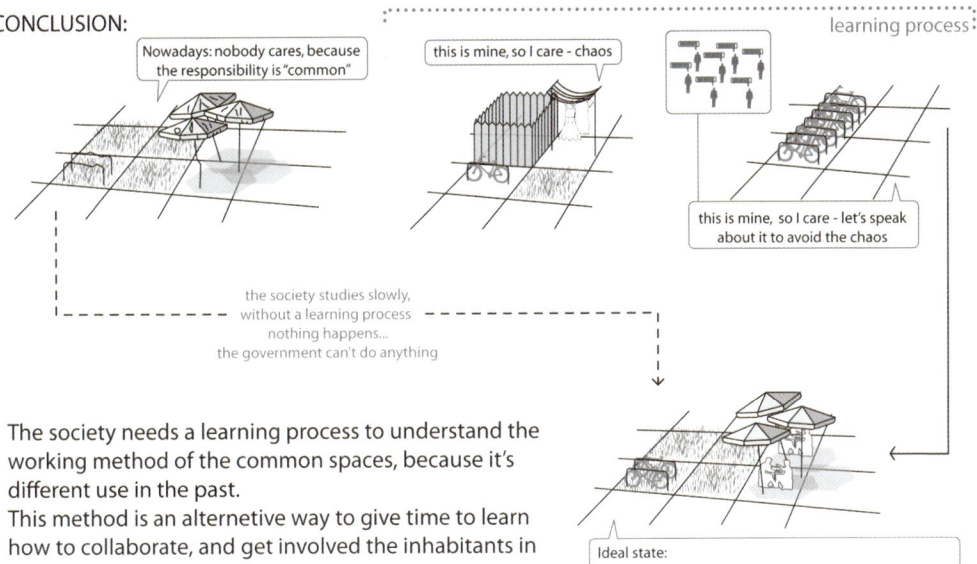

learning process

Nowadays: nobody cares, because the responsibility is "common"

this is mine, so I care - chaos

this is mine, so I care - let's speak about it to avoid the chaos

the society studies slowly, without a learning process nothing happens... the government can't do anything

The society needs a learning process to understand the working method of the common spaces, because it's different use in the past.
This method is an alternetive way to give time to learn how to collaborate, and get involved the inhabitants in the common aims.

Ideal state:
everybody cares, an expert helps to make good places

AT THE END:

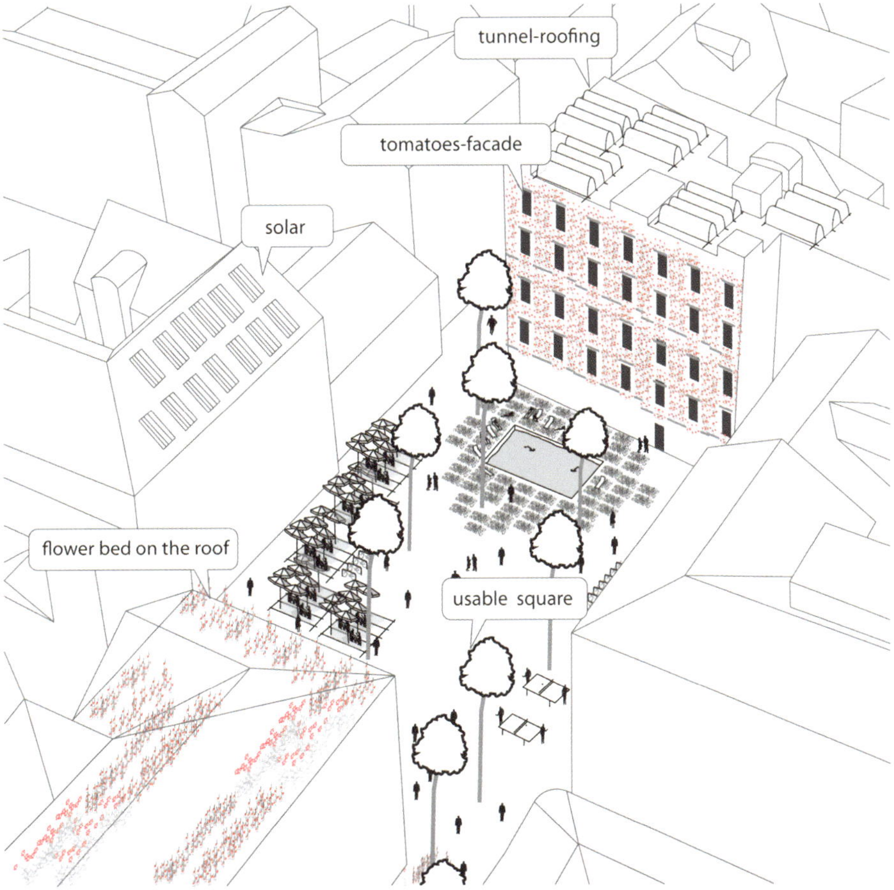

tunnel-roofing

tomatoes-facade

solar

flower bed on the roof

usable square

METHOD 2 - USING PUBLIC SPACES AS PRIVATE PARCELS - LEAVING THE CONNECTIONS PUBLIC - HOUSING ESTATE AT NÉPFÜRDŐ STREET

Present state

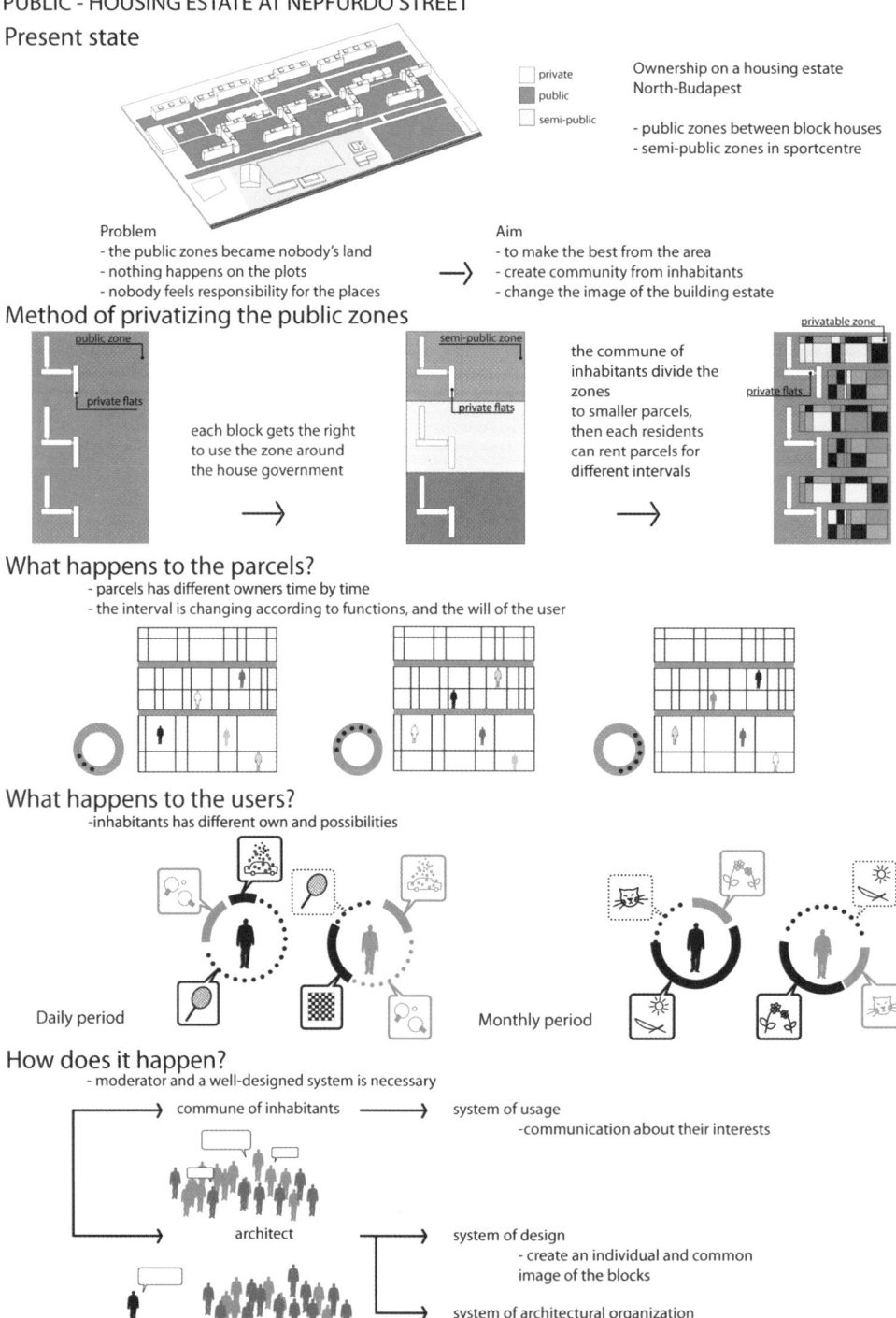

private
public
semi-public

Ownership on a housing estate
North-Budapest

- public zones between block houses
- semi-public zones in sportcentre

Problem
- the public zones became nobody's land
- nothing happens on the plots
- nobody feels responsibility for the places

$\longrightarrow$

Aim
- to make the best from the area
- create community from inhabitants
- change the image of the building estate

Method of privatizing the public zones

public zone

private flats

each block gets the right to use the zone around the house government

$\longrightarrow$

semi-public zone

private flats

the commune of inhabitants divide the zones to smaller parcels, then each residents can rent parcels for different intervals

$\longrightarrow$

privatable zone

private flats

What happens to the parcels?
- parcels has different owners time by time
- the interval is changing according to functions, and the will of the user

What happens to the users?
-inhabitants has different own and possibilities

Daily period

Monthly period

How does it happen?
- moderator and a well-designed system is necessary

commune of inhabitants $\longrightarrow$ system of usage
-communication about their interests

architect

system of design
- create an individual and common image of the blocks

system of architectural organization
- suitable place of functions
- usable spaces

BERLIN

BRATISLAVA

BUDAPEST

111

LJUBLJANA

PRAGUE

VIENNA

WARSAW

System of usage

- according to the present state (economical situation) the rate of different functions depend on actual claims
- the commune will find out, that from which function how many is necessary

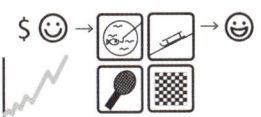

- in case of boom people have more time for entertainment

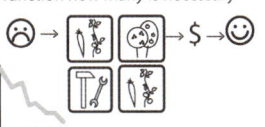

- in case of crisis people try to make money, more vegetable and fruit tree parcels are necessary, and they can't spend money on entertaining.

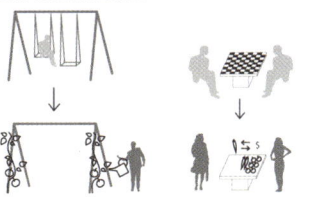

System of design

- different appearing on the housing estate: by the division of the blocks they get different identity, so one can easily find its home
  - by material: all the equipments you can rent has the same material
  - by colour: each stuff has similar colour
  - by structure
  - and so on

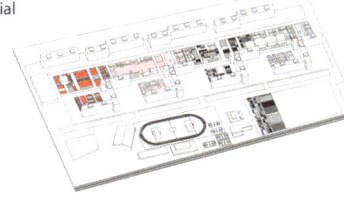

System of architectural organization

- place of functions must be a usable, smart system
  - functions disturbing each other should be placed to different sites

 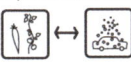 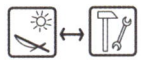

- functions which are similar, or having the same demands can be placed close to each other

need a sunny, clear plot

must be placed close to roads, result dirt and noise

sport facilities need a bigger area

need quiet place far from roads and noisy activities

-different motives and forms makes an attractive view between the boring blockhouses

close to the houses they can hang clothes, use the parcels as playgrounds, eye contact from the house is important

close to the houses and entrances there are the stations where they get the equipments, which have the same design (colours, materials)

close to the parking places there are the workshops, Where they can easily clean the cars or repair them

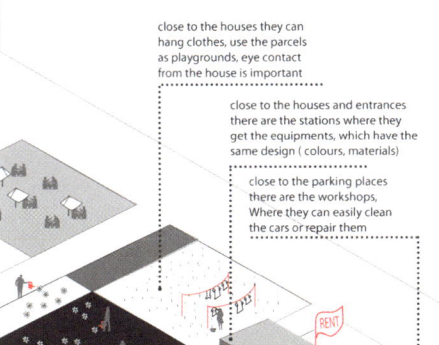

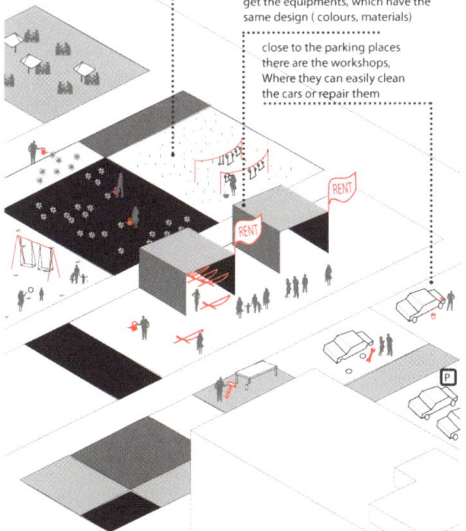

Conclusion

- expanded living space
- new possibilities for people
- useful plots
- colorful view and identity among block-houses
- communicate and react to the changing demands

Method 3 - Selling whole areas:

LaSiesta Residence and surroundings

La Siesta Residence is a newly built urban gated community in the "Buda hills". It was built up isolated from it's environment, surrounded by a high wall and guarded 24 hours/day. Surroundings are privatly owned familyhouses with small gardens.

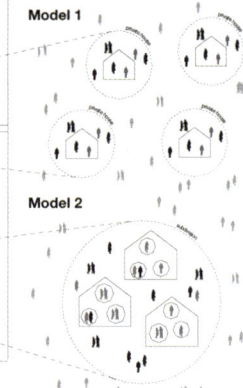

Model 1

Model 2

Problems

Model 1 - Privat houses

-residents need controlled zones, so they buid up high fences to save their goods

-gardens are to small to be widely usable

-unused gardens are often untidy

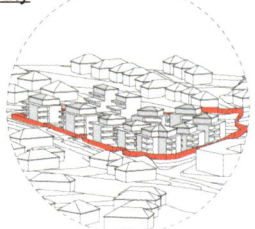

Model 2 - Gated community

-residents have a maintained, but unusable garden

-gated community was built up strongly isolated from it's surroundings

Process

1.
Residents get their street in case if they form a condominium. It means, that they can lock their street up, but they have to maintain all the place. Security and maintenance can be done even by a firm.

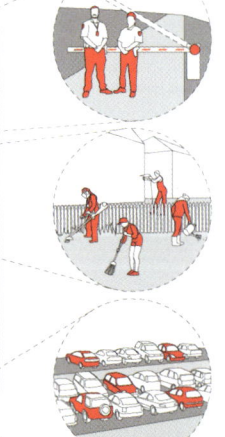

2.
Locked up area is now safe enough, so some functions can densify here, away from the houses, what makes the usage of the place more effective. Cars can park on just one plot next to the main entrance instead of parking in front of every house. There can be a bigger playground for children instead of single swings in every garden.

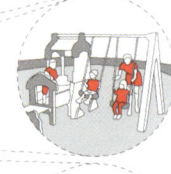

3.
When the housing community is strong enough, there's no need anymore to fence the house around. So there will be bigger free places, which are more suitables for bigger projects. Community is able to realize projects, what single families wouldn't. Just for example: they can build up their own sport centre or swimming pool, keep up a farm serving the community or invest for a mini-power station on renewable resources.

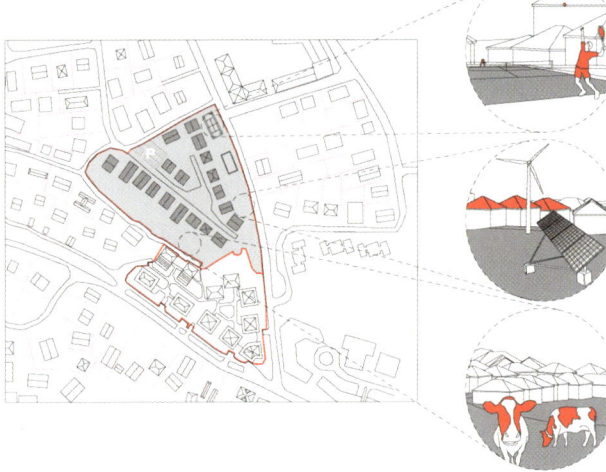

4.
And if they want, they can open their common functions for paying visitors. Those functions are practically approachable from the public zone. The income of these admissions develops the community.
Another way of making profit is to extend the houses with new storeys and new flats, and community with new members.

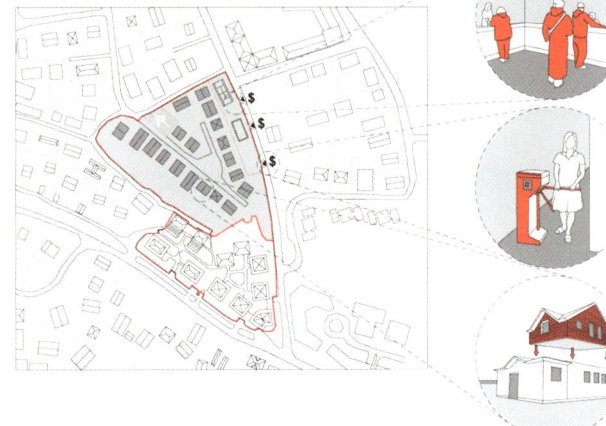

5.
Along the roads which are still public, paying services will densify. Public transport also uses these main roads. Residental and service functions will be layered, partly separated.
The income of services always develops the community where it takes place.
Isolated urban subdivision can also form it's own community-economy by opening services for paying visitors.

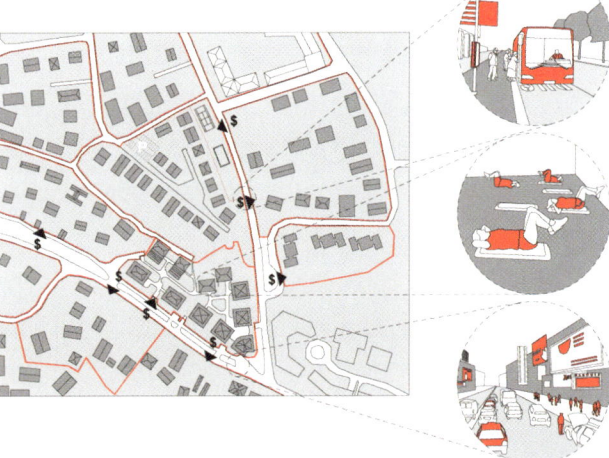

BERLIN

BRATISLAVA

BUDAPEST

113

LJUBLJANA

PRAGUE

VIENNA

WARSAW

LJUBLJANA
LIVING IN THE CITY

BERLIN

BRATISLAVA

BUDAPEST

115

LJUBLJANA

PRAGUE

VIENNA

WARSAW

Students: Andrej Blatnik | Matej Delak | Ajda Fortuna | Mojca Gabrič
Urban Jeriha | Teo Kajzer | Alenka Kramer | Nina Majoranc | Staš Mitrovič
Žiga Ravnikar | Sara Slivnik | Veronika Škof | Eva Taučar | Rok Velikonja
Vid Zabel | Klara Zalokar | Ivan Zuliani | Klemen Zupančič

Tutors: Maruša Zorec | Uroš Rustja

LIVING IN THE CITY

UROŠ RUSTJA

—

Before we consider the period of the last twenty years and focus our attention on the changes which have taken place in this period in Ljubljana, we need to be aware of the specifics of this space in comparison with other central European metropolitan cities. This concerns a peripheral space away from the European centres of power which, however, due to the meeting of cultures, is a space for communication where influences accumulate and form various syntheses. In reality this concerns a city where the Romanic and Germanic culture of Rome, Venice and Vienna intertwines with the Slavonic web of the Orient and Byzantium. Here the outer world opens up to Europe, through the Balkans which as a consequence of its ethnic and religious diversity in a geographically unified space experienced a traumatised end to the 20th century. Europe has a bad conscience because this space had become a symbol of instability and ignorance of the basic civilisation and ethical principles. But Europe is simultaneously aware that the road to its collective maturity passes only through the Balkans. The breakup of the Socialist Federal Republic of Yugoslavia in 1991 was accompanied by changes in the social, political and economic system together with the establishment of independent national states. Ljubljana became the capital city of an independent Slovenia initiating the transformation to a democratic society with a market economy. Besides transformation, the last twenty years were also a period of great technological advance resulting in intensive cultural and civilisation transformation of the way of life, communication, perception of individuality, time and space as well as the way of forming the city and space in a broader sense. In a series of discussions which took place at the Faculty of Architecture in Ljubljana we attempted to define the problems of the current development of Ljubljana and react to them by own examples. We were interested in which changes are part of those which most distinctly

CAPITAL RUNS URBANISM

PUBLIC SPACE
where is public space?

PUBLIC PROGRAMS
where is it?
who takes care of it?

CONSUMPTION
where? what? how much?

Eight key problems

influenced the develoment of
Ljubljana in the last two decades,
how we can react to these changes,
influence and change them so that
living in a central European country
of the 21st century would stand
for quality. **EIGHT KEY PROBLEMS**
were found to which we attempted to
respond by our projects. But
the starting-points of the projects
were not the city avenues, the grey
zone or a school building in
a certain place, the starting-point
for our projects were selected
RESIDENTS of Ljubljana, our target
groups, their particularities and
needs. We held conversations and
interviews with the residents, we
also made a film and based on these
studies we designed a programme for
which we found an appropriate place
in the city. With our children,
artists, senior citizens, Muslims,
students, residents of neglected
city quarters, climbers, young
families, jazzmen, actors... we wish
to show that the city is not only a
space for tourists, capital, shops,
schools and entrepreneurs, and that
the architecture does not follow
just space and a programme, but in
the first place above all people
which inhabit or cohabit the space…

TWENTY YEARS LATER

–

The changes in the political and
economic system in the early 1990s
are the consequence of a bitter
end to the economic and social
experiments of the 20th century
which were to alter reality. Alain
Badiou speaks about the passion
of the 20th century which was not
imaginary or ideological, but
a passion leading to reality. He
describes the century as a time of
deeds and decisions arising from
the conviction that it is possible
to undertake everything immediately,
here and now (Badiou, 2005).
The start of the century is marked
by a futuristic manifesto requiring
changes in society and man aiming to
create a new man for new times and
new architecture for the new man.
Gerard Wajcman chooses ruins as
the object of the 20th century
(Wajcman, 2007). If ruins are
the object of the 20th century as
a product of radical changes of
the old which is giving way to
the new, as a consequence of world
wars which futurists declare as
the sole true cleansing of
the world, then ruins also mean
the end of this period, as in case

BERLIN

BRATISLAVA

BUDAPEST

117

LJUBLJANA

PRAGUE

VIENNA

WARSAW

UNIVERSITY TOWN
living, studying

TRAFFIC
how to improve public transport?

HOUSING
lower rents?!

IDENTITY
who am I?
where do I live?

of the Berlin Wall they accompany
the opening up to the free world
- West Berlin, which was
paradoxically surrounded by a wall
like an island of free territory
- in East Germany. This act ended
the non-critical self-awareness
of the changes in man and society
which carried out its attempt at
implementation in
the cases of the socialist states of
East and Central Europe.

The specific nature of Slovenian
architectural development in
the socialist society after
the Second World War was a gradual
transition from restoration
which arose from quantity and
standardisation to the development
of a quality housing environment
based on models of the Sandinavian
countries. The individual needs of
the individual, his connection
with public space and relationship
towards nature are becoming
important. During this the key role
was played by the approach of
the architect and awareness of
personal responsibility for
a quality housing environment which
was becoming an unquestionable

ethic approach among many Slovenian
architects of this period such as
Edvard Ravnikar, Oton Jugovec, Marta
and France Ivanšek.

The subsequent transformation led to
the appropriation of state property
and re-distribution of social and
economic forces. In architecture
we noticed the search for personal
identity and expressions which
altered the specialised approach
of the architect into a persuasive
approach and his responsibility for
the quality of housing into
an egocentric need to boast of
personal author projects in space.
The decade in which we live was
immediately at the start marked by
the terrorist attack on the WTC
towers in New York and continues
with an ecological and economic
crisis. We are afraid of
the unknown enemy, bad conscience
due to personal ecological sins and
simultaneously anger due to foreign
economic experiments.

Dilemmas are opening up about
the development of the city in
a liberal market economy which is
marked by a combination of weak

Target groups of residents

mechanisms of public control, aggressive investors and undefined approaches of the field to key issues. Fatalists characterise this as the field fighting to control the uncontrollable and attempts to define what in the very principle is impossible to define. They declare the end of the public space and the end to urbanism. On the other hand, we find the pluralists who believe that urbanism should not determine, but enable, form should be generated and not formed; the author should not be a person who defines an object and interdiscipline should be what determines the process of definition. Various expert opinions occasionally agree when in accordance with their own interests and needs they support urbanism as dictated by ambitious political or economic powers.

However, individual alternatives to specialised impotence are emerging from spontaneous urban events which in past years - in fear of quality public and housing space have managed to temporarily intervene. A group of young architects called "Temp" drew attention in 2006 to the potential of the empty degraded spaces in Ljubljana and managed to renovate the abandoned wheel factory "Rog" (http://tovarna.org/) which, since this time, has been active as a cultural centre and in future it is planned that, according to the project chosen on the basis of a public tender, it will be transformed into a centre of contemporary art. Since 2004 a group of young architects called "Prostorož" (http://prostoroz.org/) has been working to transform atriums, parks, the embankments of the Ljubljanica River, children's playgrounds and streets thereby supporting the use of degraded public spaces and is revealing their hidden potential.

The change in present circumstances and creation of a new, better living environment and public space in the city is obviously possible only in connection with an involved and critical view of reality and with thinking exceeding the present. The new situation can be gradually

BERLIN

BRATISLAVA

BUDAPEST

119

LJUBLJANA

PRAGUE

VIENNA

WARSAW

DANCERS
dance center?

CLIMBERS, SKATERS, BIKERS
urban sport center?

UNACKNOWLEDGED ARTISTS
studios?

YUNG ARTISTS
creativity center?

USERS OF NEW TECHNOLOGIES
mediateque?

ALTERNATIVE CULTURE
library on Metelkova?

built with the aid of exhibitions, publications, forums, debates, theoretical theses, new projects and obviously new architectures, too. But the key remains in understanding the new and the criteria for the new. Petra Čeferin, slovenian architectural critic mentions the recently very popular and marginally problematical pose describing it as "imperative of the new" (Čeferin, 2008). The pose, which is defended by many prominent architects and architectural schools, considers the invention of a new architecture as a driving force which does not, however, think of something radically new which is totally unknown within the existing organisation of the world and at this moment cannot be demonstrated or described, but as something new which is most fascinating of all that is fascinating, the most audacious out of all that is audacious and entirely different from everything that is planned and built. The star imperative of the new does not, therefore, interfere in the existing criterion, but it takes the existing situation as a new criterion. The new is simply reduced to the existing variant and thereby closes the way so we cannot think at all about what the existing situation changes.

We can comprehend architecture as a mere moulding of functionally and programme elaborated buildings which, in accordance with the urbanist definition, are located at the planned site. The view bridging such an assumption has, in our projects for Ljubljana, opened opportunities for creating architectural projects which do not satisfy only the momentary functional needs of the users, but are able to strengthen the existing

and create a new unanticipated use of space and search for the potential of some place or group of users. The users will begin to understand the city in a similar way, not as a space of usurpation or the satisfaction of immediate needs, but as an endless range of possibilities of the use of public space, spending leisure time, recreation…, in short, own implementation in the best sense of the word. We could paraphrase our relationship towards the creation of the new with the words of slovenian philosopher Slavoj Žižek, who describes film as art which does not merely satisfy your wishes, but also teaches you to wish (Žižek, 2006). So let architecture also be such - let it not just satisfy the user's immediate wishes, but let it awaken in the user the wish for quality housing and public space.

However, it must be acknowledged that it is not possible to define in advance and clearly in what way this can be achieved. But the lack of reliable and useful definitions is what makes architecture an adventure of recurring existing situations. Dušan Pirjevec, slovenian philosopher, says that there is no reliable definition for man, because if there were, it would mean the end of man. For him man is an adventure, together with responsibility and mystery, because the meaning of human unrepeatable life is not defined in advance exactly once and for all. Architecture may not form or define space, but if it does define it, it builds boundaries (finis) and thereby takes away freedom and scope from man. Hence, architectural work should open space and the risks and temptation accompanying such a deed are possible only if they are always present and responsibility to freedom and scope (Pirjevec, 1976). We understood the architect's responsibility concerning space and man in our projects as the opening of space to target groups which we believe were overlooked in the last two decades. At the time of liberal capitalism we took responsibility for emptiness, for silence, for the view, idea, wish, memory, touch, step, child's curiosity and the peace of the elderly person, we took responsibility for the housing in the city...

DEVELOPMENT OF LJUBLJANA

—
To find the current problems and to understand them, we firstly examined the development of the city and mutual influences of the various periods. As has already been said, the origin of Ljubljana is characterised by the pass to the Mediterranean see through the "Ljubljana Gateway", which consists of the hills Grajski grič and Šišenski hrib. This passageway on the borderline of the Adriatic and Black Sea basin can also be found in the legend about the Greek Argonauts who were to carry their ship through Ljubljana from the Sava River to the Adriatic Sea. The first settlement of the territory of the Ljublanjsko barje dates back to prehistoric times and with the arrival of the Romans a Roman castrum called Emona was established on the left bank of the Ljubljanica River. A 430x540 m rectangle with the main streets of cardo and decumanus and the forum on their crossroads

having an important influence also on the development of medieval Ljubljana which, with its western fortification was supported by the remains of the ruins of Emona. Today we can find the biggest presentation of the remnants in Plečnik's layout of the southern Roman wall where he created an interesting urban and surrounding landscape composition. The later medieval and Baroque Ljubljana emerged as a triple town with three main marketplaces on the slopes of Grajski grič (Castle Hill). In the late 18th century the Ljubljanica River was regulated and is today still one of the most important pillars of city life and with the drying out of the marshland of the Ljubljansko barje it was possible to continue extending and developing the city. The city experienced greater changes at the time of the construction of the railway which in 1849 linked Vienna with Trieste, the then Austrian window to the world. The railway determined the northern boundary of the city, reinforced its temporary meaning and enabled industrialisation to flourish. Many factory complexes of the tobacco and food industry emerged on the outskirts of the then Ljubljana which after the transforming restructuring economy have remained empty and degraded zones on the outskirts of today's city centre. In recent years the city finally realised the importance of these empty industrial areas for the further development of the centre of Ljubljana and with public tenders for the transformation of the tobacco factory -"Tobačna tovarna", factories "Rog", "Kolinska" and "Cukrarna" they gradually became part of the fabric of the city.

BERLIN

BRATISLAVA

BUDAPEST

121

LJUBLJANA

PRAGUE

VIENNA

WARSAW

After the Second World War
the introduction of a planned
economy and mass industrialisation
resulted in the migration of a large
section of the rural population to
Ljubljana as well as of citizens
from other republics of the then
joint state of Yugoslavia.
The population doubled and bigger
housing estates were built on
the outskirts of the city which made
deeper incursions into
of the tobacco and food industry
emerged on the outskirts of
the then Ljubljana which after
the transforming restructuring
economy have remained empty and
degraded zones on the outskirts
of today's city centre. In recent
years the city finally realised the
importance of these empty industrial
areas for the further development
of the centre of Ljubljana and with
public tenders for
the transformation of the tobacco
factory -"Tobačna tovarna",
factories "Rog", "Kolinska" and
"Cukrarna" they gradually became
part of the fabric of the city.
After the Second World War
the introduction of a planned
economy and mass industrialisation
resulted in the migration of a large
section of the rural population to
Ljubljana as well as of citizens
from other republics of the then
joint state of Yugoslavia.
The population doubled and bigger
housing estates were built on
the outskirts of the city which made
deeper incursions into the idyllic
village backdrop of the city and
village centres were transformed
into anonymous parts of
the heterogeneous urban fabric.

With the establishment of
the independent state of Slovenia in
1991, Ljubljana became its capital

city; however it did not manage to
mould its new political, cultural
and symbolic role into
an appropriate representative public
space. The transformation into
a market liberal economic system
turned private investors and **CAPITAL**
into relevant partners during
decision-making about interventions
into the space. The key contents
for the quality of urban life,
such as **PUBLIC SPACE** and **PUBLIC
PROGRAMMES**, had simply to make way
to commercially more profitable
contents on the cruel market
of financial competitiveness.
CONSUMPTION, which dictated
the construction of bigger business
centres on the outskirts of
the city, emptied the life of
the centre, which became
a **UNIVERSITY CENTRE** designed only
for students, state officials and
tourists. The construction of
the Slovenian motorway crossroads
transformed the small state of two
million people into a big city, but
also reduced the public space to
roads and car parks, the horizon of
the world was limited to the frame
of car windows. The broader central
Slovenian region began to gravitate
daily to the city and thereby
brought an extraordinary increase in
city **TRAFFIC**. A chaotic urbanisation
of industrial and technical zones
and overpriced **HOUSING ESTATES**
of uncertain quality began to be
concentrated along the transport
belts. After all this we can ask
what de facto is today's Ljubljana?
What is its **IDENTITY?** What sort of
Ljubljana do we see in the next
twenty years? What is the potential
of the city which can be developed
in the future?

BERLIN

BRATISLAVA

BUDAPEST

123

LJUBLJANA

PRAGUE

VIENNA

WARSAW

CAPITAL REGULATES URBANISM

Unlike most other former socialist countries during the transfer of ownership of the Slovenian economy, only a small part of state enterprise had been transferred to this period to the hands of foreign owners. Fragmented ownership with a small amount of various, often also contrasting interests, appeared with denationalisation and privatisation in space. After the economic boom at the turn of the millennium, investment ventures showed considerable interest in investments into real estate and the urbanist field by its restrictions could not or did not want to follow. Investors used the lack of spatial regulation and presented their own vision of the development of Ljubljana which arose from the constantly greater commercial effect of investments. But public space and public programmes can not follow commercial logic and because nobody appeared who could represent public interest, the vision of investors gradually began to be implemented.

Besides the stadium in the city district of Bežigrad, the new passenger terminal and the residential villa Grad is a typical example of such action also the Ljubljana Kolizej, a building which lies on an important site in the very centre of the city and is protected as a monument of local significance. Despite all the clear legal obligations, the new owner did not wish to renovate the building, but allowed it to become dilapidated for so long until the relevant services would state that its renovation was no longer possible. The investor then gained permission to demolish the building and drew up an international invited competition for a new business-residential complex. The winning design, due to the oversized programme, proposed a uniform bottom part of the building with a cluster of three high-rise buildings which exceeded all urbanist norms. It disturbed the view of the castle and broke the proportion to the surrounding buildings and nearby Evangelical church. Part of the professional and other public welcomed the building with elation and registered in it many merits or even the start of the new European Ljubljana. The attempt at changes for the better may be praiseworthy, but if it is carried out at all cost it offers fertile ground for an increase in populist rhetoric which will

What determines life in the city of Ljubljana as special, pleasant and of quality?

A MAN WITH A PLAN

and a clear visions
so people listen to him.

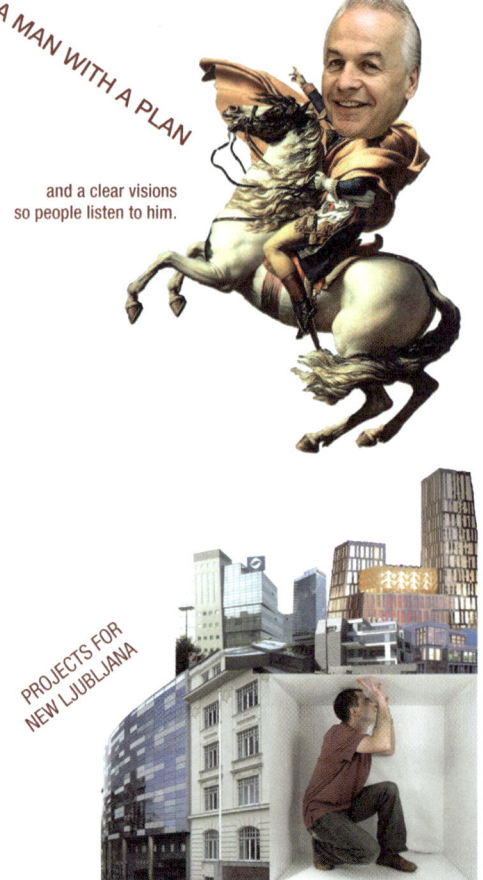

PROJECTS FOR
NEW LJUBLJANA

skilfully cover the fact that the emperor is actually naked. An example is the clear warning that when planning the space, we may not forget to respect legal norms which ensure respect of legal interest as their inadvertent lack of respect is more the qualities of a state without a legal order than the qualities of central European metropolitan cities.

At first sight it would appear that buildings such as the new Kolizej are returning life to the city centre however we soon discover that they are actually closing against the city and against public space, removing people's freedom and the city's urbanity. What determines life in the city of Ljubljana as special, pleasant and of quality? Is it not gatherings, entertainment, events, culture, games, sport, laughter…? In one word people. So the key questions are those which ask about the needs of the residents of Ljubljana, about their wishes and also where beneath the surface of monotony lies hidden the unexpected potential use of space. We looked for our users among the groups which usually tend to be overlooked in a period of liberal capitalism during interventions into space. We found them in various age categories (children require a day centre with workshops, students community life, young families apartments with common areas, older people a day centre), among various subcultures (artists require studios, young fine artists want a creativity centre, technology enthusiasts a media library, alternative culture lacks a library), among the various sport groups (dancers have no dance centre, climbers, skaters and cyclists require an urban sports centre), among the various religious groups (Muslims require an Islamic cultural centre) and the neglected suburban districts (residents of the city district of Spodnja Šiška have no community centre).

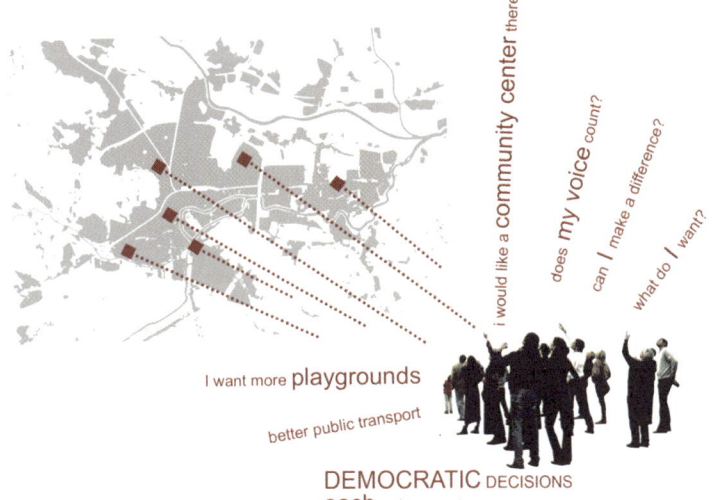

Interventions in the public space - group "Prostorož", 2009

PROJECTS

1   Day-time centre
2   Apartments for student families Housing
3   Housing
4   Housing
5   Mostovna art Centre
6   Creativity Centre
7   Open source centre Trnovo
8   Experimental theater, library Metelkova
9   Dance centre Prule
10 Urban sports Centre
11 Islamic cultural Centre
12 Šiška community centre
13 Šumi
14 Urban dens in Soteska
15 NUK II

BERLIN

BRATISLAVA

BUDAPEST

LJUBLJANA

PRAGUE

VIENNA

WARSAW

PUBLIC SPACE

What is particular about Ljubljana is its quality public spaces and proximity to green spaces. Forest and park land stretch over the hills of Grajski gric and Šišenski hrib – two extensive green areas which defined the establishment of the city in the strait between each other up to the narrowest centre of Ljubljana. Before 1991 the urbanistic plans which were drafted in 1966 and 1986 suggested a design of city branches with a concentration of built-up spaces along roadways and intermediate green wedges which would reach as far as the centre. In 1985 on the occasion of the fortieth anniversary of the end of the Second World War the Road of Remembrance and Friendship took place following the route of the barbed wire which confined occupied Ljubljana. This is an extensive landscape composition of roads, avenues, recreation and sitting area which enclose the rim around the city and offer quality public space to the residents.

Most of the important public spaces in the centre of Ljubljana have been imprinted by the seal of architect Jože Plecnik. Besides the triple bridge Tromostovje, the bridge Šuštarski most and Tržnice, he also designed the layout of the Ljubljanice River embankment which are the busiest sites of public life. But today most of the public space is occupied by parking spaces as well as the square Trg republike, a symbolic centre of Slovenian statehood and the parliament. The green wedges are being built up, and the green spaces are becoming abandoned degraded notorious spaces. The park and public spaces on the housing estates of the 1960s and 1970s are being built up by new buildings or garage houses. The urban fabric is becoming concentrated and the quality of housing is falling.

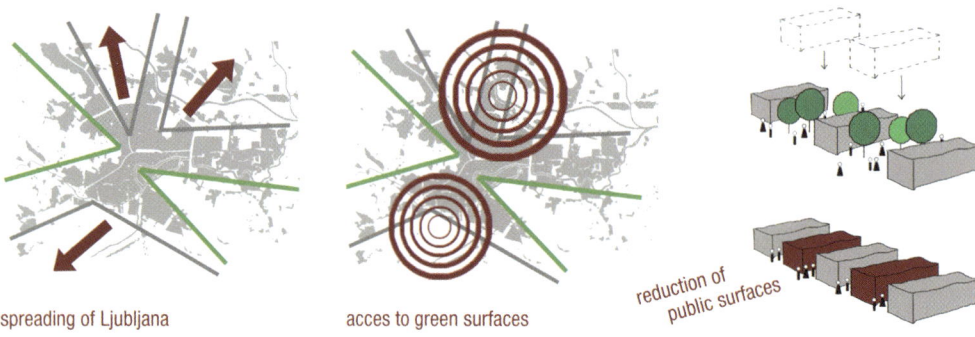

spreading of Ljubljana

acces to green surfaces

reduction of public surfaces

Mr. Darko, an engineer at the factory Litostroj, lives with his ten-year-old son, Miha, in the north-western part of Ljubljana. The housing estate has no quality outdoor playing areas because most of the residents rely on car transport. At the weekend they usually stay in the countryside at the farm of Darko's parents. The green wedges should be protected against being built up because these allow each resident to reach a public green area within five minutes. The broader area of the Islamic culture centre is dealing with the contact of the urban fabric with the green belt and its passage so that Mr. Darko and Miha can ride through the green area on a bike right to the city centre.

Parking in front of the Parlament building on Trg Republike

Parking on Novi trg in old city

ISLAMIC COMMUNITY
islamic cultural centre?

ISLAMIC CULTURAL CENTRE IN THE GREEN WEDGE | *The basic idea of urbanism lies in revitalising the five green wedges of Ljubljana. The green composition continues with Rožnik Hill, carries on under the railway and is caught between Parmova Street and the tracks continuing north. The railway remains at ground level and simultaneously acts as a barrier against the expansion of the city because it leaves the belt between the city districts of Bežigrad and Šiška open and fluid. The urbanist starting-points plan new housing, a spine along Parmova Street. In part J there is the business programme which turns into a housing part in the north. Three dominant features appear in the green belt: the Islamic cultural centre, the existing Railway Museum and a building with an expected cultural content. A road cuts into the green belt which will allow access for pedestrians and cyclists.*

The proposal of the Islamic cultural centre contains a wall structure which creates various ambiences by its layout. Light is the basic element; the space adds character and water is also important. The newly planned vegetation with which the constructed fabric grows together presents itself as the quality of the place. The dominant feature is the mošeja, which is surrounded by a low wall structure. There is an inner courtyard which communicates with the green belt. More private programmes demonstrate interconnection (apartments, medresa, hamam…). On the other side the building shows it back to the road for pedestrians to which the public programme links up (library, museum, restaurant,…).

groundfloor plan

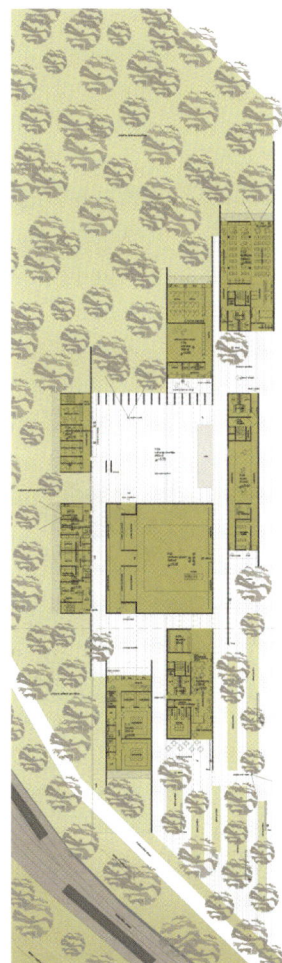

urban situation

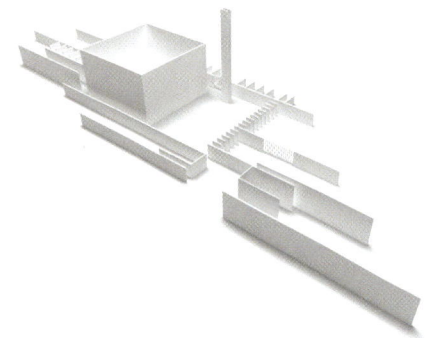

view of the atrium

conceptual model

PUBLIC CONTENTS

Local quarters such as Šiška, Bežigrad, Trnovo, Vic, Moste and Šentvid were still separate village communities with a church, rural centre, pub and marketplace at the start of the last century. Before 1991 these centres still offered residents the necessary public facilities, but after the transformation the local centres became desolate because they could no longer compete with the city centre or the new shopping centres. Today the bigger cultural institutions such as the Ljubljana Drama, Opera and Ballet, the Philharmonic, Ljubljana Festival and Cankarjev Dom with a cultural programme are mostly concentrated in the city centre. They receive far greater state grants for their activities, but their repertoire attracts only a narrow circle of city dwellers. Meanwhile there is a livelier life on the city's outskirts of alternative and non-commercial culture, music, dance and art centres such as "KUD France Prešeren", "Stara elektrarna" (Old Power Plant), Urban Cultural Centre "Kino Šiška" (Šiška Cinema), "Tovarna Rog" (Rog Factory) and "Metelkova" which just about survive from year to year on low grants.

Student Matej from the centre of Ljubljana, an avid urban cyclist, lacks a polygon for exercising, because he now has to travel elsewhere. The proximity of cycling paths, pedestrian walks and efficient public transport should be secured for housing estates outside the city centre. Local centres should also be promoted because the concentration of public and cultural facilities in the city centre is inadequate because it does not allow intensive human contact and the identification with the centre of its narrower living space. The Urban Sports Centre in the city district of Bežigrad is developing a new typology for this unusual public programme which will also be used by urban cyclist Matej.

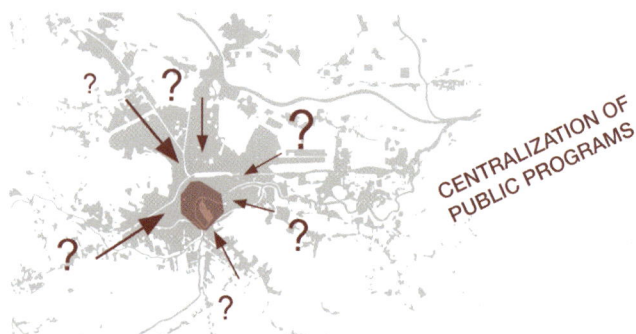

CENTRALIZATION OF PUBLIC PROGRAMS

Local centres offer residents the public facilities

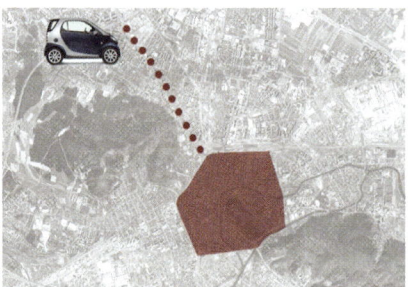

Map of public programs in Ljubljana

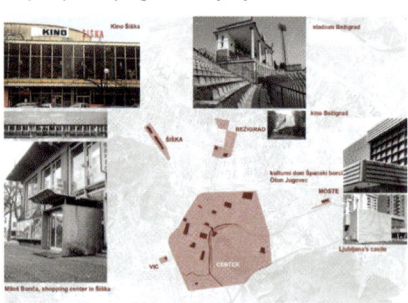

THE URBAN SPORTS CENTRE | *I chose climbers, skaters and bmxes as the target group. This group does not have a space in Ljubljana and members of these groups feel degraded by the surroundings they live in. In a survey I focused on the target group to discover what this group of people needs and what they wish for. The place which turned out to be adequate according to the survey was the area between the streets Dunajska, Hranilniškau and Bežigrad. This is land where the teaching workshops of architect Savin Sever used to stand. My target group extended to include the surrounding residents. By analysing the territory I discovered that there was no adequate green space in the surroundings where the residents could go for some quiet. This is how I arrived at the task for securing adequate space for climbers, skaters, bmxers and sufficiently large green space which could function as a park and continue on from the legacy of Savin Sever.*

CLIMBER, SKATERS, BIKERS
urban sports centre?

1st floor

section through the climbing hall

conceptual model

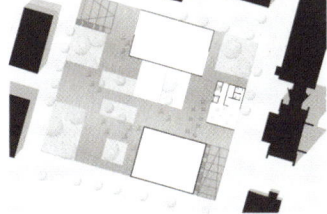

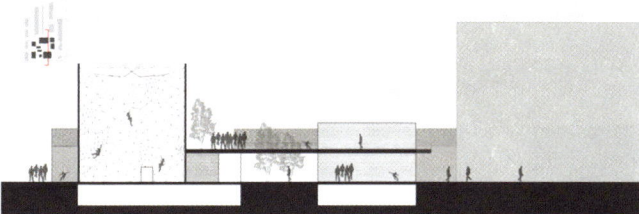

groundfloor plan

view of the public roof

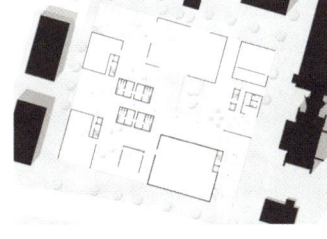

view to the Urban sports centre from the Slovenska street

CONSUMPTION

New centres and commercial facilities began to appear in the last twenty years on the city outskirts which were defined by the new construction of the motorway ring road. Before 1991 most Slovenes did their bigger shopping for food, clothing and technology in Italy and Austria, while today a considerable number of people living in central Slovenia go to the new Ljubljana shopping centres. In 1954 public warehouses were built in the north-eastern part of Ljubljana for the needs of the biggest centre of goods and transport in Yugoslavia. After 1990 the BTC goods-retail centre emerged spontaneously in the abandoned public warehouses which, after 2000, with the arrival of foreign retail chains and adequate public programmes, a cinema, entertainment and swimming pool centre, became a counterpart to the formal centre of Ljubljana. Today the BTC centre is being extended to include a children's playground, bars and restaurants, marketplace, sports buildings, high-rise business building and a hotel. As regard the size, it has become comparable with the centre of Ljubljana being only 3 km away, but due to the immediate proximity of the motorway ring road its transport link is incomparably better adapted to car traffic. The main shopping boulevard in hall A measures 350 m and contains 180 shops, unlike the street "Mestni trg" in the centre of the old district of Ljubljana which measures 370 m and contains 50 shops.

Commercial zones in Ljubljana today

Consumption in Slovenija before 1991

The young family of Tomaž and Tina with children Ana and Jaka live in the Šiška city district, but like best of all to spend their free Saturdays in the shopping centre. The shopping continues with lunch in the self-service restaurant and seeing a 3D film in the cinema. In the local centres users should be allowed to spend quality leisure time. The Cultural Centre Spodnja Šiška is attempting to get young families to spend their leisure time in the puppet theatre and in the children's playground among those of the same age.

Comparison of the walking distance and area

Commercial zone BTC City emerged spontaneously in the abandoned public warehouses

main street of medieval Ljubljana
lenght - 370 m
50 shops

Hala A - first shopping center in BTC City
lenght - 350 m
180 shops

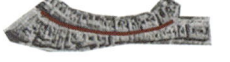

area of the city center

area of BTC City

3 km

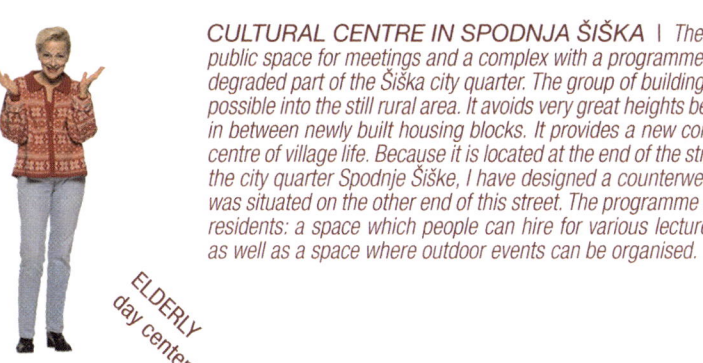

CULTURAL CENTRE IN SPODNJA ŠIŠKA | *The cultural centre is a quality open public space for meetings and a complex with a programme that brings public events to this degraded part of the Šiška city quarter. The group of buildings is built so blend in as much as possible into the still rural area. It avoids very great heights because at this time it is squeezed in between newly built housing blocks. It provides a new concept of a village nucleus as the centre of village life. Because it is located at the end of the street Medvedova, the main axis of the city quarter Spodnje Šiške, I have designed a counterweight to the former cinema which was situated on the other end of this street. The programme is a reaction to the wishes of the residents: a space which people can hire for various lectures, workshops, performances ... as well as a space where outdoor events can be organised.*

ELDERLY day center?

BERLIN

BRATISLAVA

BUDAPEST

133

LJUBLJANA

PRAGUE

VIENNA

WARSAW

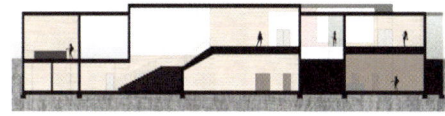

section through the entrance hall

section through the atrium

groundfloor plan

view to the atrium and exterior

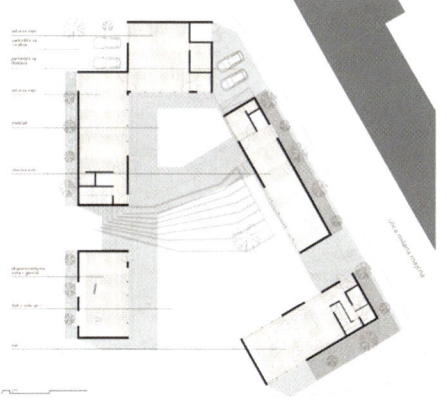

conceptual model

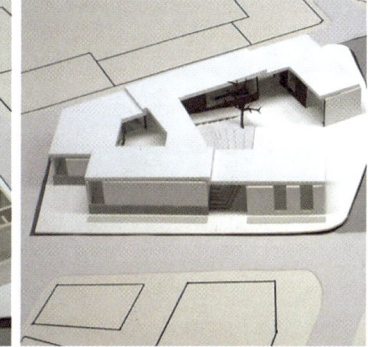

UNIVERSITY CENTRE

Ljubljana is typical of having most of the university faculties concentrated in the city centre and student life with many bars, restaurants, libraries and faculties, just as a concentration of scientific institutions which has a significant effect on the throb of city life. With the construction of new student residence halls and part of the Humanities Faculty outside the centre, as well as the foundation of the Mariborska and Primorska University, has reduced the concentration. Unfortunately, responsible officials did not know how or could not make use of the opportunities which with the extension of the university were offered, in the last twenty years, by the abandoned spaces of degraded industrial areas on the outskirts of the city centre such as the factories "Rog" and "Tabacna tovarna", which today are receiving other more commercially-orientated facilities.

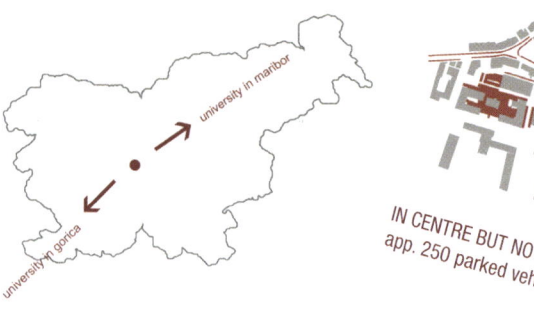

IN CENTRE BUT NO PUBLIC SPACE!
app. 250 parked vehicles on public space

Decentralization in 1975

Project for location of the former Tobacna factory

Possible concentration of new university programmes in abandoned industry heritage in the city centre

Hana, a law student, is studying in the centre near the Ljubljanica River, only a short distance from the city market. She goes to the many local cafes, restaurants and libraries. At the same time Ines is studying at the Economics Faculty in the city district of Bežigrad. The time which she could spend relaxing before lectures she spends nervously looking for a parking space instead. Darjan is studying at the Philosophical Faculty which is situated in several scattered building in the centre. They are limited by the considerable lack of space so they spend some lectures sitting on the floor. There is a lovely atrium with a park between the faculty buildings however it is difficult to get to because it is filled with parking cars. He wishes there were more activities and more space. A space needs to be found in the city centre to extend the faculties. The concentration of programmes, planning of public passageways and parkland which will link the faculty to the city can emphasise the needs of student life in the city.

Drinking coffee in the city centre | Enjoying the happenings   vs.   Eating in a lower quality cantina | How would you like to spend a break?

TRANSPORT

The Southern Railway which linked Vienna and Trieste turned Ljubljana into a transit point. Today, after the construction of the Slovene motorway crossroads the task of providing a link between Austria and Italy was shifted to passenger car transport which goes in the same direction and cuts through the second branch in Ljubljana which links Austria to Croatia. Besides better road links, which have been built in the last twenty years, the borders with Austria, Italy and Hungary have opened with Slovenia's accession to the European Union, and with the arrival of low-cost air carriers to the rest of Europe.

The motorway crossroads means that a considerable part of central Slovenia is gravitating to Ljubljana. Ljubljana has 265,000 permanent residents, 38,000 people commute to the city every week – mostly students and daily a further 157,000 who work here. Ljubljana's residents have 132,000 cars, while daily commuters bring in a further 113,000 vehicles. If we convert this figure to space, we can see that commuter's cars occupy 1.42 km^2 of the city every day. This means that the same large space as the city's nucleus moves to and from Ljubljana every day.

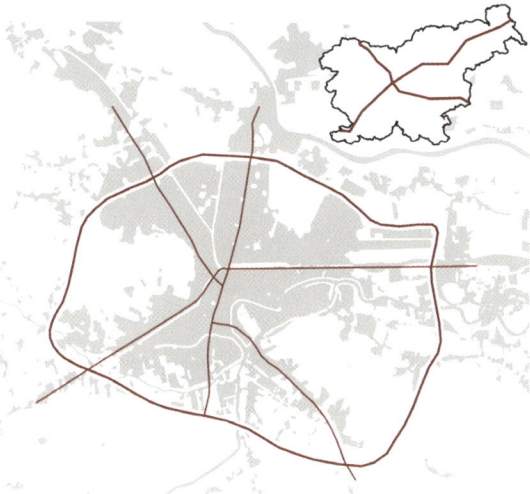

Crossing of the traffic corridors from Balkans to the Europe

Low-cost air cariers

Daily inflow of the cars doubles the amount of them in the city

Parking places in the city center

It would be possible to resolve the parking problem by public transport, but because there are no circular bus lines, Mrs. Danica must change buses twice from the city district of Dravlje on her journey to the city district of Bežigrad which takes her 50 minutes, although the distance to her destination is only 2 km. Should the weather so allow, she uses her bike. A tram and another efficient means of public transport need to be built. This does not just apply to Ljubljana, but to the entire suburban area. According to the models of Danish urbanist Jahn Gehl, the use of bikes and pedestrian zones should be promoted. Car transport should be concentrated in garage buildings on the city outskirts.

BERLIN
BRATISLAVA
BUDAPEST
135
LJUBLJANA
PRAGUE
VIENNA
WARSAW

HOUSING

The period of a planned economy and ideology of the collective spirit was replaced by the ideology of individuality. Before 1991 state policy regulated the construction of housing estates and looked after the quality of construction. Today it is up to the investor who, even if this concerns the public housing fund, is solely market-orientated. Looking at the example of the housing estate in the city district of Šiška of 1966, we can see buildings with different typology with adequate public programmes, park and common areas. Today's housing estates are orientated to utilising a site, ground plans are standardised and designed without any creativity and are far from experimenting with fluid space which we find in the work of the then Slovenian architects Milan Mihelic and Ilija Arnautovic. However right now the biggest problem of housing construction in Ljubljana is one of price, because it is possible to find a cheaper apartment in New York where average salaries are twice as high.

Regulation of the housing estates by state policy or by investor?

architect's influence quite big - variety of different floor plans
(Savsko naselje, arch. Ilija Aranutovic and Milan Mihelic, 1962)

almost none architect's influence - no changes in floor plans
(Viška soncava housing developement, 2007-2009)

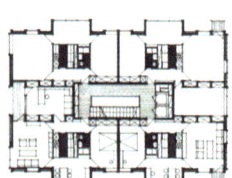

Urbanistic plan for "Šišenska soseska 6" from 1966

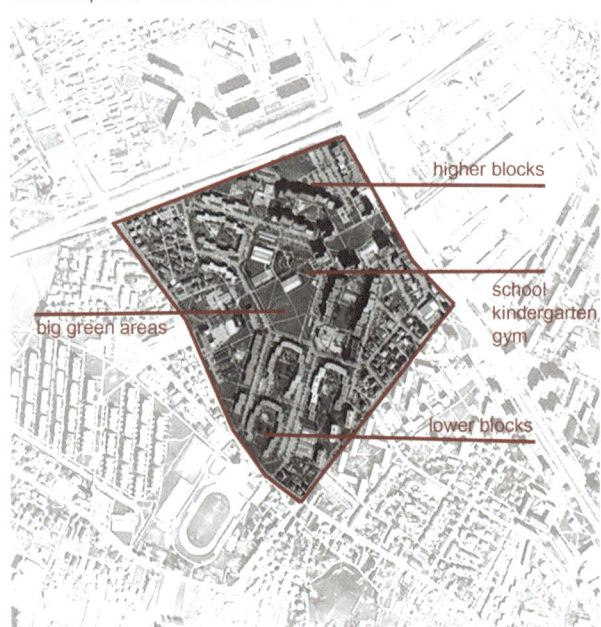

higher blocks

school
kindergarten
gym

big green areas

lower blocks

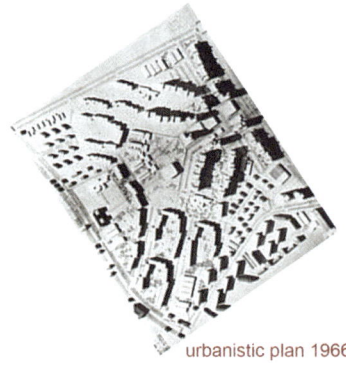

urbanistic plan 1966

We propose constructing housing communities for young families because due to price they cannot become independent and living with parents is extended late into their thirties. With the help of a loan for thirty years, they may acquire a small, but bad quality apartment or an extension to their parents' home, but they want something with a high quality and temporary which will suffice for the first ten years. The young family housing community is trying to offer young couple Jasna and Matjaž from the small town of Radovljica quality apartments in a quiet part of the city with common programmes and outdoor parkland. On the other hand urban nomads require little space – what is important is that it is in the centre of creative events. We propose building smaller parasitic buildings into the concentrated fabric of the old city nucleus. The urban slum allows young artist Staš from the city district of Trnovo to pursue his artistic work and live in the centre of events.

It is possible to find a CHEAPER APARTMENT IN NEW YORK
where average salaries are twice as high

http://www.novogradnje.com/   vs.   http://www.citi-habitats.com/

average monthly salary LJUBLJANA - 1400 EUR
two bedroom appartment - 60m2 - 240.000 EUR

average monthly salary NEW YORK - 3000 EUR
two bedroom appartment - 90m2 - 233.000 EUR

Investor, even if this concerns the public housing fund, is
solely market-orientated

Ideology of the collective spirit vs.
ideology of individuality

BERLIN
BRATISLAVA
BUDAPEST
137
LJUBLJANA
PRAGUE
VIENNA
WARSAW

HOUSING FOR STUDENT FAMILIES | *The specifics of the living habits of student families (the parent is also the student, the desire for life in a community and mutual aid) results in a concept of bringing together apartments into groups and forming a common space appropriate for playing and common care. The groups are distributed along extended corridors – playing routes where, without even planning, you can meet an inmate and establish contact. Various ground plans are possible inside the groups ranging from traditional apartments to somewhat unconventional possibilities. The housing complex ensures quality housing, maximum contact with vegetation, sufficient outdoor and indoor playing space, however a sufficiently dense settlement of the area. An area of the same built-up model is supplemented by groups of social apartments for the young where we can similarly experiment with unconventional ground plans.*

YOUNG FAMILIES
community, mutual help?

extended corridors are forming a common space

various housing groups are set by the extended corridors

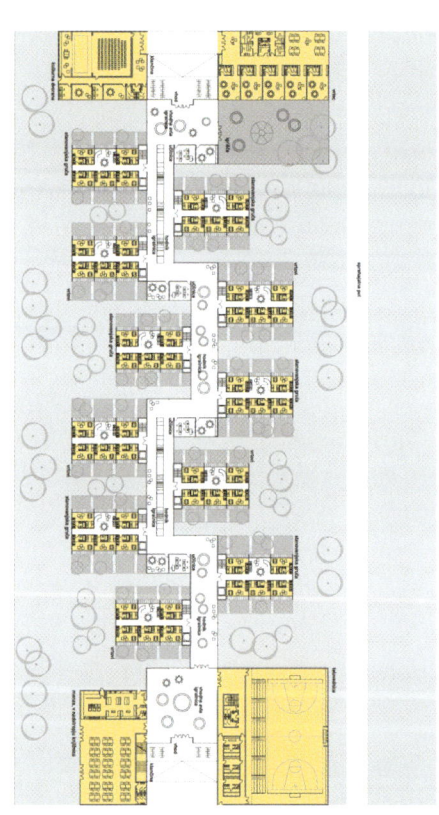

views to the common spaces

urban plan

MICRO BUILDING IN SOTESKA | *A micro building in the district of "Soteska" combines a public and private function. In one part there are "temporary dwellings" for an artist, the other part serves as its "podium". As part of the project, I wished to examine how much private space a person needs to lead a quality life and how a practical initial plan appears, and how to merge the public with the private. The building is conceived as being minimalist, practical and as functional as possible; the simple dwelling it offers a person provides all the necessary comfort, at the same time part of it acts like a public area. In the spine, which fills in a corner and is supported by the existing houses, there are primary functions on three storeys: hygiene, cooking and sleeping. The elongated panel section is designed for the secondary function of the dwelling — for rest, meeting place and work. In view of the small space, all openings are (roof and panoramic window, entrance door) extended outwards — acts as an extended indoor space. The light enters the building in various ways and contributes to diverse production of ambiences.*

BERLIN

BRATISLAVA

BUDAPEST

139

LJUBLJANA

PRAGUE

VIENNA

WARSAW

YOUNG ARTISTS
living in atelier?

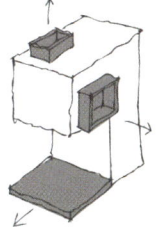

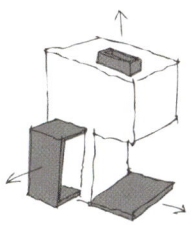

view to the micro building from Soteska street

conceptual model

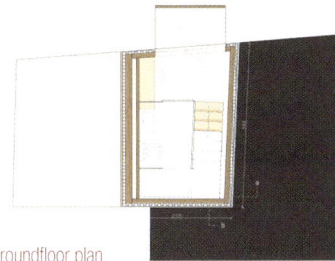

groundfloor plan

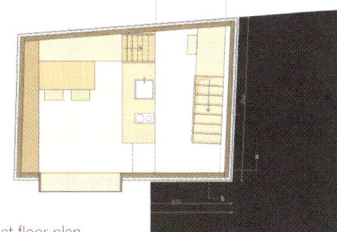

1st floor plan

2nd floor plan

section

IDENTITY

After a change in the political and economic system, as well as the system of values twenty years ago, the city was searching for its own identity and for its own role in the new state. Each change means a typical rejection of the past period and erasing of tracks which are a reminder. Before 1990 the totalitarian government prepared extensive plans and was responsible for adopting big decisions and the obedient public accepted this game without criticism. Today the public is not able or does not wish to decide about issues of personal interest itself, therefore economic and political forces are there to make decisions for them. However, the identity of space is not based on economic force, but on being aware of one's own history, culture, ethics and quality of housing.

A bad approach to buildings of cultural heritage is typical for Ljubljana. The planned renovation of the factory "Cukrarna" of 1828 and the stadium behind Bežigrad of architect Jože Plecnik is encroaching into the existing building by an oversized programme which is subject to the same commercial logic as anonymous newly constructed buildings. Buildings of Slovene modern architecture built from 1940 to 1970s fare even worse. Some have already been demolished despite the fact that they could have been put to other new use. The cultural and industrial heritage of the 20th century should be restored, not as nostalgic scenery, but revitalised by appropriate programmes. Young artist Luka from the city district of Bežigrad wants space where he would be able to create and exhibit his work, so the space must be large, cheap and linked to other artists. Studios in the industrial hall point to a possible way of restoring the industrial heritage in line with the ideas of a contemporary artist.

Demolished building from '60 by arch. Savin Sever

Stadium in Bežigrad

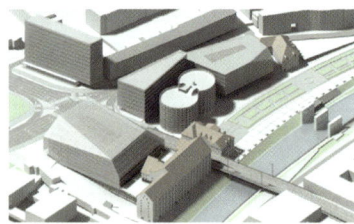

Cukrarna factory with a wining proposal

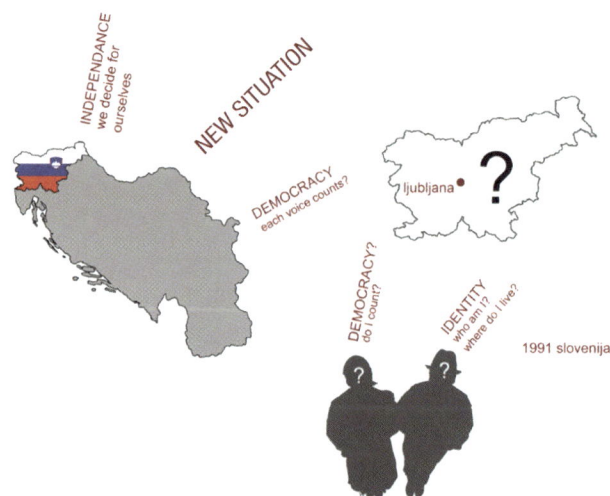

ART CENTRE | *The Art Centre with workhops and studios is designed for young artists who are searching for a place where they can create and also exhibit their work. It is located on a degraded area beside the railway. The project takes an existing abandoned hall which is turned into art gallery and railway cranes which are used as a skeleton for workhops and art studios. The basic guidelines of the project are: to preserve and renovate existing structures, to turn to advantage all their qualities and to establish good and subtle communication between old and new intervention. The main quality of the existing hall in big open space, surrounded with large glass surfaces that create very good natural lightning. The new structure is deepened into the ground to maintain the height, lightness and emptiness of the hall.*

UNACKNOULEDGED ARTISTS
studios?

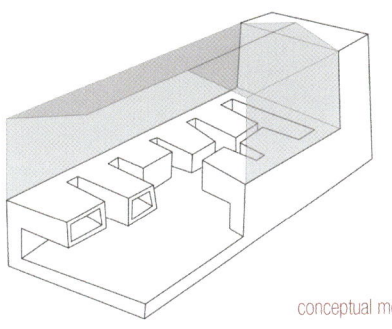

conceptual model

ground floor plan

view to the exhibition hall

section through the exhibition hall

BERLIN

BRATISLAVA

BUDAPEST

LJUBLJANA

PRAGUE

VIENNA

WARSAW

Student: Ajda Fortuna

PRAGUE
LEGIBLE CITY

BERLIN

BRATISLAVA

BUDAPEST

143

LJUBLJANA

PRAGUE

VIENNA

WARSAW

Students: Anna Anděrová | Anna Beránková | Káča Blahutová | Anna Háblová
Irina Khamidulina | Veronika Kommová | Tomáš Lindovský | Ajda Primožič
Martin Stára | Andrea Teierlová | Alena Týfová | Petr Vavřina
Pavel Vrzala

Tutors: Michal Kohout | Irena Fialová

LEGIBILITY THROUGH CONTRACTION

SEARCH FOR LIFE PATTERNS

IRENA FIALOVÁ & MICHAL KOHOUT

CONCEPT

—
The scale and complexity of the artificial environment of our cities is progressively escaping the psychological capacity of its inhabitance: the ability of man to grasp them, comprehend them and orient themselves in them and according to them. The mechanistic zooming out process, when a higher traffic density is solved by adding another lane, the increase of inhabitants by adding more storeys to a housing projects has to stop. Development of life cannot be implemented according to modernistic planners' calculation tables. Neither can any refined postmodern signage systems, any return to traditional semantics solve this dilemma!

There are some 4000 years of development behind the urban settlements where fast traffic was not a great factor and which up to today we call "classical town". One might consider the Grunderzeit city to be the last offspring of such development. Those cities were rarely bigger than 100,000 inhabitants and indeed they work more or less for settlements up to around 500,000 inhabitants. Bigger agglomerations have been coming to existence (as a rule) for about the last 50-80 years. People still need to learn how to deal with such new beasts: how to tame and organize them in a form which would work technically and at the same time emotionally enable us to call them a HOME.

We believe that the solution cannot be other than to let the growing complexity of our living requirements show, represent and stand for what they are. No matter how disturbing, unpleasant or out of control this might at first glance seem. Only in that way we may progress more sustainably and start to tie more responsibly our actions to human capacities to comprehend and appreciate them.

Human beings are willing to walk to certain services only a certain distance, drive to certain attractions only a certain length of time, have reasonable neighbour-to-neighbour relations only with a certain number of fellow neighbours. These limits have not changed much throughout our whole civilized history. We believe, that even our complex living environments are perfectly able to adapt to these coded perception needs, if only we would be willing to recognize and follow them.

We propose to name these needs by the code word LEGIBILITY. Legibility: for the person on the street, for the child on his daily route to school, for a driver commuting to work, for the jet-pilot landing at the local airport...

Our proposal for Prague - Urbanity 20 years later should therefore be read as an attempt to introduce LEGIBILITY into the planning strategies of our city. By following various critical phenomena we try to discover and apply perception criteria to the large, whole -city scale in order to improve and/or re-introduce this basic precondition of the human identification with his/her living habitat.

BRIEF OF WORK

–

The aim of the winter semester 2009/2010 work was to develop sub -themes on the basis of the work, which was done in the summer term 2008/2009 on the subject of change and future of the city. The final concept we arrived at in the summer semester tried to enhance the city legibility by splitting Prague agglomeration into 2 basic zones: City + Suburbia. The City can be further broken down naturally into the Historic city /until the end of the 18th century/, Grunderzeit city /19th and first half of the 20th century/ and Ring of settlements /2nd half of the 20th century/.

SUB-THEMES FOR POSSIBLE DEVELOPMENT

–

THE VISION OF THE CITY - THE INNER CITY versus SUBURBIA
BORDERS - research boundaries and borders between the two environments, but also within them - between their inner, structural elements; show their possible forms, historical development and international examples + their applications in Prague
RULES - research on the characters of each zone - their further internal structure, and its reinforcement through recognition and establishment of rules of natural behaviour

CHARACTER OF THE TERRITORIAL UNITS INSIDE versus OUTSIDE
Research on the order of the structural units of the city, their life, size, continuity, change, natural centres, mutual dependence versus level of independence etc.

HOUSING INSIDE versus OUTSIDE
Research on changes in life-shell patterns - the characters determining settlement, buildings, flats - there sizes, densities, character, etc.

HEAVY TRAFFIC IN THE CITY: CAR, TRAIN, TRAM, BUS, etc.
SPACES - research on transformation of urban space and the change of the character of the basic types in the transition of the different city zones

SYSTEMS - research of rules of
conduct for different types of heavy
traffic /individual and public
transport/ within each zone or
subzone and on their boundaries

LIGHT TRAFFIC IN THE CITY:
PEDESTRIANS, BICYCLES, SKATES etc.
SPACES - research on transformation
of urban space and the change of
the character of the basic types and
their transition into different city
zones
SYSTEMS - research into rules of
conduct for different types of light
traffic within each zone or subzone

GREENERY INSIDE versus OUTSIDE
Landscape in the town versus
a settlement in the landscape -
research on the transformation of
the agricultural landscape into
recreation landscape

RIVER INSIDE versus OUTSIDE
Research of changes and potential
of the Vltava River in respect of
zones; what does today's city need
the once life-giving phenomenon of
the river for?

RESULTS

–

The students involved in
the URBANITY project had various
credits/time/energy available for
their design. Their results
therefore varied from more elaborate
and grounded works to shorter
introductions of important themes
and visions.

By analysing the development of
Prague and its outskirts in the last
20 years (including e.g.
the development of apartment prices,
migration, densities, transportation

possibilities) the following overall
characteristic of Prague was
formulated by Ajda Primožič:
The tendency of the Prague citizen
is to move massively from the dense
city into the quiet and idyllic
suburban communities. These
represent (in the minds of
the migrating population) safety,
organization, low density, greenery
and peaceful lifestyle but many of
them have (in reality) turned into
the opposite. Urban growth is
uncontrollably spreading into
the surrounding landscape, dividing
it into two zones: one that is
rapidly changing as a result of
avinable public transport and the
other, which is not affected by this
fast development so much.

As the overall development of
the number of inhabitants of
Prague has not been growing and is
predicted to remain more or less
the same in thefuture, the dense
part of the city is restructuring
itself, filling in brownfield
areas and gentrifying itself. This
development of the inner city is
occurring in a more organized
manner, though it is unfortunately
accompanied by the fulfilment of
conceptually 1970s traffic plans,
which are cutting through Prague
in just a slightly less aggressive
manner than the first north-south
highway called Magistrala did thirty
years ago. Pavel Vrzala and Andrea
Teierlová were two of the students
looking for possibilities of
healing this north-south cut, which
surgically divides the historical
core of the city, founded by Charles
IV in the 14th century from its
19th century continuation. Petr
Vavřina looked at the theme of cuts,
intermediate and left over spaces,
various borders and boundaries of

the inside of Prague in a more general manner and tried to reveal their hidden potential as new diverse public spaces of the 21st century. Irina Khamidulina researched the changes, potential and role of the Vltava River in today's city together with research on the transformation of originally agricultural landscape into recreation area.

The most complex work was done by Anna Háblová, who chose the URBANITY project as her diploma theme. Based on extensive analysis of Prague's development and it's comparison with current global and regional problems and visions of sustainable development she formulated the concept of Two Zones of Prague:
Inside Prague and Outside Suburbia. Each of these zones has a different character, behaviour and development patterns. Her proposal considers two different sustainable and diversity encouraging sets of rules and visions should exist for each of them, as what is a desirable development of the inside zone is perhaps non desirable in the outside and vice versa. Her work examines boundaries and borders between the two environments and also inside each environment and formulates a vision for Inside Prague as a Polycentric City and for Outside Suburbia as Islands in Landscape. Her project includes model examples of the development of one of the polycentric centres, of the creation of the boundary between the two zones as well as of the boundary between the islands in landscape.

CONCLUDING NOTES

—

Seeing legibility as a worthwhile vision or goal of today's town-planning brings into focus also the changing character of order and the creative act under present conditions. Order as an intrinsic quality, the sine qua non, of any planning and the creative act as its basic tool.

Planning is in fact balancing vision, life processes and means. Answering the 3 basic questions: why, what, how? The final form depends on the means available and processes implemented. In fact without knowing the two latter it is hard to give any realistic form to the vision itself. In a situation of a relative formal instability and a degree of typological change which accompanies our present lives it is logical to advance with the plans in a way that include only gradual stabilization of not only the vision's formal expression itself, but also of the processes and means which condition it. In other words, one can go only that further with formally fixing the vision, how much fixed are the processes and means. In the condition of our social circumstances it means we need to learn more to work with flexibly formulated visions.
The aim of any plan is to introduce some degree of clarity and foreseeability into the environment. The traditional method how plans achieved this, was through modelling the future state. Traditional master plans capture the future "ideal"

BERLIN

BRATISLAVA

BUDAPEST

147

LJUBLJANA

PRAGUE

VIENNA

WARSAW

situation, the state when the plan fully implemented is the point □ which the town (region, society) is striving to reach. These plans were based on the following presumptions:

a) Such "ideal" point or situation indeed exists.

b) Such point is foreseeable and can be expressed in the way of a single creative act - the master plan.

c) Society has the coherence and instruments to secure the implementation of such foreseen vision of its own future.

Ad a) The fact that such a point exists includes the notion that the town growth is controllable. Randomness of future development is to a great degree excluded, or brought under considerable control. This happened usually by means of strong typological unity and great implementation diversity. The typological unity enabled every participant of the planning process (public, planner, politicians and private stake holder) basic ability to set, read and understand the overall goals of the plan. The implementation diversity on the other had allowed for a necessary flexibility. However, the requested flexibility was not such to obliterate the plan. Such approach also demanded from all the participants a high degree of tolerance. A tolerance now gone with all the written standards which govern our lives and define the conditions under which certain use or behaviour can be exercised. The standards (and their growing number and precision) set a basis for intolerance (mainly legal) and prohibit flexibility and idiosyncrasy.

Ad b) Traditional architectural plans for buildings determined only the basis guide -lines. The rest was agreed with the master builder or individual craftsman directly on the site Such approach could work only in conditions of great trust, self understood standards and big flexibility on all parts. After the written standards introduced a new state of institutionalized intolerance that our plans became unforeseeable and difficult to express in terms of physical design and are pressing more and more on the "performance-specification" way of recording. The basic question of today's planning is how does the unstable, fluid character of the medium change the character of the creative act itself? To what degree can environment legibility be generated by order, by familiarity or by other factors? To what extend does the societies system of governance reflect on these matters? How do the factors influencing the legibility change with the scale of settlements? What is the nature of the creative act at the larger scale of urban and regional plans?

Ad c) In the present Czech society notorious for it's continual series of political discontinuations it is hardly imaginable sustaining continual public support for a policy longer than 5 - 10 years (time frame exceeding 1 - 2 tenure of politicians, but also a time in which major life-changing technical devices are introduced and implemented). It is probably here that we have to seek an answer, why 20 years after dramatic political changes were introduced and virtually all Czech cities and villages got new master plans, we are still waiting for a major urban design event to be not only staged but first of all demanded.

The exercise character of
the Urbanity project and the feeble
response it had among the local city
officials only underlines this
overall social inertia.

BERLIN

BRATISLAVA

BUDAPEST

149

LJUBLJANA

PRAGUE

VIENNA

WARSAW

1 VISION FOR PRAGUE TWO ZONES - INSIDE, OUTSIDE

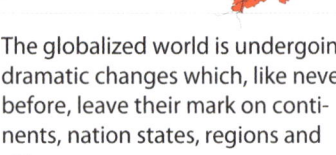

GLOBAL AND REGIONAL PROBLEMS AND TRENDS

The globalized world is undergoing dramatic changes which, like never before, leave their mark on continents, nation states, regions and cities.

Decrease of population, well balanced by immigration into level stagnation, is the reason for reducing and not spreading city. Nevertheless in combination with growing of living space causes uneconomical development and spreading city into landscape, which is no more sustainable and should be replaced by more efficient use of existing urban areas and definition of whatever borders of city. Also every weekend commuting into countryside and back into city weights environment and causes traffic problems. Is the nature around Prague inconvenient?

Demographic changes require a rethinking of the conventional 3-life-phase understanding. Socially and economically it is not accountable to exclude the elderly for about one fourth of their lifetime from society action? Diversification of lifestyles and cultures in combination with growing migration demands new living environments. Raising awareness of personal health will be a mega future market which dramatically changes consumerism and the demand for healthy environments. The conceptual age and moral consumerism in contrast to mass consumerism asks for customized and healthy products with a politically correct origin. Abstract technological developments, accelerating mobility and the interplay of local and global make every day's life more and more complex and complicate personal orientation and identity formation. The new organisation of businesses to open systems requires fundamental changes in work habits. The climate will change dramatically if the pollution of the planet is not expressly reduced. Reversal of resources will lead to global conflicts if no change in economical orientation is put foreword.

STAGNATION OF POPULATION

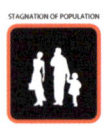
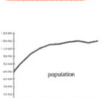

desintegration of the city

contraction of the city

WEEKEND COMUTING

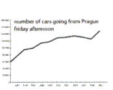
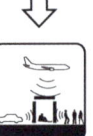

contemplation in urban density

nature nearer city

LIVING SPACE

increase of living space

efficient development

DEMOGRAPHIC CHANGE

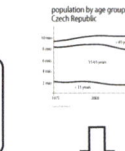

integration into economic cycle

integration into every day's life

HEALTH SOCIETY EVOLVES

health consciousness

organic agriculture

clean industries

wellness + fitness

TECHNOLOGY CONVERGENCE

NBIC

future science

new energy

new medicine

new materials

GLOBALISATION - LOCALISATION

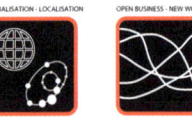

local - global

individualism - local integration

global connectivity

OPEN BUSINESS - NEW WORK

traditional split

future split

hybrid environments

hybrid environments

ENERGY+RESOURCE REVERSAL

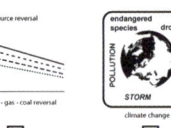
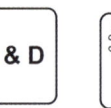

resource reversal

water - oil - gas - coal reversal

R & D

foster efficiency

renewable energy

polycentrical

CLIMATE CHANGE

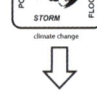

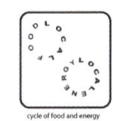
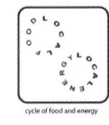

climate change

cycle of food and energy

cycle of energy efficiency

SUSTAINABLE PLANNING AND CONSTRUCTION POLICY

holistic urbanism

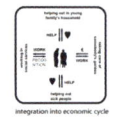
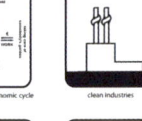

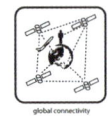

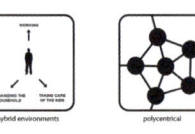

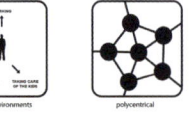

HISTORIC CENTRE

CULTURAL PROPERTY

19. CENTURY CITY

AREAS OF CONSISTENT USE

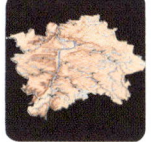

PARKS IN THE CITY

TOPOGRAPHY

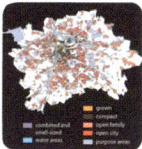

HOUSING ESTATES

STRUCTURE OF DEVELOPMENT

TRANSPORT

DEVELOPMENT OF ADMINISTRATIVE BORDERS

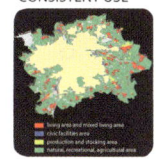

LANDSCAPE

AREAS OF CONSISTENT USE

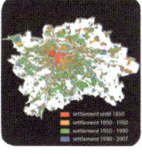

SUBURBIA

DEVELOPMENT OF SETTLEMENT

BERLIN

BRATISLAVA

BUDAPEST

LJUBLJANA

PRAGUE

VIENNA

WARSAW

ABSTRACTION OF CITY STRUCTURE

state of matter

ABSTRACT SECTION

existing border of Prague

historic centre of Prague | 19. st. city | housing estate | empty places | expanding villages without concept | storage facilities degradeting nature

dense city

proposal

pressure on recultivation border of Prague | new border of Prague

second zone of Prague

P+R

historic centre of Prague | 19. st. city | public transport, P+R nature nearly centre | border park | villages in landcape | more efficient storage facilities

dense city

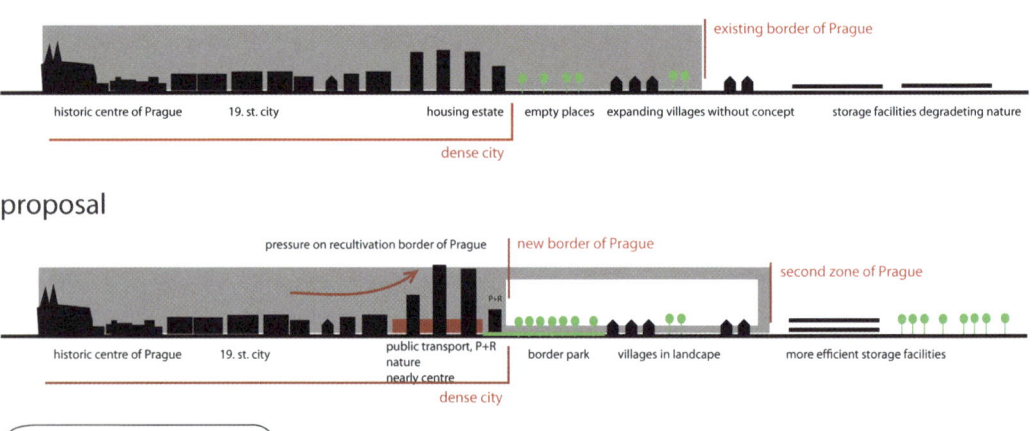

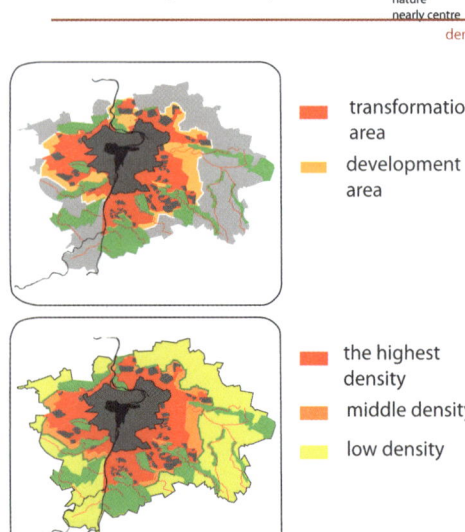

■ transformation area

■ development area

The main proposal is result of understanding the city like matter with holes of parks and crumbs of suburbia coupled with general and global problems and trends in the world. The aim of the proposal is to gently grab the city and give its comprehensible meanings. The aim is to say what things are and accordingly with it work and establish new rules. The aim is finding simple and understandable concept influencing as much layers of city as possible. All aims will be achieved by dividing the city into two zones.

■ the highest density

■ middle density

■ low density

4 VISION FOR PRAGUE TWO ZONES / PROPOSAL

THE MAIN AIM OF THE PROJECT IS READABILITY AND SUSTAINABILITY OF PRAGUE

IT IS ACHIEVED BY DIVIDING THE CITY INTO TWO ZONES - INSIDE PRAGUE AND OUTSIDE SUBURBIA

FIRST ZONE - INSIDE PRAGUE
➡ CONTRACTION

SECOND ZONE - OUTSIDE SUBURBIA
⇨ EXTENSION

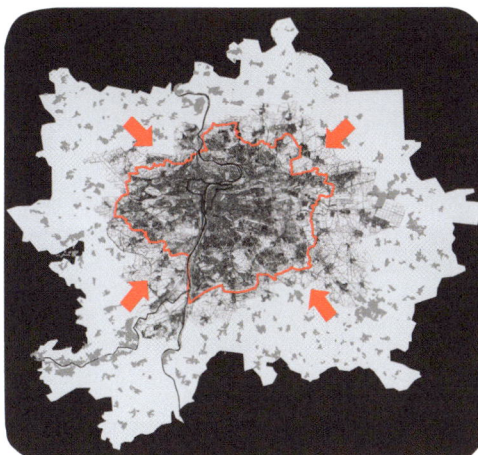

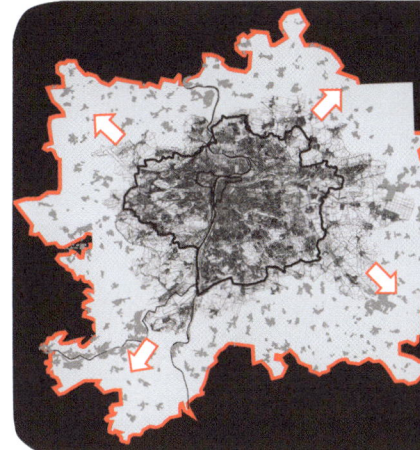

The first zone is the Prague and consists of the dense (continual) city including sufficient reserve. The borders will be smaller than existing one, which were established in 1974 because of expecting big increase of population and land was at one dash removed from Land Resource. The second zone will be porous areas depended on the city, but without possibility to identify itself with the Prague because of need to look for its own identity.

In spite of feeling, that suburbia should be the whole Bohemia, the borders of the second zone are defined like administrative borders of municipalities containing more than 50% of to the city commuting people. Each part will have each own rules. In the first zone will be restricted cars and supported public transport, in the second will be protected nature and restricted spreading of villages. For each zone will be found its own concept.

FIRST ZONE PRAGUE

SECOND ZONE SUBURBIA

BERLIN

BRATISLAVA

BUDAPEST

153

LJUBLJANA

PRAGUE

VIENNA

WARSAW

5 VISION FOR PRAGUE — POLYCENTRIC CITY / PROPOSAL

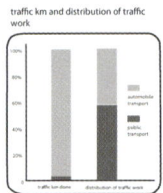

traffic km and distribution of traffic work

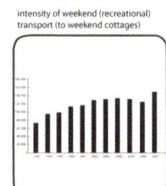

intensity of weekend (recreational) transport (to weekend cottages)

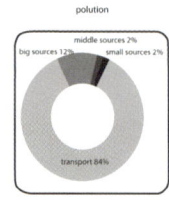

polution

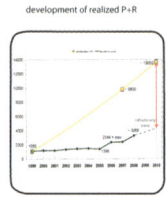

development of realized P+R

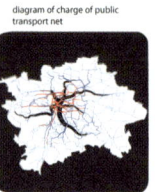

diagram of charge of public transport net

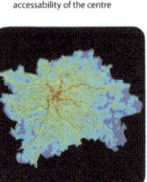

accessability of the centre

HISTORICAL CORE

Historic centre of Prague will stay under the strict control, so in this case it is not possible much to influence increas of people living in the centre. Only by upgrading existing parks and local centres.

DEVELOPING ZONE

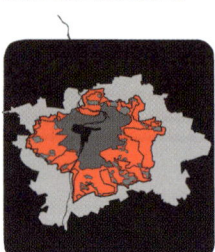

Circle between protective zone of historical centre and new boundary including housing estates will be the most developing area in the city.It will frofit from the closeness of the centre andfrom the closeness of the border park and landscape. It will be good conected with the centre and with whole area by the circle - train.

POLYCENTRIC AND SUFFICIENT DENSITY

People living in the city don´t need as much extensive greenery, as high quality centres in neighbourhood.   Centres depend on accessability and density. That is the reason why to design new line of public transport.

Circular metro will conect border parts of denser city including housing estates and dead zones. It will create more polycentrical city,densify the city, create new potencials and rise number of P+R. Circular metro comes through diferent areas. Some are underground, some comes lengthtways existing roads, some comes through dead places and peripheries.

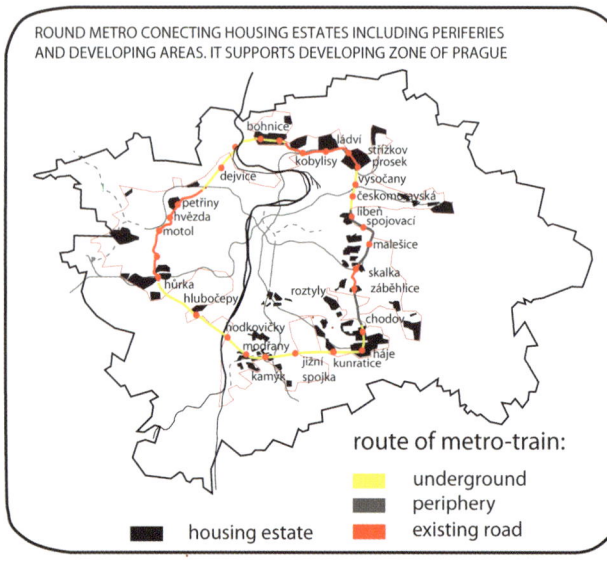

ROUND METRO CONECTING HOUSING ESTATES INCLUDING PERIFERIES AND DEVELOPING AREAS. IT SUPPORTS DEVELOPING ZONE OF PRAGUE

route of metro-train:
- underground
- periphery
- existing road

housing estate

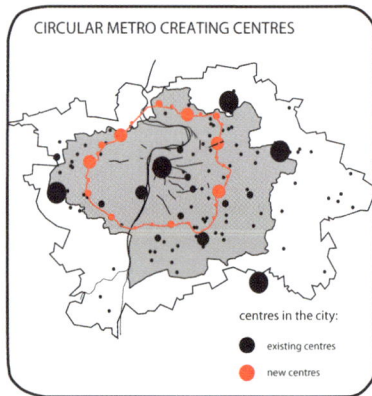

CIRCULAR METRO CREATING CENTRES

centres in the city:
- existing centres
- new centres

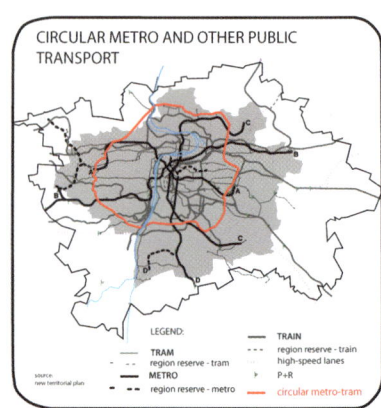

CIRCULAR METRO AND OTHER PUBLIC TRANSPORT

LEGEND:
TRAM · region reserve - tram · METRO · region reserve - metro
TRAIN · region reserve - train · high-speed lanes · P+R · circular metro-tram
source: new teritorial plan

Student: Anna Háblová

Skalka as a stop of circle metro and crossing between A and E metro. Skalka as a potential of quality living with quality centre and quality parks.

cirkular metro
Skalka station

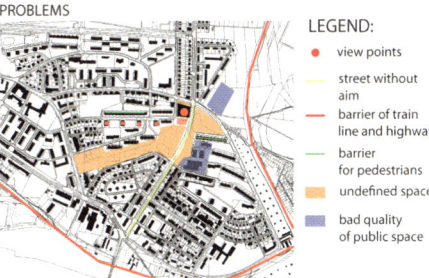

PROBLEMS

LEGEND:
- ● view points
- ▬ street without aim
- ▬ barrier of train line and highway
- ▬ barrier for pedestrians
- undefined space
- bad quality of public space

- trafic accessability - enaugh greenery - area of family houses - proximity of forest - good permeability for pedestrians	- not compact area - housing estates - bad quality of centre - need of bigger centre - not defined spaces
S	**W**
O	**T**
- free space - greenery - potencial of people	- too extensive development with not living spaces will disvalue calm place for living

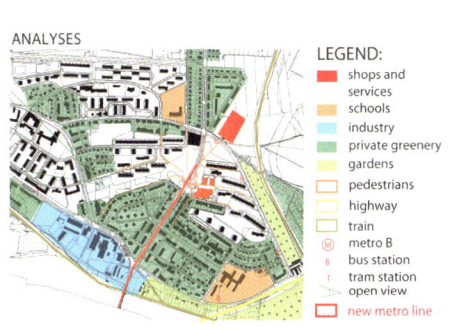

ANALYSES

LEGEND:
- shops and services
- schools
- industry
- private greenery
- gardens
- pedestrians
- highway
- train
- Ⓜ metro B
- Ⓑ bus station
- Ⓣ tram station
- open view
- new metro line

It is need to create new conditions for area transformation - more economical and ecological. This proposal tries to show variants, which are aiming to consolidate area and create quality centre.

stark centre   amenable periphery   completion areas   grid - lines   grid - spots   flowing blocks

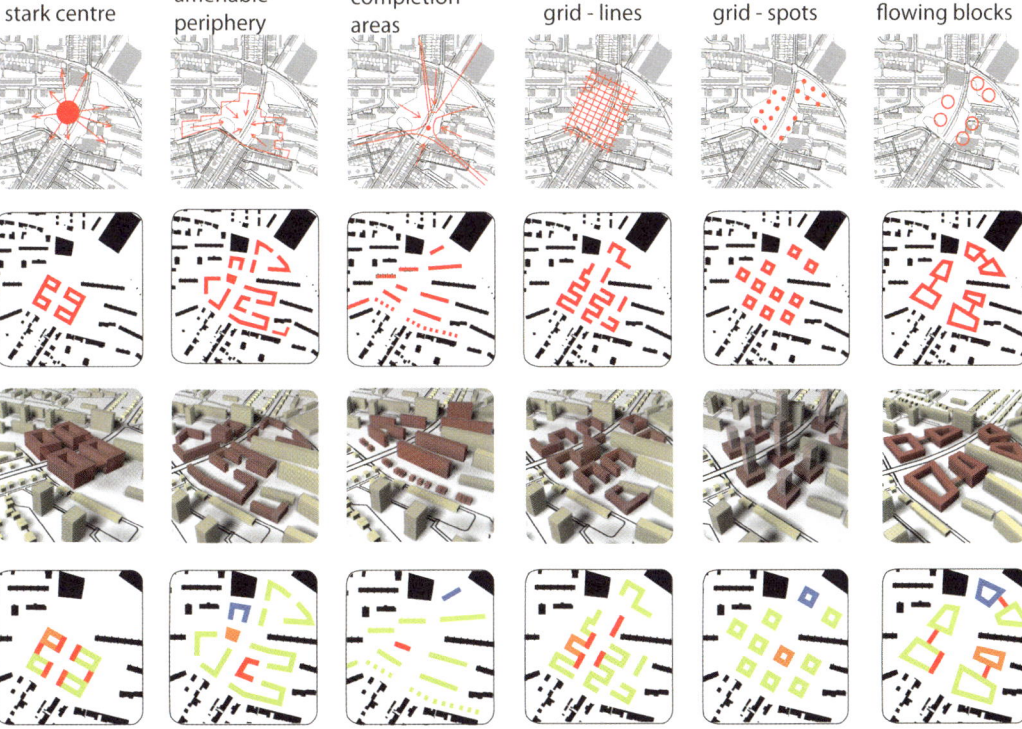

155

RESEARCH ON SUBURBIA OF EASTERN PRAGUE

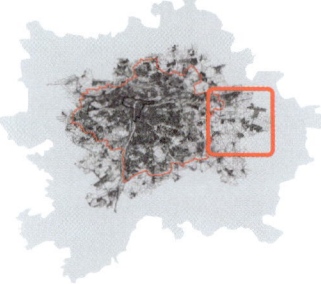

Without increase of inhabitants in Prague, nature subsides and built-up areas grows.

Agricultural land consumption was between 2000 – 2007 49 ha/day. (For confrontation Austria 35 ha/day, Switzerland 10 ha/day.)

This research tries to discover causes and consequences of urban sprawl. It was chosen 5 villages from eastern Prague. All possible characters and signs in villages were marked by positive and negative symbols. From this evaluation get out idilist village Dolní Počernice and the worst-case Újezd nad Lesy. From this know-ledges get out the proposal.

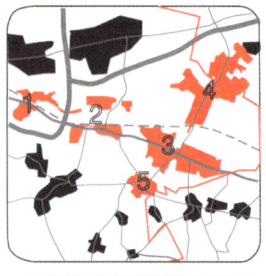

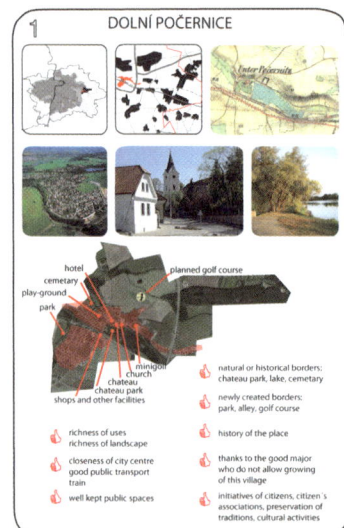

1 DOLNÍ POČERNICE

hotel
cemetary
play-ground
park

planned golf course

minigolf
chateau
chateau park
shops and other facilities

- natural or historical borders: chateau park, lake, cemetary
- newly created borders: park, alley, golf course
- richness of uses
- richness of landscape
- history of the place
- closeness of city centre
- good public transport
- train
- thanks to the good major who do not allow growing of this village
- well kept public spaces
- initiatives of citizens, citizen´s associations, preservation of traditions, cultural activities

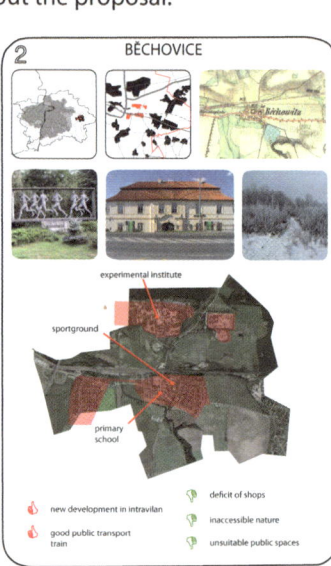

2 BĚCHOVICE

experimental institute

sportground

primary school

- new development in intravilan
- good public transport
- train
- deficit of shops
- inaccessible nature
- unsuitable public spaces

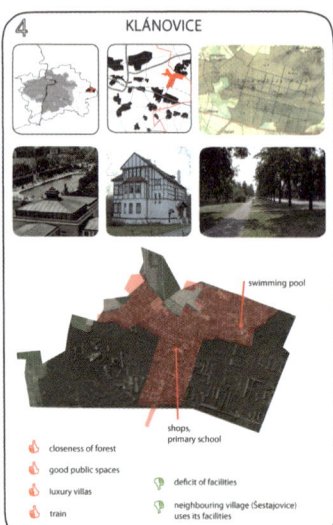

4 KLÁNOVICE

swimming pool

shops, primary school

- closeness of forest
- good public spaces
- luxury villas
- train
- deficit of facilities
- neighbouring village (Šestajovice) uses its facilities

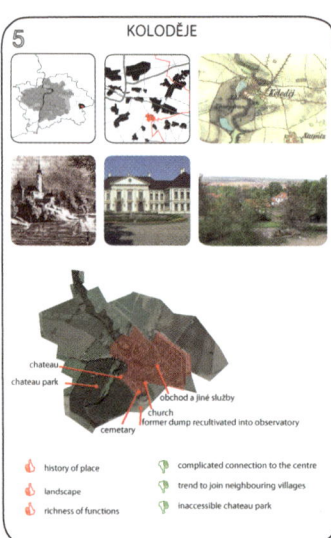

5 KOLODĚJE

chateau
chateau park

obchod a jiné služby
church
former dump recultivated into observatory
cemetary

- history of place
- landscape
- richness of functions
- complicated connection to the centre
- trend to join neighbouring villages
- inaccessible chateau park

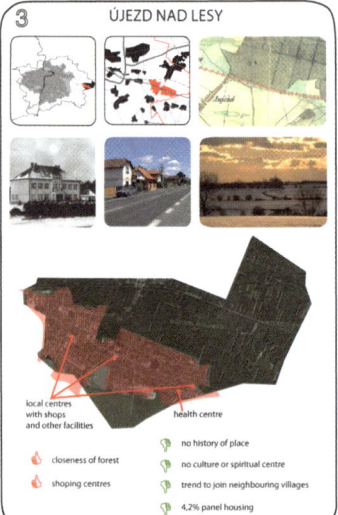

3 ÚJEZD NAD LESY

local centres
with shops
and other facilities

health centre

- closeness of forest
- shoping centres
- no history of place
- no culture or spiritual centre
- trend to join neighbouring villages
- 4,2% panel housing

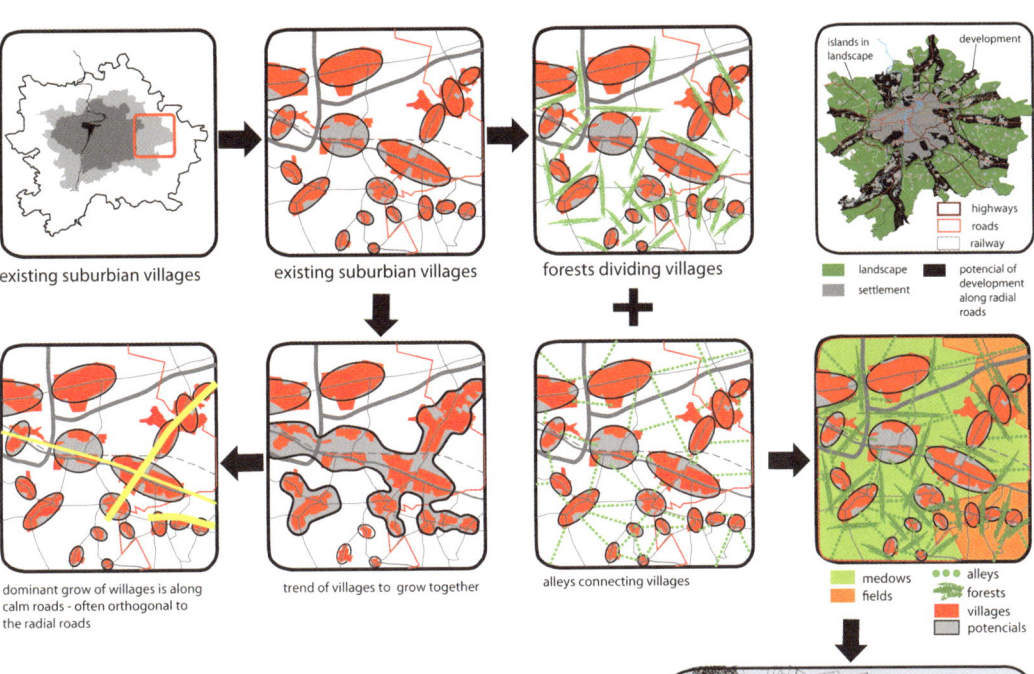

existing suburbian villages

existing suburbian villages

forests dividing villages

islands in landscape   development

highways
roads
railway

landscape
settlement

potencial of development along radial roads

dominant grow of willages is along calm roads - often orthogonal to the radial roads

trend of villages to grow together

alleys connecting villages

medows
fields

alleys
forests
villages
potencials

ISLANDS IN LANDSCAPE

Prague (in history and also now) is cyclical undergoing changes of urbanization and reurbanization. It seems that it is time to solve problems of suburbanization, but it is also time for reurbanization preparations. It means to create in the city conditions of area trans-formation and offer more economical and more eco-logical alternate. It is also need to have buttres in our system of law for instruments of land planning.It is need tax policy, which will disadvantage un-built areas before built-up areas.

One of suburbia trend is rapid growing and joining of villages. They miss centres with facilities. Most of things depend on quality mayor.My only part is design of space,trying divide and same connect villages. Divide by forests and connect by alleys.

Nature will be preserved and intravilans will be used effectively.

Land will be removed from Land Resources and changed into zones of forests between villges and alleys conecting them.Remaining land will be changed into meadows and fields.

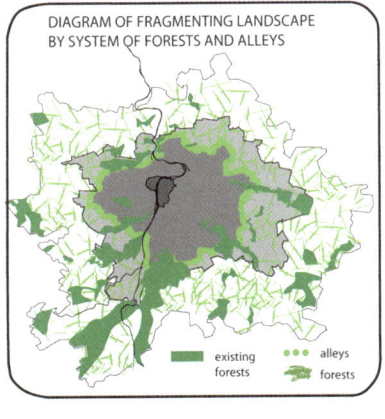

DIAGRAM OF FRAGMENTING LANDSCAPE BY SYSTEM OF FORESTS AND ALLEYS

existing forests
alleys
forests

VISION FOR PRAGUE   BORDERS / PROPOSAL

First zone of prague is created on administrative borders of municipalities, which contains dense city.

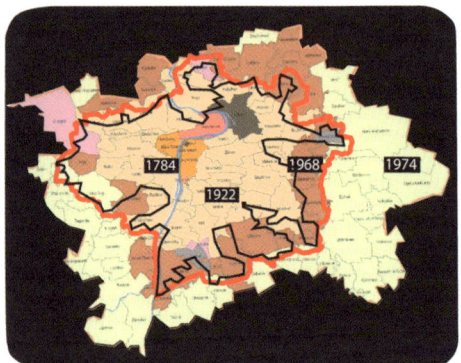

NOT BORDERS, BUT BOUNDARIES

The boundary will be like interface.It will consists of dense edge of city and intensive landscape.

Dense edge of city will be supported by circular metro, making possible to develop old housing estates with peripheries. One part of Intensive landscape will be Border park imitating the new administrative border of Prague. The aim of it is to make accessible beautiful nature around Prague. Doesn´t matter, if it will be only path for walking and cyclists.

PRINCIP OF INTENSIVE LANDSCAPE

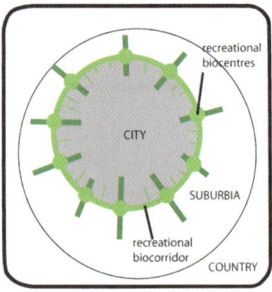

PRINCIP OF BOUNDARY

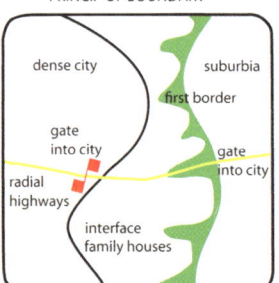

This project concentrated on eastern Prague solves above all definition of continual Border park in concrete area. It does not copy administrative border, but is naturally passed through lands-cape. Above all it copies existing paths, alleys and parks. Part of Prague boundary is (together with Border park) also interface,formed by former villages, integrated into Prague, and dense zone, opened on highways by symbolic gates.

BORDER PARK IN SYSTEM OF FORESTS

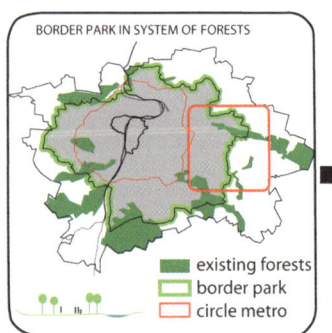

existing forests
border park
circle metro

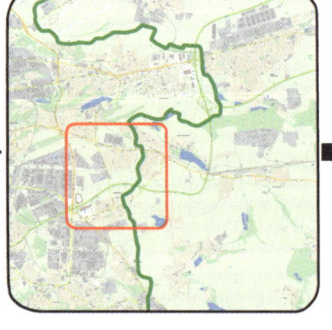

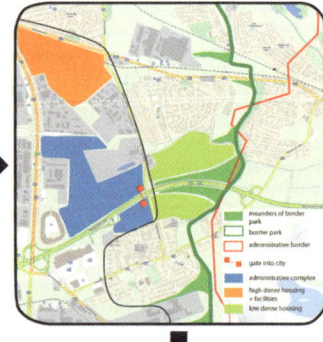

STATE OF MATTER

INSPIRATION

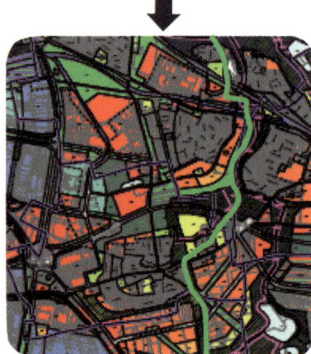

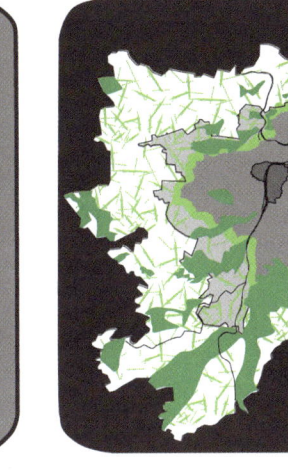

BOUNDARY BETWEEN TWO LANDSCAPES

Second zone will be created on administrative borders of municipalities, which contains more than 50% inhabitants comuting to the Prague.

Boundary between suburbia and country will be designed itself by changing landscape of second zone. The difference between both landscapes will create feeling of new boundary.

GRADATION OF LANDSCAPES

1 dense city

2 suburbian landscape with mozaik of forests and meadows

1

2   3   4

3 suburbian landscape with mozaik of forests and fields

4 country with agriculture landscape

DIAGRAM OF FRAGMENTING LANDSCAPE BY SYSTEM OF FORESTS AND ALLEYS

STATE OF MATTER

INSPIRATION

CONSEPT OF CITY DENSIFICATION

CONSEPT DESCRIPTION

Consept of this project starts from the analysis of posible approaches of the city densification. We can set up few types of changes that leads to city evolution.

The first approach is the extensive growth. It uses free places on the edge of existing structure and adds new physical structure. It's effect is enlarging the city, but mostly not enlarging the density as itself. In history was this approach in most cases positive, but it has also it's limits. Nowadays is the extensive growth fastened by advanced transportation, so it's hardly connectabe by man. That may cause some problems.

Next type is intensive growth. It's caused by growing demands on the use of the location. As the city grows, it needs bigger squares, streets, buildings and structures. The intensive growth maximalizes potential of quality locations in the city and makes them turn into new centers.

Other approach is the city renewal. It starts in locations that are used no more, or that they are used unsufficiently, than it creates bigger value for the location. The potential of such localities is in it's sell value and it's existing connections to the surrounding city, that makes them interresting for new development.

The most complicated approach is the connection adding. The existing borders with low use are broken and changed to vital boundaries. It's mostly very hard to break such borders in the city, because other approaches can be much easier for the same purpose. But it has much bigger potential. Boundaries combine the potential of surrounding localities and multiply them.

Prague has big potential in it's unused borders. This project tries to reveal it by searching for negative borders in the dense Prague and showing possible potential of such localities.

CITY DENSIFICATION

INTENSIVE
Intensification creates new centers and maximalizes potential of places with good connection and good location in the city.

EXTENSIVE
Extensive densification uses free places in the city for new development and adds new values to the present state. It also enlarges land use.

RENEWAL
Renewal densification searches for locations which are not sufficiently used. Than it improves the present state and creates bigger value for this location.

CONNECTING
Connection areas in the city breaks existing borders and change them to boundaries. The potential for adding new layer to existing structure can be released.

POLYCENTRIC CITY

DENSE CITY

QUALITY CITY

RELEASED POTENTIAL

EXAMPLE - PŘÍKOPY STREET

1300

1850

1950

NOW

EXAMPLE - VIENNA RINGSTRASSE

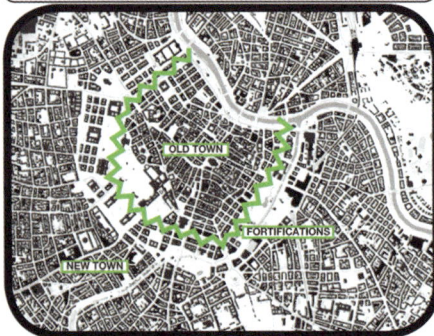

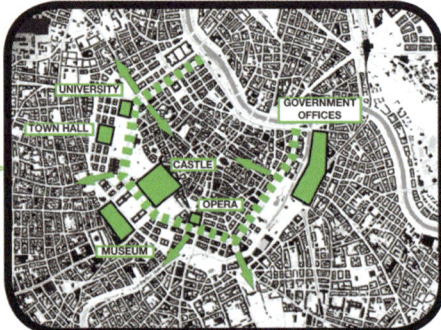

1300

1880

1920

NOW

MAIN TRAFFIC ARTERY

RINGSTRASSE NR.2

PRESENT STATE - RUSH STREET

ILLUSTRATION - BOULEVARD

RAILROAD SYSTEM IN VRŠOVICE

GREEN CORRIDOR IN CITY CENTER

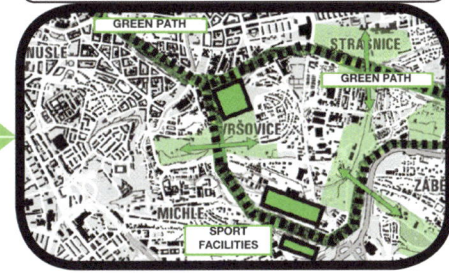

PRESENT STATE - RAILROAD

ILLUSTRATION - MULTIFUNCTIONAL PARK

PARK LETNÁ - SOUTH SLOPE

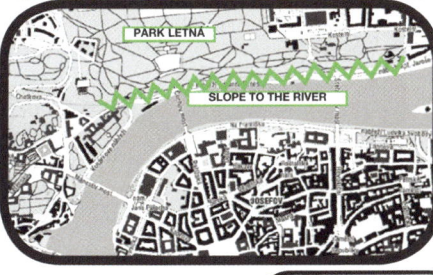

PARK CONNECTED TO OLD TOWN

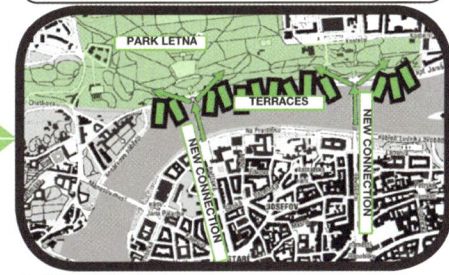

PRESENT STATE - INACCESSIBLE SLOPE

ILLUSTRATION - PUBLIC TERRACES

BERLIN

BRATISLAVA

BUDAPEST

161

LJUBLJANA

PRAGUE

VIENNA

WARSAW

PRAGUE IN-OUT. VLTAVA.

1. WHAT IS THERE NOW?

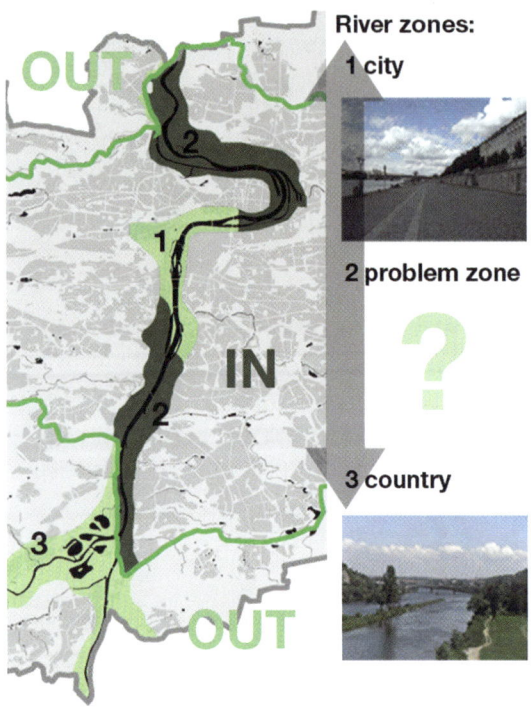

River zones:

1 city

2 problem zone

3 country

2. ANALYSIS OF PROBLEM ZONE

natural environment, river is a communication line, fine views, attractive for rest	low cross-country ability, brownfields, uninhabited territories, closed private areas, flooded areas
attractive space for residence, work and rest for different ages, for tourist and dwellers	enlargement abandone tritries, decrease life quality level, insurmountable barrier, border

3. WHAT IS PROBLEM?

This zone is IN the city but it looks like a country side. It does not belong to nature and it does not actively use like a city zone. It is loosed area. City develops faster then river zone. Now abandoned river zone needs **REVITALIZATION**.

4. RULES

zone 2 should be city in looks

ZONE 1   ZONE 2   **IN OUT**

ZONE 1   ZONE 2   **IN OUT**

river zone is not border

dip

5. FILLING ZONE

PRAGUE - THE CHANGE AND FUTURE OF THE CITY
NORTH-SOUTH HIGHWAY PROPOSAL

ANDREA TEIERLOVÁ
PAVEL VRZALA

ANALYTIC PART

SCHEME ZÁKOS 1974

Scheme of the Basic road system (ZÁKOS), started in 1974 and partly buildt, then in 1990 stoped, because it wasn't good for Prague. Sanation of historical parts of the Prague and building highways through the centre was the parts of ZÁKOS. Due to this facts the cars replace the people in the city.

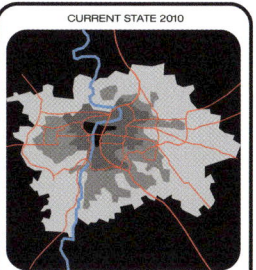

CURRENT STATE 2010

After 1990 the plans of ZÁKOS was changed. Projected sanations of historical centre was canceled, part of the comunications was changed into the tunnels (now in progress). The whole project of transportation in Prague is still unfinished and the whole system doesn't work

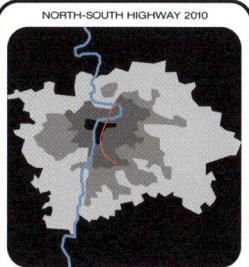

NORTH-SOUTH HIGHWAY 2010

The North-South Highway is the most frequently used road in the Czech Republic. There is over 100000 cars per a day. The surroundings of the road is not a living city. The North-South Highway goes through the city centre, there is no other way for going through the Prague in north-south direction.

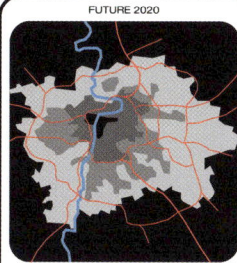

FUTURE 2020

After finishing the road plans the North-South Highway will be not important for transit traffic. It will be possible to change the road back to the city street. It is important to realise that the city is made of people and for people, not for the cars. Prague needs public spaces of good quality.

CONCEPT

one level transport

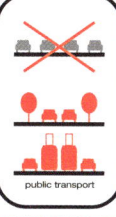

public transport

two way roads

speed limits

different users

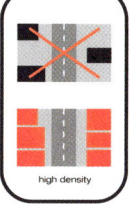

high density

SUSTAINABLE CITY LIVING SPACE IS MORE IMPORTANT THAN FREE WAY FOR CARS IN THE STREETS

163

PROPOSAL

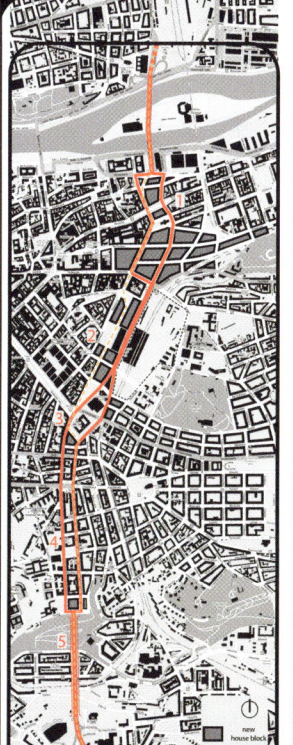

new house block

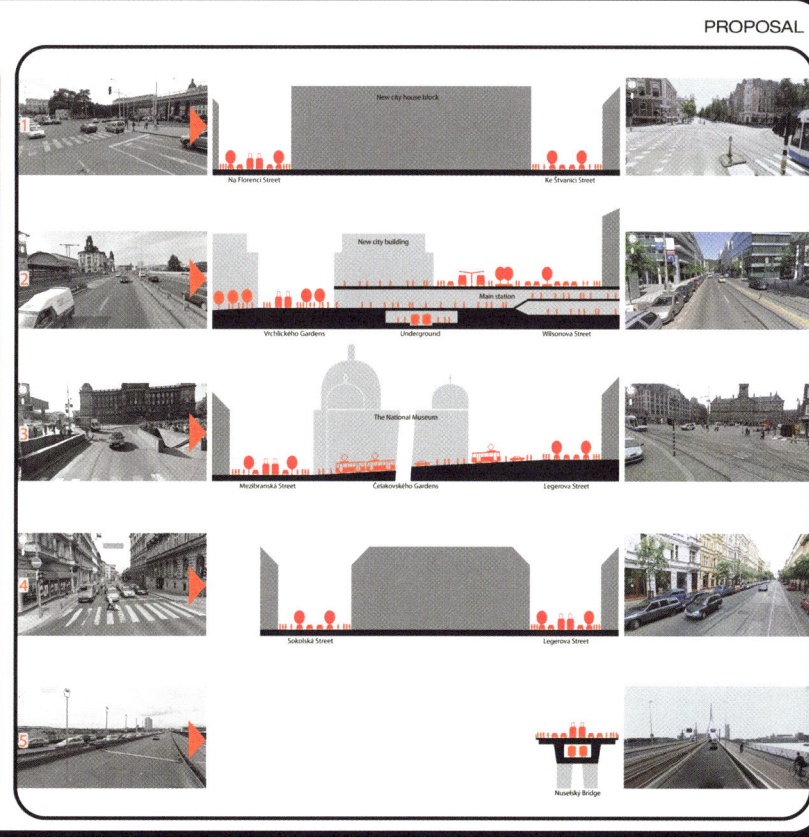

VIENNA
SLOW CAPITAL

BERLIN

BRATISLAVA

BUDAPEST

165

LJUBLJANA

PRAGUE

VIENNA

WARSAW

Students: Stefan Aursulesei | Adnan Balcinovic | Sebastian Bauer
Clemens Hasler | Wesley Ho | Christiane Hütter | Roland Icking
Christiane Irxenmayer | Mariedl Kleemann | Sarah Köck | Jasmin Leonhard
Daniela Mitterberger | Gunita Pavlovica | Lukas Pazmandy| Adina Radway
Lukas Rückerl | Frank Schwenk | Roland Stolz | Philipp Soeparno
Teresa Traunsteiner | Aron Tsang | Mechtild Weber | Michaela Wonisch
Marc Werner | Isabell Wolke

Tutors: Stefan Gruber | Lisa Schmidt-Colinet

VIENNA: SLOW CAPITAL?

STEFAN GRUBER

A SHORT HISTORY OF THE WORLD'S MOST LIVABLE CITY—OR ON THE RISK OF THROWING OUT THE PROVERBIAL BABY WITH THE BATHWATER

—

Overnight on May 2.1989, Vienna found itself once again in the centre of Europe. After existing on the impervious edge of a divided world between East and West for half a century, Vienna awoke. Its long beauty sleep was disrupted by the beginning of a vibrant development that is referred to as the second Gründerzeit[1]. But any attendant enthusiasm was also mixed with resentment: both the sudden pressure to act and the need to competitively position Vienna amongst European capitals shattered the city's long-held mantle of comfort.

The following years were filled with continuous debates, plans and speculations: What was the future of the city, the effect of this geo-political shift? But twenty years later, planning policies that initially seemed like gradual adaptations appear in retrospect as a radical break: a paradigm change from 'Soft urban renewal' (Sanfte Stadterneuerung) to urban expansion (Stadterweiterung), from essentially ecologic concerns to economic ones[2], from city planning to mere urbanization[3].

Over the course of the 20th century (and nearly uninterrupted rule by the Social-Democrats) Vienna has earned an international reputation for city planning that consistently regulates private interests in the name of welfare and the public good. Think Red Vienna. During the inter-war period, the city constructed 64,000 housing units, including many social facilities in only 10 years. Vienna still commends itself on these accomplishments. But 1989 and the opening to the East has led Vienna to embrace an approach to planning where the multiple interests at stake are simply moderated in favour of economic prosperity, city marketability and international competitiveness. We could subsume these developments under the global trend of neo-liberalism, and claim that Vienna, relatively speaking, represents a rather moderate case. Nonetheless, the ideological turn - though never clearly spelled out by the still-ruling Social-Democrats - is crucial for understanding Vienna's current success in international city ratings. And it is in a state of suspension between the aspiration to be a global player once again and nostalgia for the days of quaint urban life that Vienna finds itself climbing the ranks of the world's most desirable cities to live in. Just this spring Mercer rated Vienna no. 1 in their "2010 - Global - Quality of Living Report"[4] in its second consecutive year. Yet Vienna's current state, seemingly combining the best of all worlds, is fleeting, its triumph deceptively shortsighted.

As with large ships, cities react slowly, continuing to drift one way long after the helm has been pulled around. This delayed response often impedes distinguishing between cause and effect. The questions now are how today's decisions will affect Vienna in twenty years, and how we can learn from the recent past?

SOFT URBAN RENEWAL

—

"Wien ist anders" ("Vienna is different") proclaimed the city in the early 80's, in an attempt to brush up its backward image. Indeed, post-war Vienna was anything but the dazzling metropolis it had been at the turn of the century. Then, Vienna ranked fourth among the world's largest cities (the equivalent to New York City today); by 1945, however, its population shrank by a quarter, stagnating up to 1989[5]. Unlike many European cities which used the reconstruction efforts after WWII as an opportunity to reorganize themselves according to modern and functionalist principles, Vienna's historic city fabric was spared; it made do instead with quick repairs. Only few large scale projects typical of the 60's and 70's ever materialized in Vienna: the UN headquarters, a subway and a 20km long island regulating the Danube. Each of them met with broad public resistance. Meanwhile, inner-city housing conditions remained obsolete. Almost two-thirds of apartments were without private bath or shower until 1970[6]. And the desolate situation in historic quarters further encouraged the bourgeoisie's flight to suburbia.

The combination of all these factors prepared the ground for Vienna's soft urban renewal movement. At the same time an international backlash against modernist planning led to the rediscovery of the historic city. Kevin Lynch in "The Image of the City" (1960), Jane Jacobs in "Death and Life of Great American Cities" (1961) and Aldo Rossi in "L'architettura della città"(1966) all argued for the merits of urban morphologies grown over time, as well as a return to referencing historic models. For Vienna in particular, the rehabilitation of its Gründerzeit quarters was an opportunity to counteract negative growth. After all, Vienna's proclamation of its "difference" might have been more than a vain advertisement campaign. Instead, it expressed the city's confidence in its ability to capitalize on the current condition.

In the meantime, the process leading to the so-called "Viennese model" of soft urban renewal was arduous. Twenty years passed from early rehabilitation experiments, such as the Blutgasse project in Vienna's first district[7], until an official urban development plan took up the ideas in 1984. Soft urban renewal obviously wasn't conceived at the drawing board. It started bottom-up with students, artists and activist groups. They appropriated dilapi-dated buildings and reclaimed the historic city as a venue for alternative lifestyle and urban (sub)culture[8]. Early initiatives gained momentum and created public awareness for environmental issues in the city. These in turn triggered further projects. The Planquadrat project is a popular example[9]: within one perimeter block of Vienna's fourth district[2], a row of houses was assigned to be demolished to give way to a widened road. The city suggested that the opening would provide access to a new public park, placed at the centre of the block. An ORF television team chose to

BERLIN

BRATISLAVA

BUDAPEST

167

LJUBLJANA

PRAGUE

VIENNA

WARSAW

document the transformation process. Soon, however, the journalists became a driving force in organizing the inhabitants and initiating counter proposals. Four years of discussions later, the block was remodelled. Old buildings were restored. The inner courtyard was gutted from parking lots, fences and shacks. Today the Planquadrat is still a public oasis that is maintained by neighbours and unusually well-frequented; the open, green courtyard providing light and recreational space is further equipped with a communal kitchen reminiscent of "Red Vienna's Hof -projects".

Although similar projects have existed in Vienna since the fifties, the various initiatives only converged in the "Super summer" of 1976[10]. Coop himmelb(l)au had been invited to curate a series of temporary interventions on the Naschmarkt as part of the "Wiener Festwochen" (the Vienna festival). Along with fellow architects, such as Haus-Rucker-Co, Missinglink and Superstudio, their "playground for citizens" aimed at converting passive observers into active participants and giving people a sense of ownership of the city. They succeeded as at the end of the festival, activities were spontaneously transferred to the former municipal abattoir St. Marx in order to prevent its demolition. The festival's final rock concert grew into a summer-long squat attracting 200.000 visitors. And though the bulldozer at the end of the summer couldn't be stopped, the events had long-lasting effects. It stressed the public claim for co-responsibility and necessity for civic participation in processes that shape the urban environment.

It also taught the city to rather embrace activists than fight them. In fact, all resilient Arena squatters were eventually offered alternative spaces for living or cultural venues. The authorities' sensitivity and ability to channel dissident forces into urban regeneration efforts became a subtle but important trait of Viennese planning policies.[11]

THE BIG PLAN OF SMALL STEPS

—
Local experience was complemented by global events. The oil crisis crushed the blind belief in an automobile future. The Club of Rome announced the global limits to growth.[12] This tempered Viennese's inferiority complex, propelling them into the role of a potential avantgarde. Vienna did have experience with devising strategies to address finite resources. Marrying nostalgia for picturesque cityscapes with an ecological cause turned soft urban renewal into a sound political agenda. In 1976 mayor Leopold Gratz commissioned the elaboration of a comprehensive city development plan that would provide a coherent vision and connect the many bottom-up driven measures to add up to more than the sum of its parts. Ratified in 1984, the so-called STEP84 was referred to as the "big plan of small steps". Combining municipal coordination with public participation, Vienna's urban renewal program required new instruments for implementing its goals. One crucial measure was the creation of decentralized planning and consulting bureaus

situated within each neighbourhood[13]. From here, city officials could immerse themselves in the local milieu and follow initiatives on a daily basis.

Over time, 4.700 buildings with 201.000 housing units would be renovated, reducing the percentage of "sub-standard apartments" from 39% to 14%[14].The greatest challenge would be to rehabilitate neighbourhoods without displacing its population. The city's political objectives were clearly outlined in the STEP84's introduction: Improving living standards and environmental condition in the city (also to counteract urban flight); reinforcing social equality and solidarity (through an even accessibility to infrastructure); promoting cultural urban diversity including the protection of cultural heritage; and balancing the cities' relation to its territory, thereby encouraging civic participation and self-determination. With such an emancipatory focus, planning took on a broader socio-political dimension. It is striking how current the claims of 1984 sound today in an age of ubiquitous political and corporate commitment to sustainability. Had Vienna continuously developed and refined its strategies, it might now be at the forefront of ecological urbanism[15]. But for better or worse, 1989 would radically alter Vienna's course.

BIG STEPS AND MANY PLANS

–

The fall of the iron curtain presented Vienna with an unexpected opportunity to position itself as a gateway between East and West. Both the border opening and the following wars in former Yugoslavia prompted significant immigration. Vienna suddenly grew[16]. Yet reactions were ambivalent. The mood in Vienna at that time is probably best captured by this single decision: in 1986 Vienna applied to host the World Expo'95 in tandem with Budapest. The event was intended as a political gesture and a city promotion of global magnitude. But now that history had turned in favour of such twinning, the Viennese got cold feet. They cancelled the event in a referendum. However, as if Viennese were unwilling to pass on the world expo's benefits, they went straight on to realize the post-expo scenario. The resulting Donau city, as it stands today, is symptomatic for post-1989 urban planning in Vienna. Inspired by Paris-La Défense and Mitterand´s foible for grand architectural projects, the Donau city was to become Vienna's second "city" and finally perform the leap across the Danube. A series of corporate high-rises would represent the city's newly acquired financial influence and ambitions in a global city competition. More critical than the project itself however, was the way in which the original master plan was eventually implemented. In their scheme Krischanitz and Neumann envisioned an even mix of programs combining offices, housing and cultural or educational facilities laid out on a regular grid with open blocks and punctual high-rises. In response to the site, the public realm was organized on two levels, the ground level dedicated to cars and ample vegetation; the upper one, consisting of bridges and terraces leading through the tree canopies, reserved for pedestrians and

BERLIN

BRATISLAVA

BUDAPEST

169

LJUBLJANA

PRAGUE

VIENNA

WARSAW

building access. But the plan was compromised from the very start. The development of the 17,4 hectare area and 1,650,000 m3 construction volume was given single handedly to the private WED-developer (Wiener Entwicklungsgesellschaft für den Donauraum). The city, anxious to lure big investors to Vienna, left the location, shape and height of buildings "to be negotiated"[17]. From then on, changes to the master plan were justified with economic arguments. The result is an uncoordinated array of oversized towers mostly accessed from the underground car park.

The left-over public spaces remain deserted and exposed to dramatic down winds. Housing on the site eventually had to be subsidized by the city as its development wasn't lucrative enough. It was also pushed to the least attractive (and least valuable) edges of the site. Meanwhile, funding for the cultural or educational programs is still missing. Thus, as a constant reminder of frail public governance, the centre of Vienna's second "city" remains a giant, empty pit. In 2001, a second master plan competition was called in an attempt to rescue the situation. Dominique Perault (coincidentally the architect of Mitterand's Très Grande Bibliothèque de France) was commissioned to revitalize the urban ensemble. The centre piece of his response is two twin-towers, higher than any other building in Vienna and uncomfortably evocative of New York's World Trade Centre. Due to the recent recession however, it seems funds will only suffice for one of the towers and if one is optimistic to fix up the public space…

Though the largest in size,

the Donau city is not Vienna's only example of flawed new developments: the Millennium Tower, the Gasometer City, Monte Laa and the Wienerberg City have all lived through similar histories[18]. Developments range between 130,000 and 240,000m2 of usable area in size; all are situated at the urban fringe. The two latter examples stand out in that they plainly disregard the city's imperative to only develop sites connected to public transport and which aren't dependent on car access alone. All projects furthermore share a huge proportion of shopping, although Vienna already offers the highest ratio of retail area per capita in Europe. Meanwhile inner-city shopping streets struggle with vacancies. Shopping mall developments obviously attract large investments with particularly high turnovers, and the city has gone as far as subsidizing housing in order to provide the critical mass of inhabitants or customers that would make certain types of retail viable[19]. Has Vienna's illustrious social housing tradition become an indirect subsidy of shopping malls for which actual demand doesn't exist?[20] Is welfare being defined here as ensuring overall economic prosperity independently of its distribution?

VIENNA, TWENTY YEARS LATER

—

Vienna's most recent urban development plan, STEP'05, affirms the ideas of soft urban renewal. It pleads, however, that city planning today must first and foremost assure regional location development and intercity competitiveness. As if these two notions were mutually exclusive, it emphasizes the idealism of 1984's development plan and its simultaneous lack of focus on economic strategies. In contrast to the political beliefs stated at the beginning of the STEP84, in its 2005 counterpart both mayor Häupl and Stadtrat Schicker merely describe the impact of the current economic situation. The plan is broken down into thirteen key areas of action or "hotspots on which the city will focus efforts"[21]. The overall vision connecting these areas however remains vague. Splintering increases flexibility to respond to particular conditions and interests. The downside of course is the risk of making developments a matter of negotiation. Prior examples have revealed repeated discrepancies between the municipality's intentions and actual implementations. One thus has to ask where the incapacity to regulate and direct urbanization comes from.

Though Vienna's recent focus on regional relations seems reasonable, it far exceeds the city's scope of influence. Other instruments would be necessary to plan and act at the scale of Centrope, a region ten times the size of Holland's Randstad. Despite the ambition to position itself at the crossroads between the former East and West, Vienna still awaits a highway connection to Brno and Prague. Twenty years later, when crossing the Czech-Austrian border, one is dumped from a four-lane-wide motorway into a country road.

VIENNA: SLOW CAPITAL

—

Under the current conditions of raging financial crises and the end of fossil energy resources looming (once again), we might halt and wonder: what is it that makes Vienna one of the most desirable cities to live in today?
Is it the urban developments and projects of the past twenty years? Is it really the new signature highrises and shopping centre dispersed at Vienna's urban fringe? Or is the wealth they attract and produce? If it is simply Vienna's geo-political situation, how does Vienna differ from cities like Berlin, Prague or Budapest? What are Vienna's tangible or intangible characteristics that will sustain its success twenty years from now? Here I would like to propose an alternative leitbild for Vienna, one that reassesses Viennese values and embraces its most essential feature: slowness. It is slowness in its broadest sense that is Vienna's greatest asset—much more than the generic representations of financial power and its dire attempts at global competitiveness. And in an odd paradox, committing to this slowness as a way of life might make Vienna even more competitive in the long term.

Slowness, when attributed to a city, suggests not only a laid-back life style, but also gradual rather than impulsive change and developments. Long-term repercussions are favored over short-term benefits. Influences are taken from local and culturally-specific factors rather than global trends. Slowness is sustainable and

BERLIN

BRATISLAVA

BUDAPEST

171

LJUBLJANA

PRAGUE

VIENNA

WARSAW

ecological, advocating short distances and respect for existing urban fabric and building matter. Slowness is a privilege, one that maybe only the "world's most desirable city to live in" can afford, and at the risk of losing its rank yet maintaining its quality.

The leitbild of "Slow Capital" advocates an urban development that is strategic in its speed and focus. It plays on the double meaning of capital. It suggests that the quality of life in a city might also be determined by its capacity to resist certain movements and concentrate on its unique attributes instead. Global rankings on the contrary are concerned with parameters that are comparable and thus per definition generic. Werner Rosinak, a Viennese traffic engineer who has been advocating deceleration as a strategy for Vienna since 1990, uses Vienna's tramways as a paradigmatic example for the benefits of slow development:[23] While in the 50's most modern cities such as Los Angeles embraced the automobile future by ridding themselves of their tram system, Vienna failed to follow the trend. By the time it realized what was going on tramlines had become sustainable and progressive once again. The red trams are an essential feature of Viennese street life. More importantly, Vienna's tram system has marked out arteries of high infrastructural density and can thus effectively counteract sprawl.
Pre-1989's low-pressure environment bred a planning culture able to transform the city despite demographic and economic stagnation. Why shouldn't one be able to inverse the situation and continue to develop the city gradually despite the current pressure? The slow capital strategy doesn't aim to put Vienna asleep, stagnate its economy and freeze its development. Much rather, slowness has to be injected strategically in order to maintain and reinforce Vienna's utmost strength and sign of quality of life, in spite of steady growth.

Vienna's recent past has demonstrated the apparent inevitability of large projects (aka Bigness) following the principles of economy of scale. The vision of "Vienna: Slow Capital" however challenges the ostensible incompatibility of large-scale building complexes with dense, historic urban conditions. Can Bigness act as an urban catalyst for the regeneration and densification at the scale of a neighbourhood? Can big investments be channeled into Vienna's Gründerzeit quarters without throwing out the proverbial baby with the bath? "Vienna: Slow Capital" calls for a critical revision of Bigness and its inclination to "fuck context"[24]. As an antidote to Rem Koolhaas' assertion that "only Bigness instigates the regimes of complexity that mobilize the full intelligence of architecture and its related fields"[25], Vienna's soft urban renewal has shown how minimal local measures can produce a stunning intelligence, irreducible complexity and systemic change. Thus the leitbild of slow capital aims at reviving an approach to urbanism in which a series of strategic interventions produce synergetic effects on the city as a whole. Slowness here should neither be understood as a general nostalgia for historic cities, nor as a populist resolution. Rather it is a radical realism, a realistic assessment of Vienna's strength and weaknesses combined with a radical commitment to a feature that is immune to zeitgeist and fashion. Slowness is no guarantee for spectacular architecture; it's effects however will be irresistibly seductive.

----

1 The German term Gründerzeit refers to the period of massive industrialization and economic upswing in the mid-19th century. In a short time entire neighborhoods were developed by private investors producing splendid palaces for nouveau-riche citizens, but also infamous rental ghettos for the working class.

2 See: Kurt Stimmer und Gottfried Pirhofer, „Pläne für Wien: Theorie und Praxis der Wiener Stadtplanung von 1945 bis 2005", Stadtentwicklung Wien 2007. p.74

3 Amongst others Pier Vittorio Aureli makes the difference between "civitas - the origin of the term 'city' - and urbs - a term transformed by Idefonso Cerda's popular neologism, urbanization, in 1867. Civitas is the political institution that signifies the collective will of a community to inhabit and coexist in one place. Urbs is the infrastructure that ultimately materially supports this choice" in Pier Vittorio Aureli "The city as political form", Visionary Power, NAi Publishers, Rotterdam 2007. p.17

4 "http://www.mercer.com/qualityoflivingpr#City_Ranking_Tables" http://www.mercer.com/qualityoflivingpr#City_Ranking_Tables

5 Between 1918 and 1945 Vienna's population shrank from 2.1 Mio inhabitants to 1.6 Mio. After a slight increase from 1945-71 it dropped by 5.5% to 1.5 Mio inhabitants until 1981.

6 See: Kurt Stimmer und Gottfried Pirhofer, „Pläne für Wien: Theorie und Praxis der Wiener Stadtplanung von 1945 bis 2005", Stadtentwicklung Wien 2007. p.86 (http://www.wien.gv.at/stadtentwicklung/grundlagen/pdf/planungsgeschichte-01.pdf)

7 The Blugassen rehabilitation was criticized as too luxurious, because unjustified amounts of public funds were spent for the benefits of few individuals. The original inhabitants were forced out and replaced by yuppie intellectual and artist crowd.

8 A detailed account of the history of soft urban renewal is given by Christiane Feuerstein "Anfänge der sanften Stadterneuerung in Wien. Die Entdeckung der alltäglichen Stadt" in: Christiane Feuerstein, Angelika Fitz "Wann begann temporär? Frühe Stadtinterventionen und sanfte Stadterneuerung in Wien", Springer-Verlag, Wien 2009. Also see: Leopold Redl, „Über den Alltag der Stadterneuerung" in: Stadt im Durchschnitt, Böhlau, Wien 1994

9 See: Helmut Voitl, Elisabeth Guggenberger, Peter Pirker "Planquadrat. Ruhe, Grün und Sicherheit - Wohnen in der Stadt" Wien 1977

10 See: Christiane Feuerstein, Angelika Fitz "Wann begann temporär? Frühe Stadtinterventionen und sanfte Stadterneuerung in Wien", Springer-Verlag, Wien 2009

11 See: Siegfried Mattl, Das 20. Jahrhundert, Pichler, Wien 2000. p.89. Also see: Hazel Rosenstrauch „Ostcharme mit Westkomfort" in: Wien wirklich, Verlag für Gesellschaftskritik, Wien1992

12 See: Donella H. Meadows, Dennis L. Meadows, Jørgen Randers, et al. "Limits to Growth: The 30-Year Update", Chelsea Green; 3rd edition 2004, 1st edition 1972

13 Local plus one mobile so-called Gebietsbetreuungen exist today in Vienna

14 See: http://www.bestpractices.at/main.php?page=vienna/best_practices/housing/urban_renewal&lang=de

15 In Mercer's Eco-City Ranking 2010 Vienna only holds place 44. http://www.mercer.com/qualityoflivingpr#Ranking_Eco_Cities

16 Between 1990 and 1993 Vienna grew by 110,000 inhabitants, mainly due to immigration and counterbalancing 20,000 that moved to its periphery

17 See: Reinhard Seiss „Wer baut Wien? Hintergründe und Motive der Stadtentwicklung Wiens seit 1989", Anton Pustet, Salzburg 2007. p.20

18 Ibid.

19 Ibid. p.23

20 Of course there are exceptions to the rule and Vienna has produced some remarkable social housing projects since the nineties, though most of the examples are located in dense urban environments. Inevitably their ingenuity emerged partly out of contextual constraints.

21 Rudi Schicker „Vienna - The Opportunities and Tasks of Urban Development" in STEP05, Vienna City Administration MA18 Vienna 2005

22 The title „Vienna: Slow Capital" corresponds to the one of two design studios the author has led as a professor at the Academy of Fine Arts Vienna during the academic year 2009/10. The studios were co-taught with Lisa Schmidt-Colinet and part of a collaborative project with six other Central European Universities called "Urbanity - twenty years later"

23 See: Werner Rosinak, Viennaline, in: Bleibt Wien Wien? Falter Verlag, Wien 1995

24 Rem Koolhaas, Bigness, in: S,M,L,XL, Monacelli Press, New York 1998

25 Ibid.

BERLIN

BRATISLAVA

BUDAPEST

173

LJUBLJANA

PRAGUE

VIENNA

WARSAW

NEGOTIATING BIGNESS AND SOFT URBAN RENEWAL

LISA SCHMIDT-COLINET

PROJECTS FOR "VIENNA: SLOW CAPTAL"

—
Recent urban developments in Vienna expose the difficulties of large -scale master planning. Though Vienna's current master plan clearly defines individual target areas of future urban development, it remains unable to convey an overall vision. In response, this project proposes a leitmotif envisioning Vienna as a Slow Capital. As an image, "Vienna: Slow Capital" is clear and evocative, open enough to engender a variety of tactics. The project questions a top-down approach towards city planning. Instead it explores the potential of strategic local interventions influencing the city as a whole and adding up to one coherent vision.

This project extended over the course of three semesters: A first research semester was dedicated to comparing Vienna's urban development before and after 1989. It explored the effects of Vienna's new geopolitical position on planning regulations and urban form. This led to the proposal of a leitmotif for Vienna: "Slow Capital". The following two semesters investigated possibilities of further densifying Vienna's historic city fabric, and reconciling pre- and post- 1989

strategies, which are Soft Urban Renewal and Bigness. These two distinct urban paradigms have defined Vienna's development before and after 1989: During the years of stagnating population the city had focused on the renewal of the existing Gründerzeit fabric. Under the pressure to grow and to compete with the neighbouring cities after 1989 focus shifted towards large projects, supposed to attract further development, hence located at the periphery. Through their location and their size, theses recent projects became self -referential, claiming to be cities within the city. Isolated from any context they were not able to attract a critical mass.

The leitmotif "Vienna: Slow Capital" postulates to pause for a second, to rethink the rush to develop and to reconsider existing qualities and competences. Slowness also evokes an image of intense and slower ways of using the city, to live in close contact with the neighbourhood. Therefore the studio aimed at projects that interact with the surrounding differently, that create porosity towards the neighbourhood, proposals that are integrative rather then exclusive. Challenging the gravitation of large implementations towards the periphery and introducing large programmatic input into the urban fabric, questions their inherent characteristic to be introverted and isolated from its surrounding. Vienna's model of Soft Urban Renewal has the ambition not only to refurbish the built structure, but also to consolidate existing neighbourhoods. This expertise has the potential to establish a productive dialogue between big implementations and the existing

fabric of the city. A Negotiation between Bigness and Soft Urban Renewal had brought up projects that interweave architecture and the city differently and thus contribute to "slower" forms of living and working.
Using this conflict as a generative device, one semester put emphasis on strategies for integrating large projects at the scale of a neighbourhood; the following focused on architectural proposals and their implications for the surroundings.

VIENNA, 20 YEARS LATER
- A DOCUMENTATION AND EVALUATION

For a deeper understanding of recent developments, research was extended to the planning history of Vienna back to its foundation, relating architecture and urban development to political, cultural and technological events. To illustrate the new dynamics caused by the fall of the Iron Curtain and Austria's accession to the EU, each student further focused on a particular phenomenon.

Potentials and risks of the changed status of allotment gardens, for example, were explored by Roland Stolz. The permission, introduced in 1992, to inhabit allotment gardens all year round, showed the cities' effort to provide new housing space for a rising population. Other students were reviewing large-scale implementations, emblematic for Vienna's rush to develop, such as the Donau-City: Mechthild Weber disentangled this complex development and illustrated, how an overall master plan faded into the background.

Building onto the findings of this first semester, the following two semesters developed specific projects exploring the potential of slowness for the city.

NEGOTIATING BIGNESS AND SOFT URBAN RENEWAL. STRATEGIES FOR A NEIGHBOURHOOD.

Questioning the apparent incompatibility of the two paradigms, Bigness and Soft Urban Renewal, the studio brief proposed the implementation of large projects within dense Gründerzeit neighbourhoods. The resulting conflict inevitably imposes a critical revision of Bigness. It challenges its isolation from the surrounding and demands flexibility to change and adapt over time.

The studio aimed at interventions that operate between architecture and urbanism, working on multiple scales: strategies had to be defined to make large implementations operate as urban catalyst for a sustainable renewal, to strengthen the existing neighbourhood. Spatial proposals had to articulate the relation of enclosed and commonly shared space of the street, thus between private and public realm. Exploring the territory between Bigness and Soft Urban Renewal, the studio both used and subverted Bigness.

Three neighbourhood areas were selected, located within the dense fabric of the Gründerzeit:

Fünfhaus and the area south of the Meiselmarkt, both in Vienna's 15th district and the northern part of the 10th district. The areas are located near large developments of the Westbahnhof and the new Central-station. They have not been targeted for urban development, and have not yet undergone gentrification. In the shadow of these large developments, the defined areas have the chance to experiment with transformations of their urban fabric and to revise the characteristic perimeter block.

Departing from the close observation of the urban environments, students came up with the definition of the programme (30,000-40,000 sqm were given as a figure), which create additional value for the neighbourhood residents. Location, or spots of intervention, had to be defined: the proposals ranged from highly-densified implementations e.g. unusually located within the street, towards fragmented and dispersed interventions that integrate the public realm of the city.

"Playground 15" is reclaiming the street as a place for meeting and playful activity. Taking into consideration a lack of programme for the young population of the district, a small network of streets is proposed as a shared surface for the neighbourhood. Freed from parking cars and transformed into a topographical landscape, the space of the street becomes a playground. The street as a central element of the project extends into three buildings. There, it turns into a parking-gorund, a surface for indoor-leisure activities and ground for student homes. Slowness triggers innovation on different scales: on the everyday level, slowing down traffic through the undulated surfaces invites to use the street differently. Hence, the proposal

allows for a slow transition from a parking ground towards other activities, challenging possibilities of the inclined ground. In a longtime perspective, a lively street will effect the adjacent vacant ground-floor spaces. Frequented with passers-by, varying in age, interests and time schedules, the abandoned shops may turn into interesting locations again. Thus, the project aims first at changing the conditions that cause the decrease of ground-floor usage, rather than implanting new programmes directly.

The presence of vacant ground-floor shops is one of the most urgent problems of Vienna's Gründerzeit areas. Dominated by housing, the areas have lost their quality as mixed-use districts; previously-existing relations between small shops, workshops and inhabitants have dissolved. Shops suffer from a lack of business; large areas are used as depot spaces or garages. These no longer contribute to the bustle of the street. The idea of slowness proved to be productive in several proposals, to increase the quality of the street and to re-establish a strong interrelation between the buildings, ground floor spaces and the street.

The project "Density and Dispersion" identifies the open space of numerous empty building lots in the area as a quality for the neighbourhood rather than as potential land for construction. An agreement between the city and the investor-a kind of barter-could allow for the high densification of one dedicated site in order to keep gaps throughout the district free from buildings. Thus, the project asks the question: What are the conditions we can impose on investors, when the city offers profitable inner-city building plots in exchange?

Using the leitmotif of Slowness, "The Green Network" is based on a long-term strategy, giving time for the complex negotiations between the tenants, private owners and the city. Precise research on ownerships and tenants was the basis for a proposal, which in small steps and phases, regroupes plots and creates synergies between the interests of different tenants. The strategy allowed for densification within the courtyard of one block, and intensification of green, crossing block and neighbourhood. The presence of parks, which are difficult to access and hidden backyards contribute to a perceived lack of greenery in the district. The project used this discrepancy to propose minimal interventions enhancing the visibility and connection of the existing green spaces. Regrouping leftover spaces and unused plots allows the establishment of a communal -green. In addition, vertical terraces give the possibility of private gardening.

The Viennese Gründerzeitblock is characterized by the multitude of ownerships. Projects that restructure an entire block must involve tenants, private owners, and the planning department. This kind of intervention challenges the existing planning instruments. It demands an extension of the authority of the Gebietsbetreuung (a service institution, established by the city in 1974, in the course of the Soft Urban Renewal) as

a mediating instrument. Even though the city has a strong interest in reconversions of blocks, it is the complexity of this process, which prevents them happening on a larger scale.

The projects of that semester focused on the mutual influence of large implementations and the interests of an existing neighbourhood. In a third chapter, the antagonism of Bigness and Soft Urban Renewal allowed for a revision of Bigness on the scale of buildings.

BIGNESS: THE RUINS OF TOMORROW?

Vienna is currently experiencing intense inner-city shopping development. Enormous amounts of retail space are constructed even though the market is saturated. Following this development, the generic programme of shopping was chosen as the starting point for this third studio. Departing from the surplus of retail space and its unpredictable economic situation, shopping was considered as an initial programme, unstable and therefore temporary. Complemented by offices and the more stable programme of housing, the projects had to develop a building strategy to house different programmatic consistencies.

Slowness demands a stronger interaction with the urban context; therefore the program challenges the predominant typology of the introverted shopping mall. The projects had to redefine the relation of retail space to the surrounding: Following a commercial logic on the one hand, additional value for the neighbourhoods had to be created

BERLIN

BRATISLAVA

BUDAPEST

177

LJUBLJANA

PRAGUE

VIENNA

WARSAW

on the other hand. Which typological innovations can be generated by the implementation of Bigness within the dense historic context? How can its characteristic to be introverted be turned around? Can the relation of programmatic entities become strong enough to make an enclosing envelope obsolete? To find answers to these questions, students first developed a "proto-typology", a diagrammatic organisation of given programme. In a second step those were confronted with the specific local environment and had to establish a dialogue.
The chosen site was located in the 10th district, next to one of the important arterial roads connecting the south of Vienna with its centre. Currently the area is occupied by a large supermarket and parking.

Students developed different foci. Some projects used the leitmotif "Vienna: Slow Capital" to articulate a long-term strategy for buildings which anticipate change and are able to transform and adapt. Other projects stressed the typological transformation of shopping surfaces, challenging their potential to actively contribute to the neighbourhood.

Clemens Hasler proposed an open ground floor, where circular pavilions are surrounded by the space of the city. Referring to existing market structures in Vienna, the privately owned commercial surfaces are reduced to sales-areas, whereas the pavement of the city covers circulation and in between spaces. The 19th century Gründerzeitblock establishes a clear distinction between the space of the street as public and the inner courtyards as private.

As a counterproposal, this project allowed strolls through the block, thus relating to the local context and connecting the neighbourhood.

Philipp Soeparno understood the proposed site as a fragment of the city. His proposal became a model for the city itself, posing the question: How do we achieve a city that anticipates change, growth and shrinkage? In addition to the mixed usage, his project aimed at a melange of buildings, differing in size and lifespan. Soeparno proposed the coexistence of two opposing models: Concentration of volumes through large buildings which are extremely robust in terms of their structure and possible usage, next to fragmented smallgrained structures. The almost neutral large volumes allowed divers programmes to take place, but also different models of ownership and tenants. A large retail warehouse can house a market, loft-spaces, apartments. The adjacent smaller, light buildings, can easily be transformed, torn down and or rebuilt. This surrounding is not articulated as an architectural proposal. A series of rules and building regulations defined the size of the parcel and building lines. These building lines should guarantee a quality of throughways and diagonal crossings and allow for a differentiation of the in-between spaces related to the direct surrounding. The analysis of the site and its environment had illustrated the mutual influence of divers ground-floor programmes and the activity of the public realm. Taking into account these interdependencies, Soeparno defined density, height and set-backs depending on the programme: As commercial space produces - and is

dependent on - a higher frequency
of people, streets become larger,
whereas intimate streets are
considered more convenient for
housing. The project proposed to
relate two approaches to sustainable
planning: light structures, reduced
to what we actually need, coexist
next to the neutral envelope, which
provides all possibilities of usage,
and where architecture becomes
infrastructure.

In the course of the three
semesters, the studio came up with
alternatives to master planning.
The projects escape the apparent
categorizations of architecture
versus urban planning, design versus
strategy. These are projects that
work both on a spatial level and at
strategic level of the city.

BERLIN

BRATISLAVA

BUDAPEST

179

LJUBLJANA

PRAGUE

VIENNA

WARSAW

This illustrated timeline chronicles Vienna's urban development from its roman origin to today, twenty years after the fall of the iron curtain. Political, social and cultural events (both local and global) are juxtaposed with contemporary forms of urbanization and architectural projects. Together they establish possible links, cause and effect relationships between the forces at play in shaping our built environment.

Students: Adnan Balcinovic | Clemens Hasler | Christiane Irxenmayer
Lukas Pazmandy | Adina Radway | Roland Stolz | Philipp Soeparno
Mechtild Weber | Michaela Wonisch | Marc Werner

BERLIN
BRATISLAVA
BUDAPEST

181

LJUBLJANA
PRAGUE
VIENNA
WARSAW

THE RINGSTRASSE

1858   1860   1862   1864

Allerhöchst genehmigter Plan   der Stadterweiterung

Heinrichshof 1861-62
Theophil Hansen

Groundplan

The Heinrich-Hof of the
baron Heinrich Drasche
mirrors the social and
economic status of its
owner. It gave example
for many Ringstrassen-
palais.

beim Beginne des Jahres

THE RINGSTRASSE FIRST PART 1857-65

LIBERALS
ELECTION 1861

Poverty and housing
shortance

Dr. Andreas Zelinka

1860   1862

1858

1864

The Donau City project is emblematic for post-1989 developments in Vienna. Both its genesis and current outcome illustrate the challenge of new and very large developments (aka Bigness). This research traces back original intentions, negotiations and decisions between the multiple players involved. It ultimately questions the role of the architect and develops three future scenarios: The one of an optimist, the one of a radical pragmatist or a visionary technocrat.

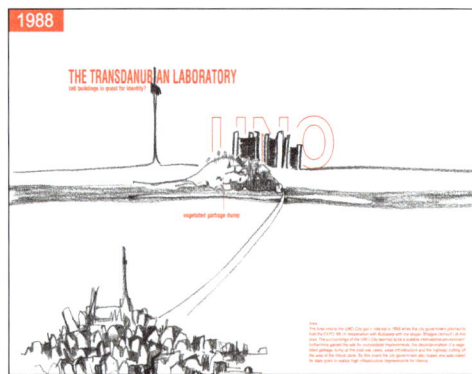

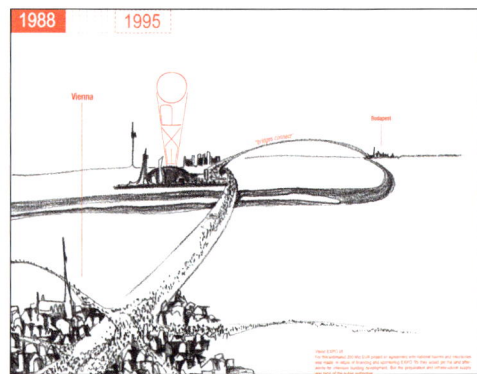

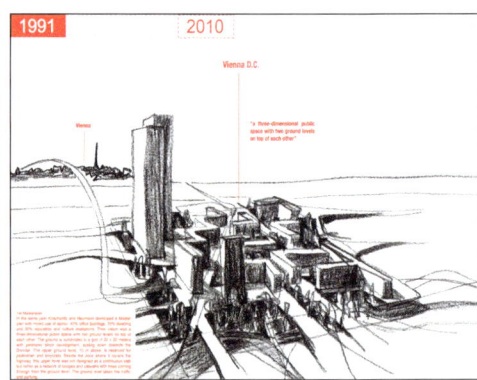

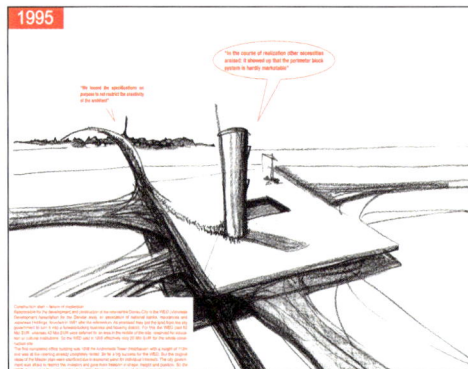

overlaid masterplans / the architect as an idealist?

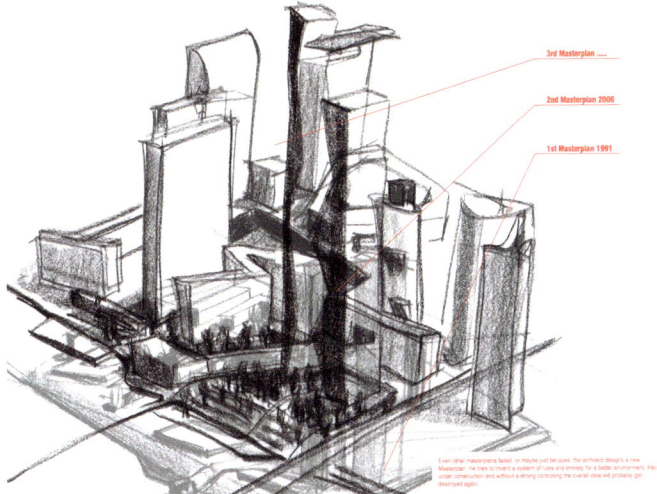

3rd Masterplan

2nd Masterplan 2006

1st Masterplan 1991

unrestricted capitalism / the architect as supplier?

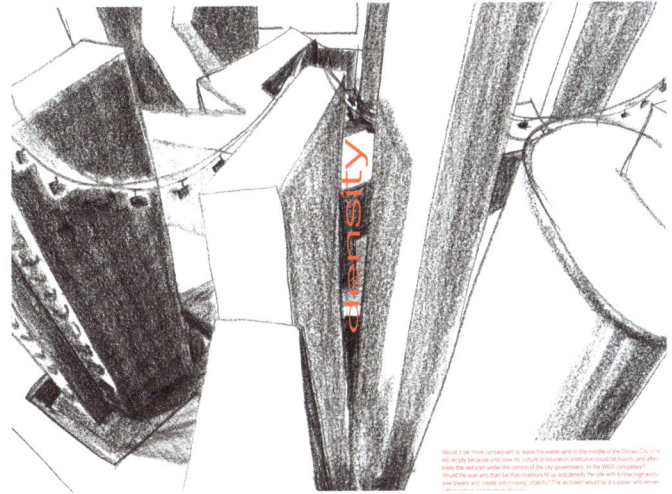

pragmatic optimism / the architect as inventor?

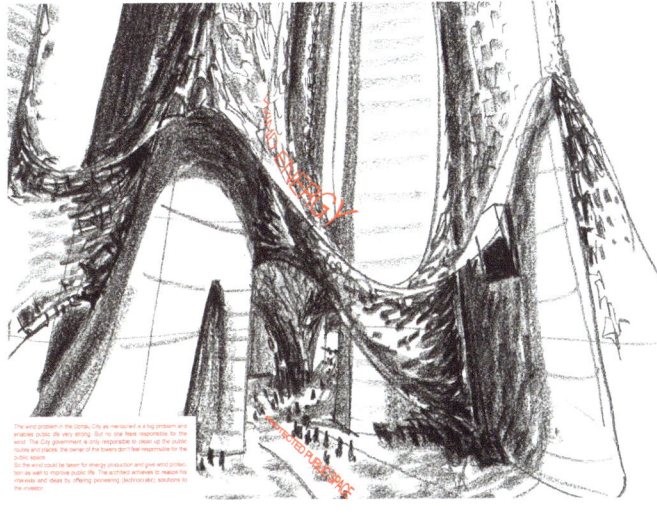

BERLIN
BRATISLAVA
BUDAPEST
183
LJUBLJANA
PRAGUE
VIENNA
WARSAW

In response to the sudden immigration of 1989-1993, Vienna allowed allotment gardens to become permanent residences. While immediately relieving the housing market, it produced other deficiencies on the long term. Once innocent garden associations have become Vienna's gated communities. Access to the private neighborhoods is restricted. Yet its inhabitants demand infrastructure to be paid by public funds. Based on trade-off scenarios the project proposes a series of possible developments.

1920 - 0 m²

1985 - 35 m²

1992 - 50 m²

2010 - 60 m²

2020 - 80 m²

2020 - 80 m²

2050 - 120 m²

2050 - 120 m²

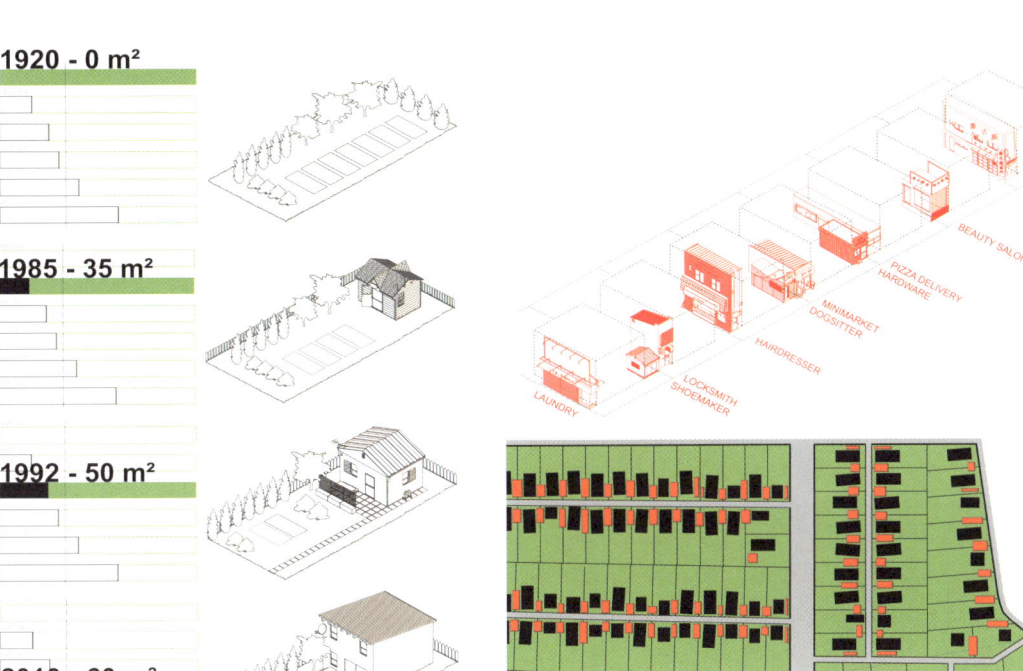

LAUNDRY
LOCKSMITH
SHOEMAKER
HAIRDRESSER
DOGSITTER
MINIMARKET
PIZZA DELIVERY
HARDWARE
BEAUTY SALON

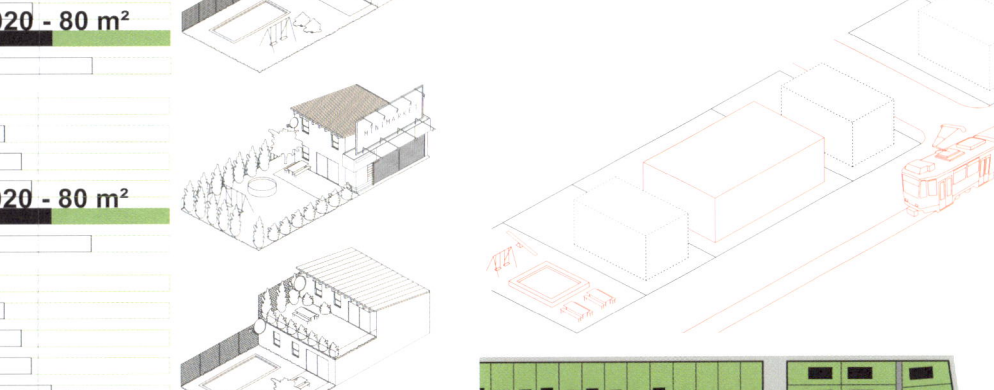

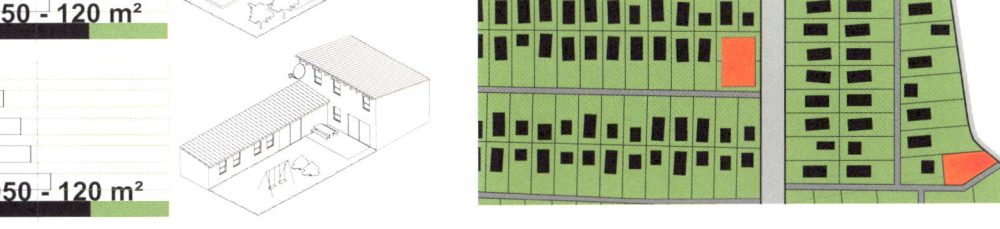

BERLIN

BRATISLAVA

BUDAPEST

185

LJUBLJANA

PRAGUE

VIENNA

WARSAW

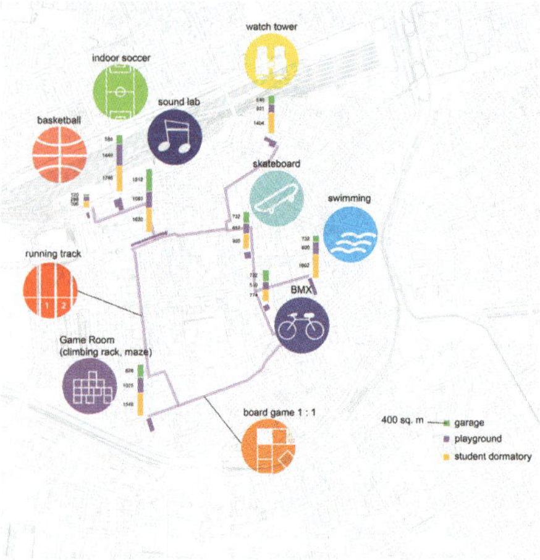

type of user   type of surface

pedestrian

bike

car

speed

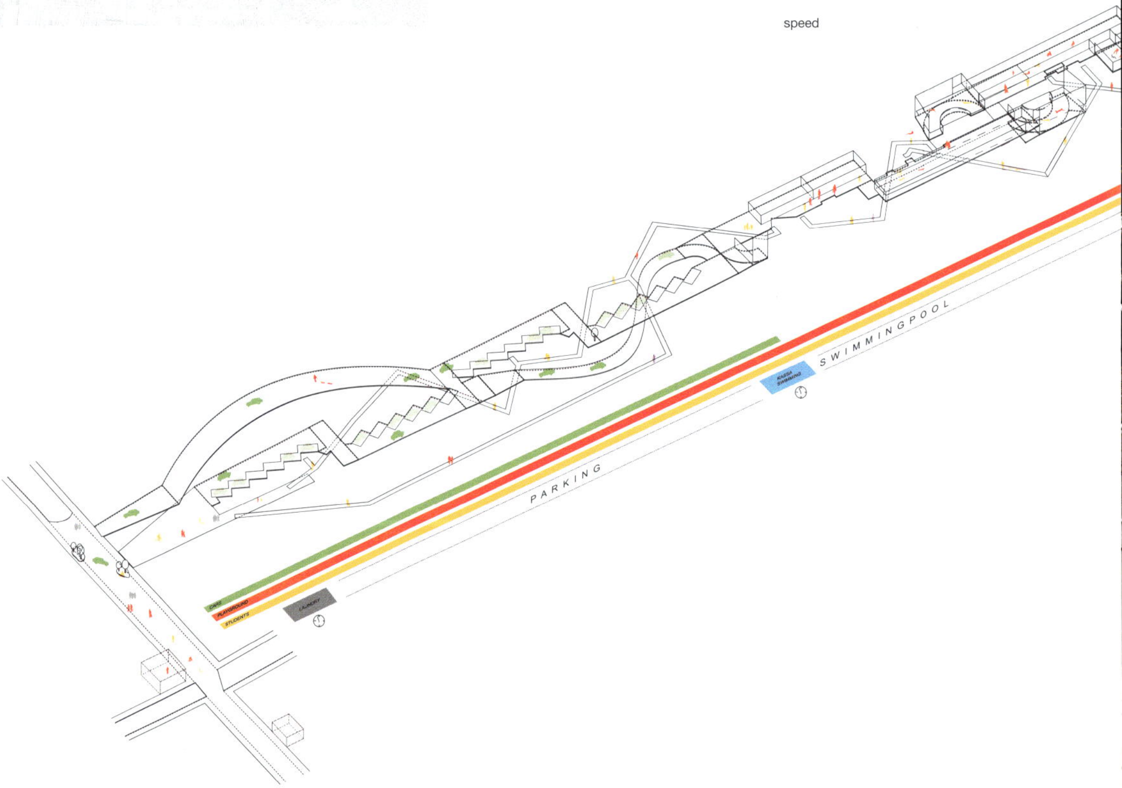

SWIMMINGPOOL

PARKING

watch tower

indoor soccer

sound lab

basketball

skateboard

swimming

running track

BMX

Game Room
(climbing rack, maze)

board game 1 : 1

400 sq. m — garage
playground
student dormatory

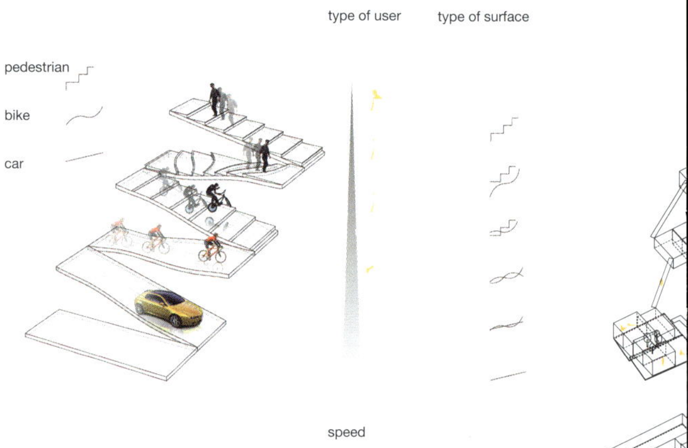

"Playground15" aims at freeing neighborhood streets from parking cars. It converts
selected roads into a network of linear playgrounds. In exchange it places multi-
story car parks in a series of small empty lots. These buildings are conceived as
hybrid typologies further housing leisure facilities and student-accommodation. The
design extends the public sidewalk, blurring in-and outside. The folded topography
regulates accessibility and differentiates programming. The architectural intervention turns into a catalyst activating the neighborhood streets.

Students: Wesley Ho | Mariedl Kleemann | Jasmin Leonard

BERLIN

BRATISLAVA

BUDAPEST

LJUBLJANA

PRAGUE

VIENNA

WARSAW

STUDENTROOMS   STUDENTROOM

TO   HAVE

S T U D E N T R O O M S

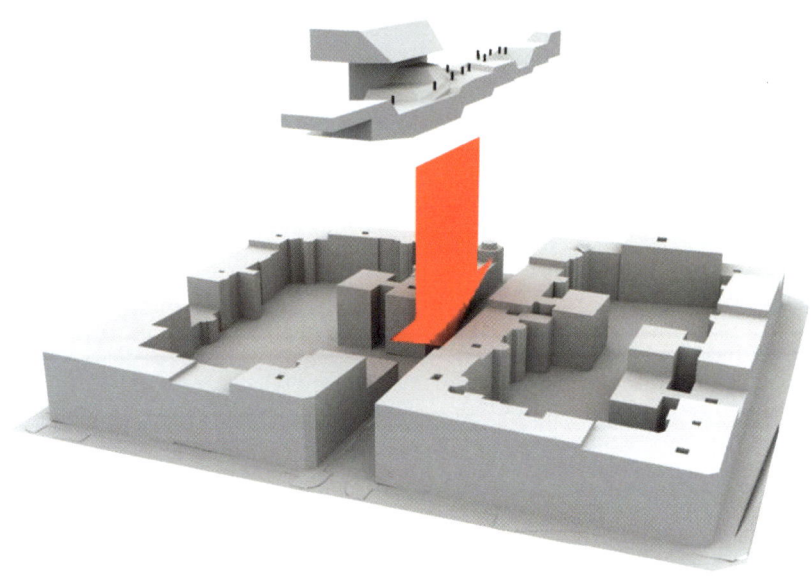

The proposal challenges the opposition between figure-ground, perimeter block and street, building and infrastructure. In response to many vacant stores, it puts forward a scenario in which certain streets are filled with linear low-rise buildings. While the roofscape remains publicly accessible, a whole new set of spaces and relations to the public realm emerge. The project expands the catalogue of urban experiences and produces differentiation at the scale of the neighborhood.

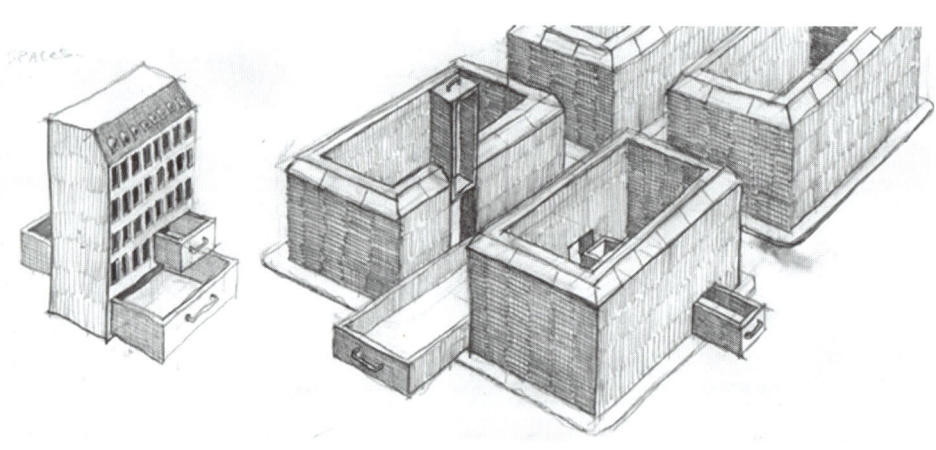

Students: Stefan Aursulesei | Roland Icking | Gunita Pavlovica

BERLIN

BRATISLAVA

BUDAPEST

189

LJUBLJANA

PRAGUE

VIENNA

WARSAW

WORKSHOP
OFFICE
OFFICE
PARKING

SPORTS
OFFICE
OFFICE
PARKING

MEDIATHEK
OFFICE
OFFICE
PARKING

YOUTH
OFFICE
OFFICE
PARKING

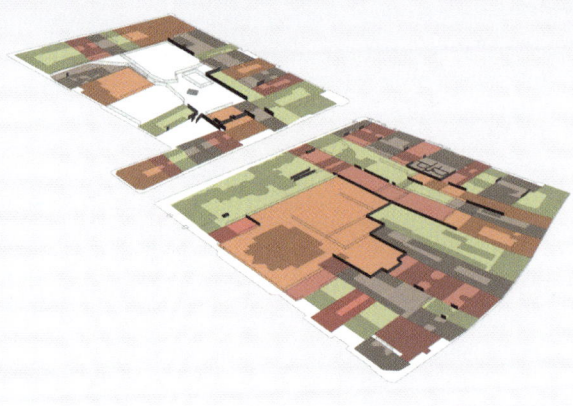

land subdivision, ownerships and accessibility

inhabitants and green area/person

Students: Sebastian Bauer | Christiane Hütter | Daniela Mitterberger

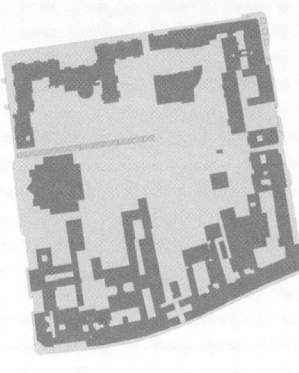
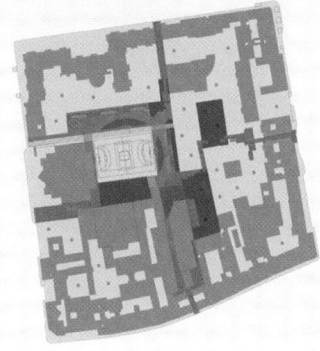
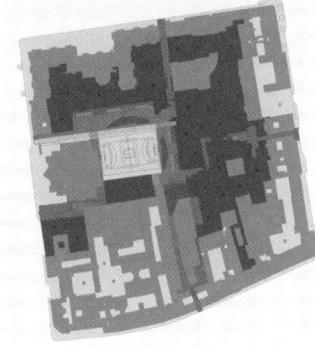

surface treatment   2015   2020   2025

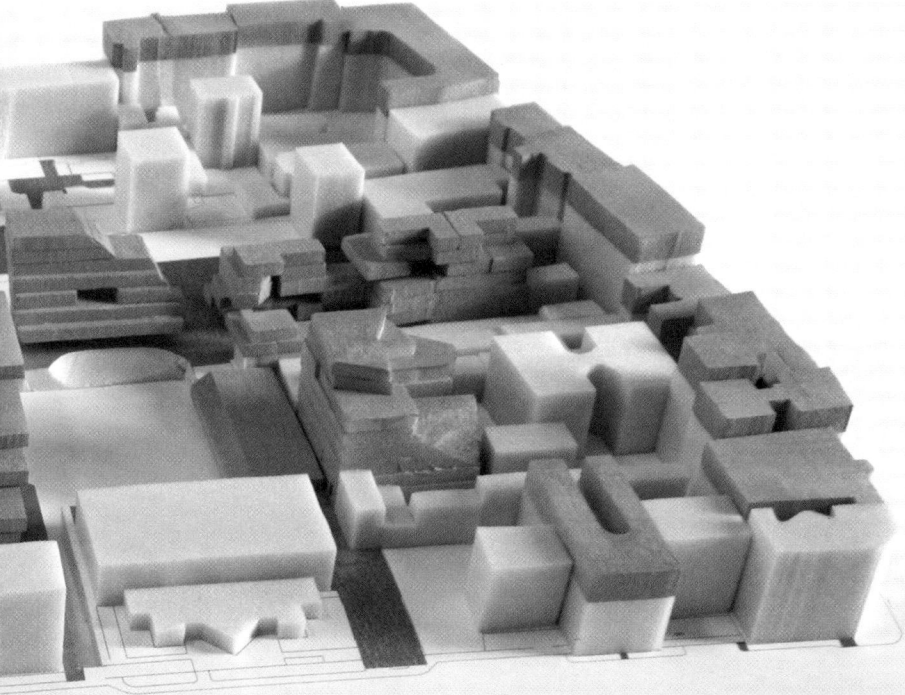

This project exposes the latent potentials of garden fragments by connecting them into a network of greenery. A meticulous analysis of surface treatment, ground ownership and potential sites for densification leads to a phasing strategy that will gradually reconfigure building mass and connect voids. Profits from new constructions allow purchasing leftover green spaces, eventually weaving a network of paths and rendering the perimeter block porous despite further densification. Gutted from cars, fences and shacks the inner courtyards of the perimeter blocks become an essential feature of the neighbourhood.

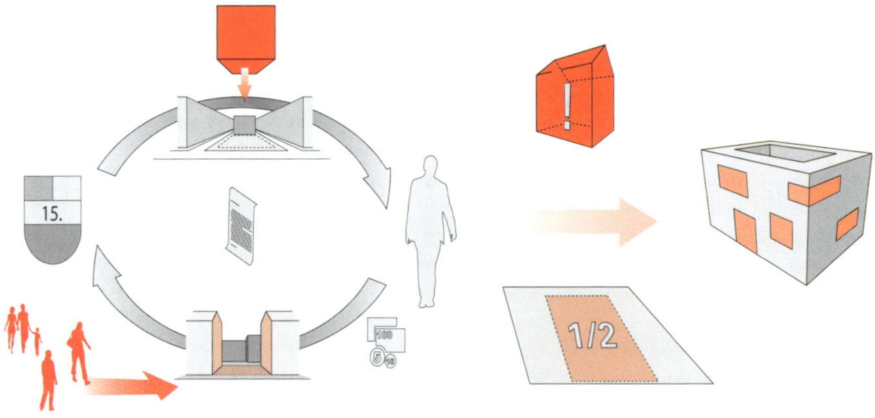

15.

1/2

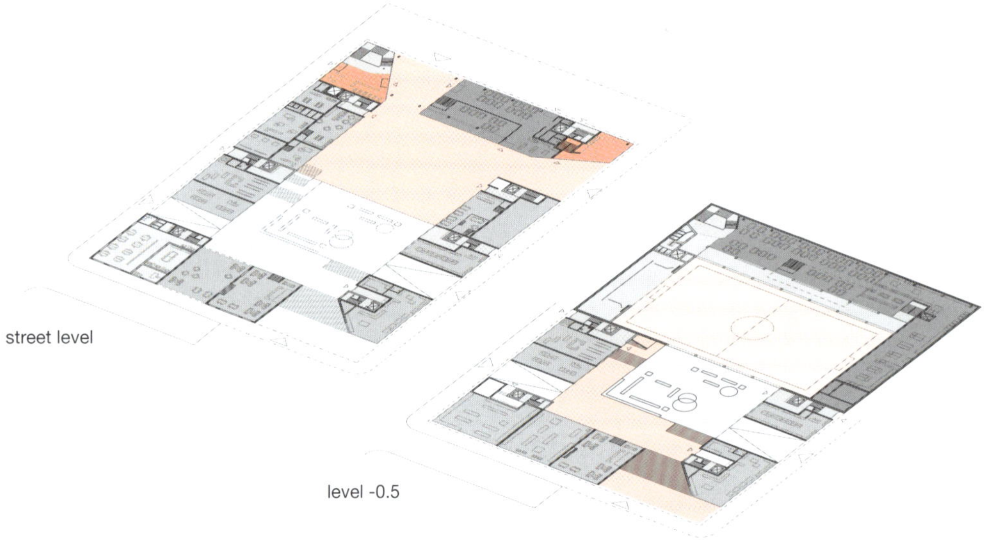

street level

level -0.5

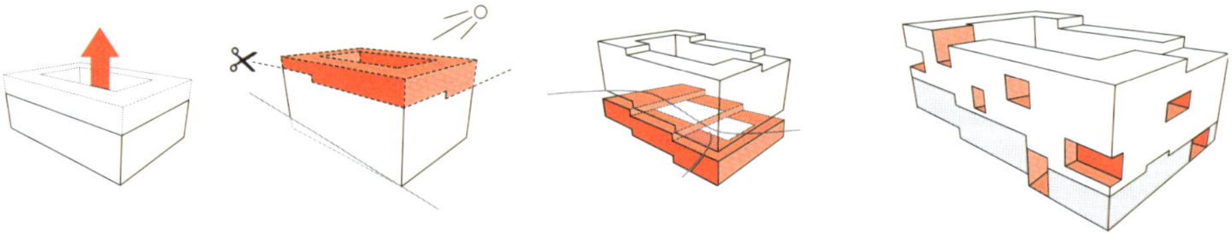

How can the informal qualities of building gaps in a neighborhood be experienced and preserved? In a barter arrangement the project develops an entire housing block on the current location of a public, yet second-rate plaza. In exchange the investor is bound to make the separate vacant lots publically accessible. Further the inner courtyard is to remain open to its surroundings. Inhabitants are given a series of intimate yet shared outdoor spaces through voids carved out of the building mass. These voids are reminiscent of the dispersed building gaps.

BERLIN

BRATISLAVA

BUDAPEST

LJUBLJANA

PRAGUE

VIENNA

WARSAW

193

■ vacant plots
new function
for the neighbourhood

■ voids
semi-private,
semi public and
public program

This project merges two common shopping typologies: the mall and the market. Thus it blurs the critical distinction between private and public urban space. Covered by a one-story carpet of courtyard houses the mall functions as a coherent whole, yet its perimeter remains porous. The ground floor is permanently accessible, while it is maintained by shop owners. In section the project is a figure-ground inversion; what is solid on street-level become hollow on top.

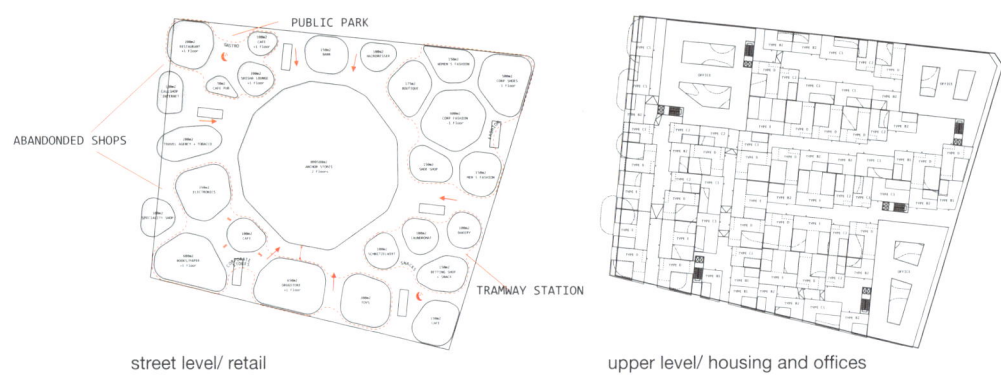

street level/ retail

upper level/ housing and offices

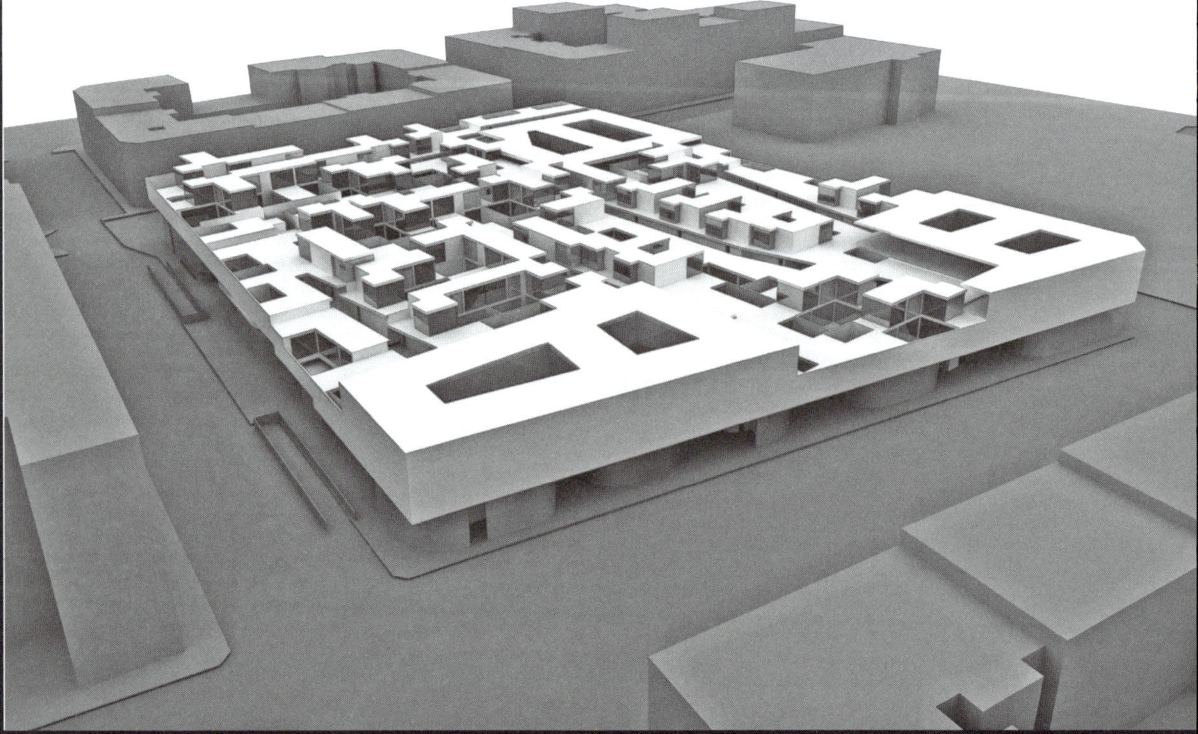

Student: Clemens Hasler

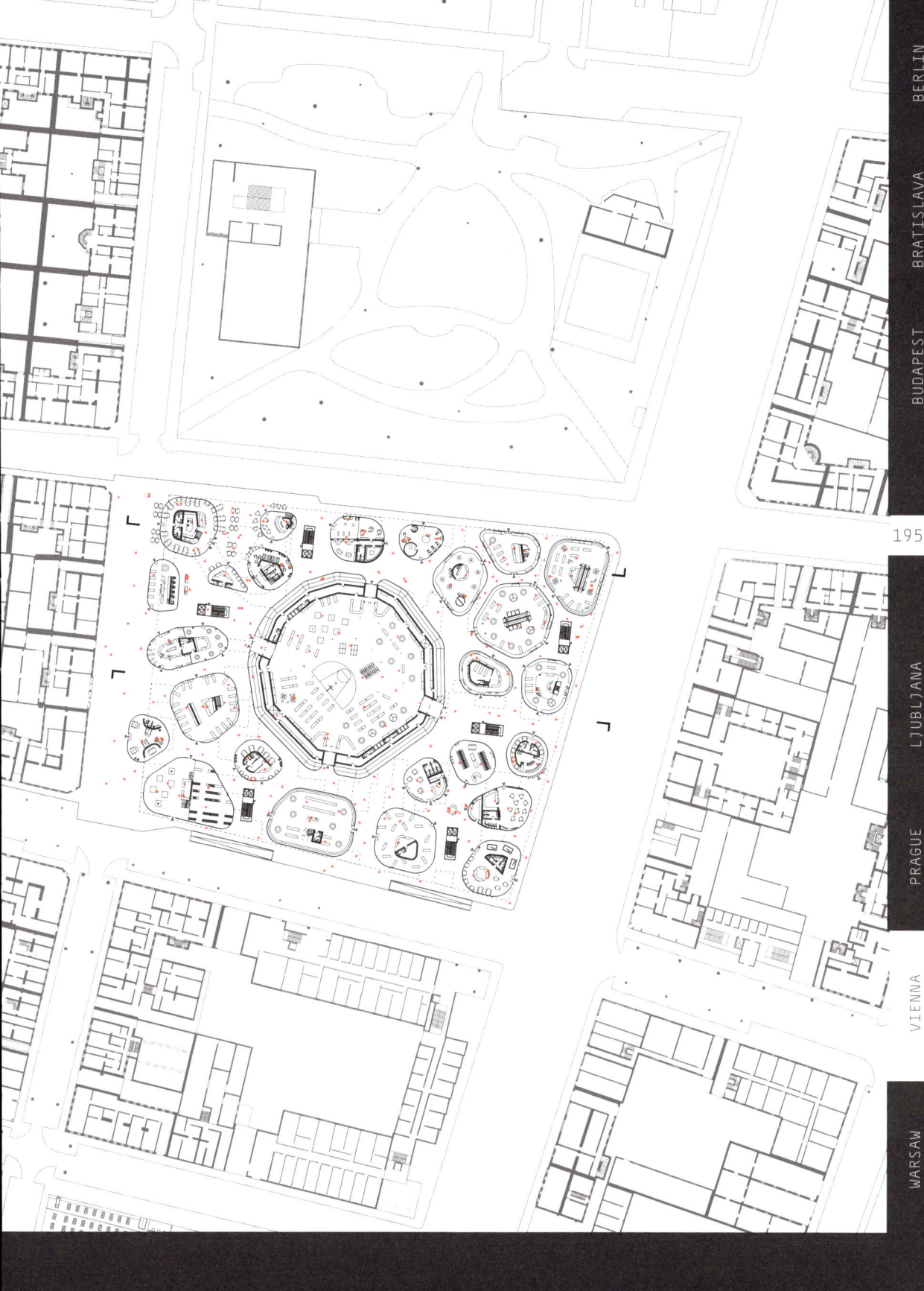

BERLIN

BRATISLAVA

BUDAPEST

195

LJUBLJANA

PRAGUE

VIENNA

WARSAW

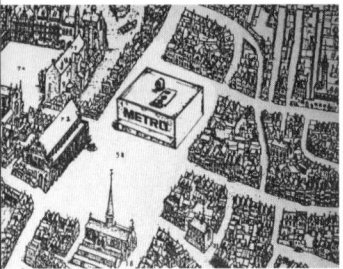

What is urbanity? A balancing act between regulation and flexibility, permanence and change, design and planning. Thus this project defines two types of components: large building blocks with a carefully designed structure that allows for maximum programmatic flexibility; and the subdivision of land into very small lots that, along with a few zoning rules, allow for transformation over time. The combination of these two scales, large buildings and small lots, flexibility in space and time is a contemporary response to the flexibility provided by the Gründerzeit block. It promises to produce a robust and vibrant neighborhood.

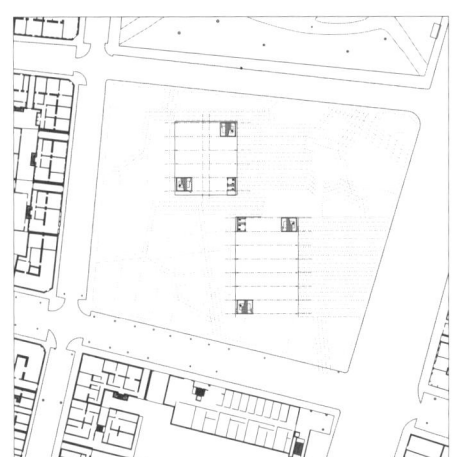

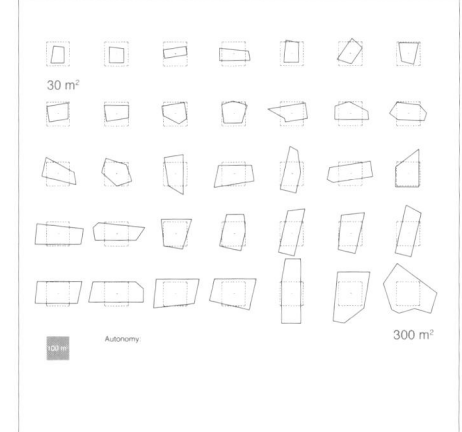

lot layout and position of large building blocks

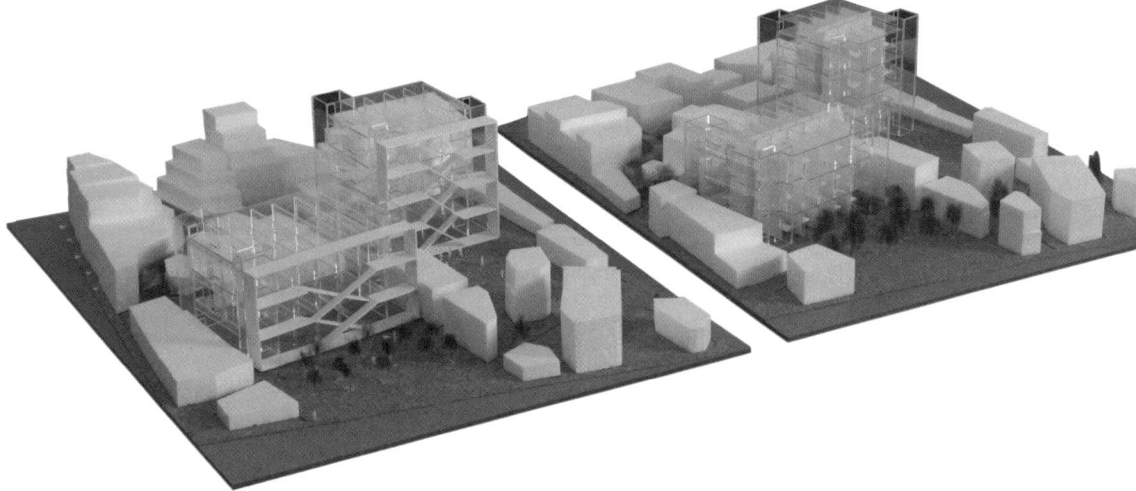

transformation scenarios over time

office

office

housing

shopping

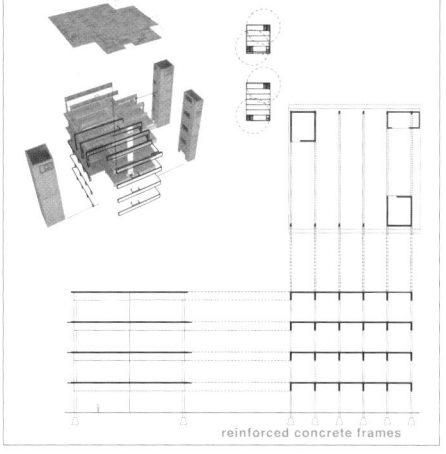

reinforced concrete frames

BERLIN

BRATISLAVA

BUDAPEST

197

LJUBLJANA

PRAGUE

VIENNA

WARSAW

WARSAW
CITY PARKOUR

BERLIN

BRATISLAVA

BUDAPEST

199

LJUBLJANA

PRAGUE

VIENNA

WARSAW

Students: Piotr Kilanowski | Joanna Koszewska | Aleksandra Melion
Dorota Nagowska | Marcin Brzeski

Tutor: Sławomir Gzell

WHY THE WARSAW PARKOUR?

SŁAWOMIR GZELL
—
Besides a period of quiet/planned development, every city experiences dramatic events which alter its history or at least its appearance. This is also true of the events which occurred in Warsaw. Besides the usual disasters (fires, epidemics, floods), Warsaw was also subjected in its history to many wars and faced numerous periods of war. In 1656 there were even two battles over Warsaw (with the Swedes, who robbed it of everything, and even pulled up the paving in the castle), and then there were wars with other assailants recurring in 1794, 1831, 1863, and 1920 (at the time the Red Army attack was repelled), 1939 and 1944 – if we were to name only the bloodiest and most destructive. So it is no surprise that the marks of these events, and the Russian occupation, which lasted more than the entire 19th century, and then the communist government from 1945 to 1989, are still visible today in the structure of the city, its buildings and in the behaviour of its residents. In the analysis of today's transformation of the city, the most fundamental is the most recent period which we can examine immediately.

—
The Second World War was ending. Warsaw's war losses accounted for cca 85 % of everything found in the city. The city lost 850 thousand of its population. In the winter of 1944 and early 1945 Warsaw was a huge, depopulated sea of rubble with burned out shells of houses. However, in this period, on 3 January 1945, a resolution was passed to restore Warsaw and 9 days later a resolution on keeping Warsaw as the country's capital city.

On 14 February 1945 the Biuro odbudowy Stolicy (the Office of the Restoration of the Capital City) (BOS) was established. Work went at a fast pace. The planners, who prepared the restoration, worked from pre-war designs and designs drafted in conspiracy, were ready as early as 4 March. On this day BOS submitted the "General Plan of the Capital City". The start of the restoration work involved the removal of 20 million m3 of rubble. Then up to 1950 work continued in building the fundamental features of Warsaw's spatial structure which to this day are projected into its plan and the lives of its residents. It is worth to at least briefly examine the conditions of the origin of these solutions.

Firstly, we know of the opinions of Jan Olaf Chnmielewski and Szymon Syrkus, planners who in 1934 drafted the project entitled "Functional Warsaw", one of the most interesting works of the CIAM period, and after the war they played the main role in the BOS. They wrote: "in the chaos of the existing cities, the interests and needs of the large human masses are totally overlooked – but the radical recovery cannot be carried out without the mobilisation of the land lots". These opinions gave rise to the Decree of 26 October 1945 "On the communalisation of land lots on the territory of

Warsaw". This decree gave "free rein" to the planning of a new modern city but, at the same time, severed the traditional system of urban space. The further plans of Warsaw reinforced this "free" method of the planning and construction of the city. This finally gave rise to a ring of residential quarters constructed from the 1960s around the city centre which became the subject of an extensive social protest. Today part of these housing estates is rightly described as socialist slums.

Secondly, the restored Warsaw should have been different than the pre-war city. An indication of this resounded in the statements of politicians from early 1945. It was proposed that the new Warsaw be built on the principles of a city - a landscape with quarters and residential estates with freely constructed housing which were to stand in the sun and vegetation - all in contrast to a pre-war capitalist city.

The existing concept of restoration began to take on new forms from 1949. The socrealist idea began to apply which was instroduced as compulsory doctrine. Only the quarter located in the centre was build according to this plan, Marszalkowska Dzielnica Mieszkaniowa (Marszalkowska Residential Quarter) /MDM/ with the Palace of Culture and Science /PkiN/ - and this is where it all ended because the political coup in 1956 also signalled the demise of socialist realism.

It is worth mentioning more about MDM and PKiN because both these buildings arouse lively discussion in Warsaw to this day. The Palace of Culture and Science (once understandably called Joseph Stalin's Palace of Culture and Science), "a gift of the Soviet nations to the Polish people', the biggest Polish example of the period of Socrealism, determined for decades the urban space in the centre of Warsaw, its panorama and awareness of trips by rural schools about what is beautiful. No building in Warsaw is so close to the post-modernist search for the connection between the present and history which is confirmed by the willingness with which Robert Krier took up the task of decision-making in 1991 in the tender for the buildings to be constructed around the Palace. Today there is nothing to indicate that the situation concerning the Palace should change, especially because it was recorded as a listed building two years ago.

Unfortunately, no idea appeared in place of Socrealism, rejected in 1956, to logically create a plan and appearance for Warsaw. The principles of the Athens Charter returned, but the return of prefabricated housing estates came in caricature and amorphic form. The focus was on quantity - the policy of the government and communist party to "provide" everyone with a flat killed the quality of the constructed houses and the quality of architecture. Warsaw flowed over into the surrounding fields. Its population was as large as it had been before the war, but took up more space. Problems arose with getting around the city, with the construction of an extended technical infrastructure and supplying the population. Such was the state of Warsaw until the next political upheaval in 1989.

It must be recalled that the Old Town remained unaffected by all the political upheavals which had been restored in the early 1950s. It was accepted by the BOS employees. It was accepted in the times of Socrealism because it was close to the slogan about architecture in its "national form and socialist contents". Finally it received the blessing of Cherles Jencks who placed it among the ancestors of post-Modernism in the current of "straight revivalism".

—
3
As has already been stated, on 26 October 1945, the Council of Ministers issued a decree by which all private land on its territory was transferred to the city of Warsaw. It basically referred to the needs of the people and necessity to make a quick decision about the restoration of the city. Simultaneously, the buildings were left in the hands of the present owners which stood on the territory removed from them. So Warsaw joined the family of socialist cities, meaning such cities in which the resident was not and could not be the owner of the territory on which he lived. He did not have to pay real estate tax, but was required to maintain a house with tenants paying rent which was not determined by market mechanisms, but by the state which was adjusted to the low income of the tenants. Because the rent was basically lower than the costs of repair, the result was obvious – entire quarters ended up in ruins and in a short time it was possible to undertake "bulldozer reconstruction". They were replaced by prefabricated houses, usually five – or eleven-storey buildings. The traditional streets disappeared, housing estates and quarters began

to resemble one another. People stopped caring where they lived. Hence this is how in socialist Warsaw the socialist Varsovian was created becoming indifferent to the affairs of his city.

—
4
In 1989 we regained independence and the capitalism we had been waiting to achieve for fifty years. In the general concept it was to be the cure for all the ills of the city and its residents. It was to be the same as it had been till now only everyone was to be rich and could do what they wanted. Right from the very start the need was denied to make plans in Warsaw because these are a means of coercion, and it was claimed that what the law does not direclty prohibit is permitted. So there was nothing strange that in a situation of transformation and the weakening of city administration these slogans bore fruit – hundreds of buildings appeared around Warsaw constructed without a plan or building permit. Simultaneously, planners began competing in the "modernisation" of plans. Words appeared such as zoning, monitoring, negotiation and participation, unfortunately they were incorporated into the texts of plans without it being understood what they actually mean and it was (is?) a rather sad "superficial westernisation" of our profession. In the space it is accompanied by the construction of buildings serving purposes unknown in a socialist city, mainly banks and other financial institutions. These are accompanied by business centres on the outskirts of the city. These "money cathedrals" are rather bad imitations of Big Architecture, look cheap because they are built by foreign capital in the country and city which is still an increased

investment risk while there is a lack of Polish capital.

All this can be seen in Warsaw. In general terms, a phenomenon can be observed in Warsaw typical of a western European city called "gentrification", the growth of social stratification and decline and marginalisation of an area of old housing. Specific processes are taking place in the Śródmieście quarter where the poor residents and marginal groups are being forced out by foreign capital which is looking for a better, prestigious location in the city centre. New housing estates located in the outer belt of the city are inhabited by more highly educated people. They have no regard for their surroundings which is shown by their daily mass "commuting" to the city centre.

And one more thing is characteristic of the last twenty years in Warsaw: no new public areas have appeared and the ones that exist are not sufficiently protected.

—
5
Consideration of new public areas needs to begin with an analysis of their needs. It is obvious that all people need them: both young and old alike. It would also be good if they all could be together although every social group required slighlty different space.

It can also be observed that in an expanding city public space takes on the appearance of a belt, as a square is no longer the most common seen form. This is due to the increasing mobility of the population, active encounters and a retreat from staticity. What is also important is the constant joint creation of common areas: the planner provides us with an activity framework as the participants of city life constitute its contents. Nobody wants to be passive and activity is appreciated.

The utilisation must also be considered of what loses its existing value for new needs. The recycling of space and finding constantly newer areas of utilisation for the needs required by groups of residents (and even individuals) is becoming a necessity. So what arises is what we call a liberating Emergent Structure which is the result of the dynamic behaviour of the human masses, Dynamic of the Crowd. Today's principle of urban planning must also take into account (besides other new problems) that the planned urban landscapes cannot merely be a pla-ce for architecture to illustrate motion in a better and worse way. They must be an expression of motion, circulation because today we are heading for a world built with suddenly emerging projects rather than long calculated ones. The human aspect of things must also be considered: common areas must attract, may not be boring, monotonous and perhaps they should not be planned with too much care - all this is the subject of the attempts carried out today.

The Warsaw Parkour Project comes as an answer to the abovementioned requirements. It contains everything we wanted to achieve: it is a new space in Warsaw as never envisaged before, thanks to the diversity of the routes it is designed for all sections of the population of Warsaw and can be actively utilised by them the individual paths pass through

BERLIN

BRATISLAVA

BUDAPEST

203

LJUBLJANA

PRAGUE

VIENNA

WARSAW

various fragments of the city,
resulting in their activation and in
the reurbanisation processes of
the destroyed fragments.

The Warsaw Parkour is something new
in our city. It is the public area
of the 21st century Varsovian.
–
The primary goal of 'Warsaw Parkour'
project was to optimize and extend
the existing public spaces involving
existing and extended grid of green
areas. The design treats about new
possible connections (paths,
streets, walkways, footbridges,
views etc.) between existing and
desired public areas through
the city including a certain number
of attractive locations on
the way. Spaces such as biking
tracks, streets, walkways in
surrounding forests, amusement
squares, public greenery, open air
exhibits, small architecture of
commerce or leisure. The connections
are designed in the form of so-
called 'Parkour' - a kind of sport
regarding crossing the city in
an unusual way through unusual
locations. Parkour lines are
designed to cross the city using
the mentioned-above public spaces
and green areas. Individual parkours
cross the city in the form of
straight connection from point A to
point Z on the opposite side of
the metropolitan area. In several
points parkour lines cross each
other in a certain important space,
creating a junction knot, where
additional retail spaces, small
shops, bars, cafeterias and such
are erected.
These are located as nodes on
the crossroads of parkours and
on the borders of the downtown
administration zone. All knots are
connected with another parkour line
surrounding the city center and

connecting all parks and public
spaces located in the city center
border limits. The "knots" with
their commercial, administrative
and retail functions are designed
to activate the life around, also
offering additional working places.
The parkour path avoids traditional
forms of moving through the city. It
is designed to re-use back alleys,
building interiors, garage roofs,
height differences and such, at
the same time each parkour is
divided to 3 similar paths differing
in difficulty and complexity:

• Fast (extreme, sportive)
• Medium (familiar, friendly)
• Slow (natural, ecological).

Since the Parkour is an attractive
proposal of spending time using
public space, zones added to it
should improve the common identity
amongst citizens. Such situation
gives an opportunity to propose new
style of activities and forms for
spending free time. This responds to
future needs of the given place for
inhabitants as well as newcomers.

The project diversifies green areas
(woods, parks, green squares,
gardens, tree alleys), apart from
each other pointing out fields
already existing, those to be built,
zones to be protected and lines
dividing them. In all those types
of zones points of the existing
and potential concentrations of
activities are marked.
The intention is to search for
existing places to re-define or
improve and to add new forms of
public space where they need to be
arranged.

Organizing new places of activities
the project accords to the principle
of the poly-centrality, locality,

reinforcing the identity with close surroundings, raising awareness of common recreational places and their qualities. This aims to highlight the potential role of multiple equal zones creating activity and community centres. It is helpful to decentralize the town's structure and bring facilities close to every citizen.

The final intention of the project is to invite all the future users and investors, who would be interested, to join the process. If planning or fulfilment of this project would help to establish a better dialogue between the interest of users, decision - makers and initiators - investors, it would already be a part of the general idea - linking.

The city in 1989.

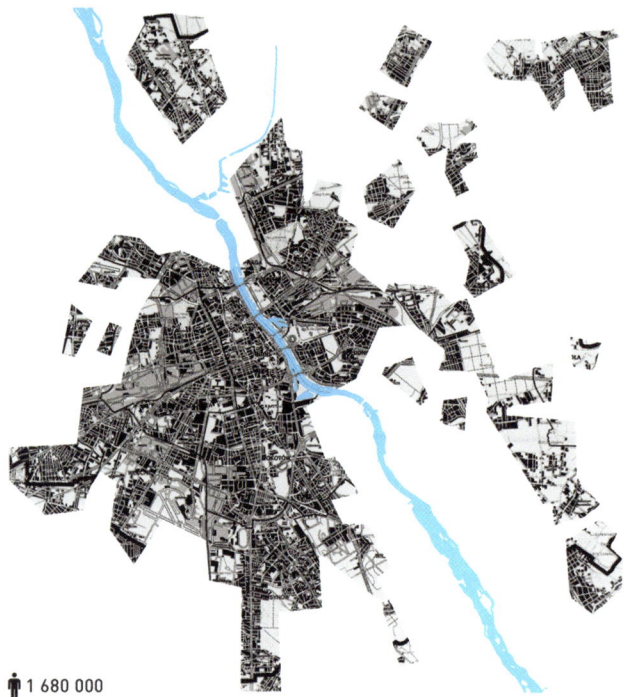

LAND USE STRUCTURE:

SEMI DENSE
IN DOWNTOWN

+

DISPERSED SOCIAL HIGH-RISE
BUILDINGS OUTSIDE THE CENTER

👤 1 680 000

The city in 2009.

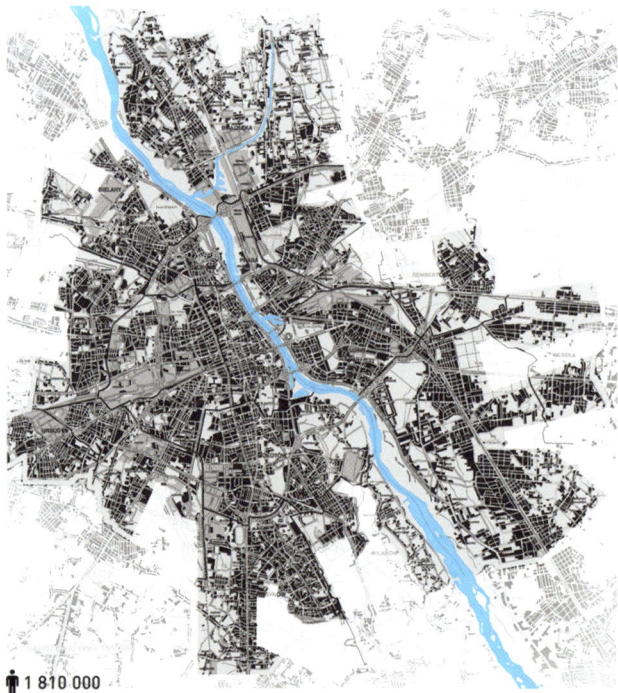

DENSE, HIGH-RISE, DIVERSED
...but **CHAOTIC** and
UNCOORDINATED

IT'S EASY TO DO BUSINESS,
BUT HARD TO **LIVE** HERE

👤 1 810 000

Students: Piotr Kilanowski | Joanna Koszewska | Aleksandra Melion
Dorota Nagowska | Marcin Brzeski

Transformation 1989 - 2009

Intensive development of the downtown district. Big business dominates the space with a number of new iconic high-rises.

Warsaw skyline

BEFORE 1989

20 YEARS LATER

'ONZ' junction in the center of Warsaw

BEFORE 1989

20 YEARS LATER

Twenty years of consistent retreat regarding Warsaw public space.

Main junction in the heart of the city

BEFORE 1989

20 YEARS LATER

UNPUBLIC SPACE IN THE CITY
- INACCESSIBLE,
- UNATTRACTIVE,
- DISORGANISED

BERLIN
BRATISLAVA
BUDAPEST

207

LJUBLJANA
PRAGUE
VIENNA
WARSAW

The city with green areas in regional scale - the goals for the future:
DELIMIT THE URBAN SPRAWL!

GREEN REST AREA → SYSTEM of
PROTECTED NATURAL AREAS

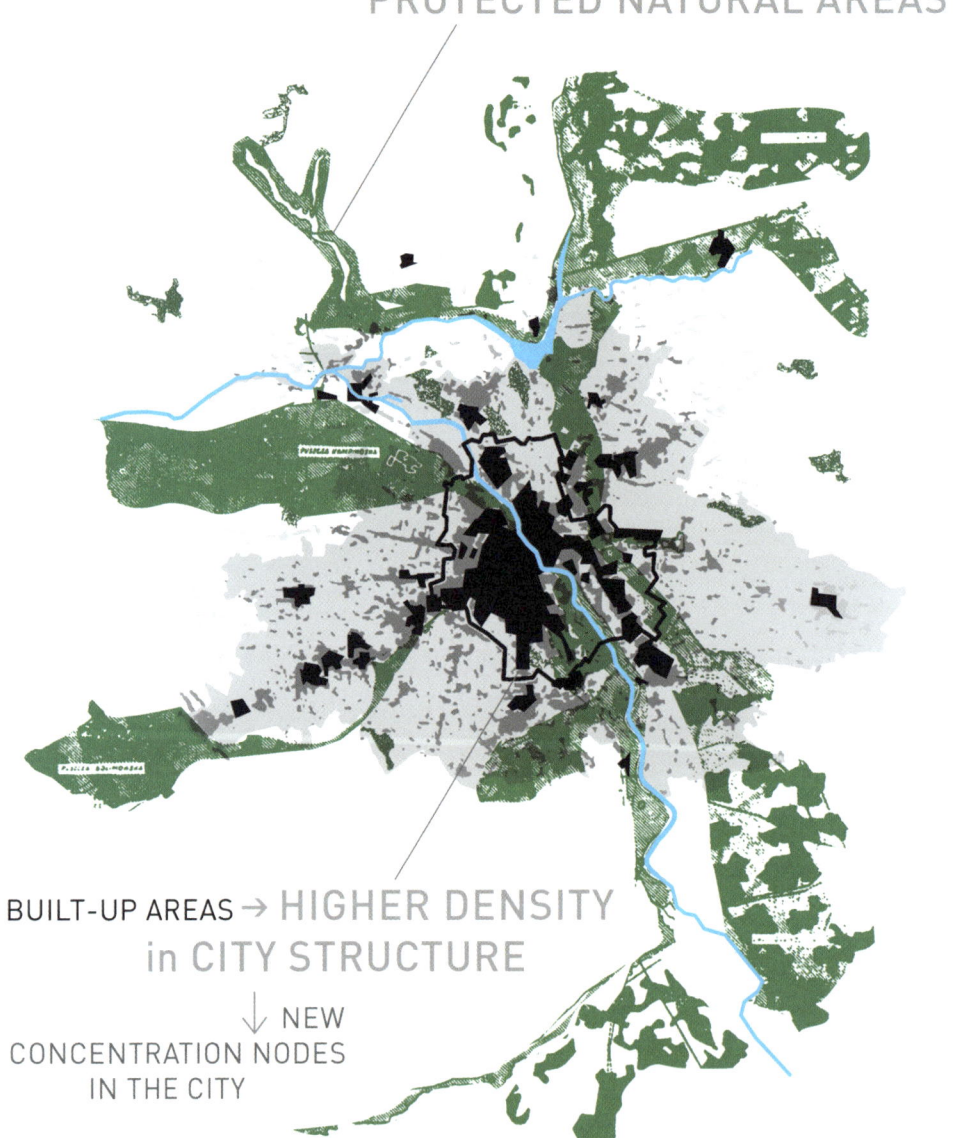

BUILT-UP AREAS → HIGHER DENSITY
in CITY STRUCTURE

↓ NEW
CONCENTRATION NODES
IN THE CITY

The city greenery as a chance for Warsaw

EXISTING GREEN AREAS
ORGANISED AS PARKS, PRIVATE
GARDENS OR CITY-FORESTS

↓

GREENERY NETWORK
ORGANISED AS A **SYSTEM**

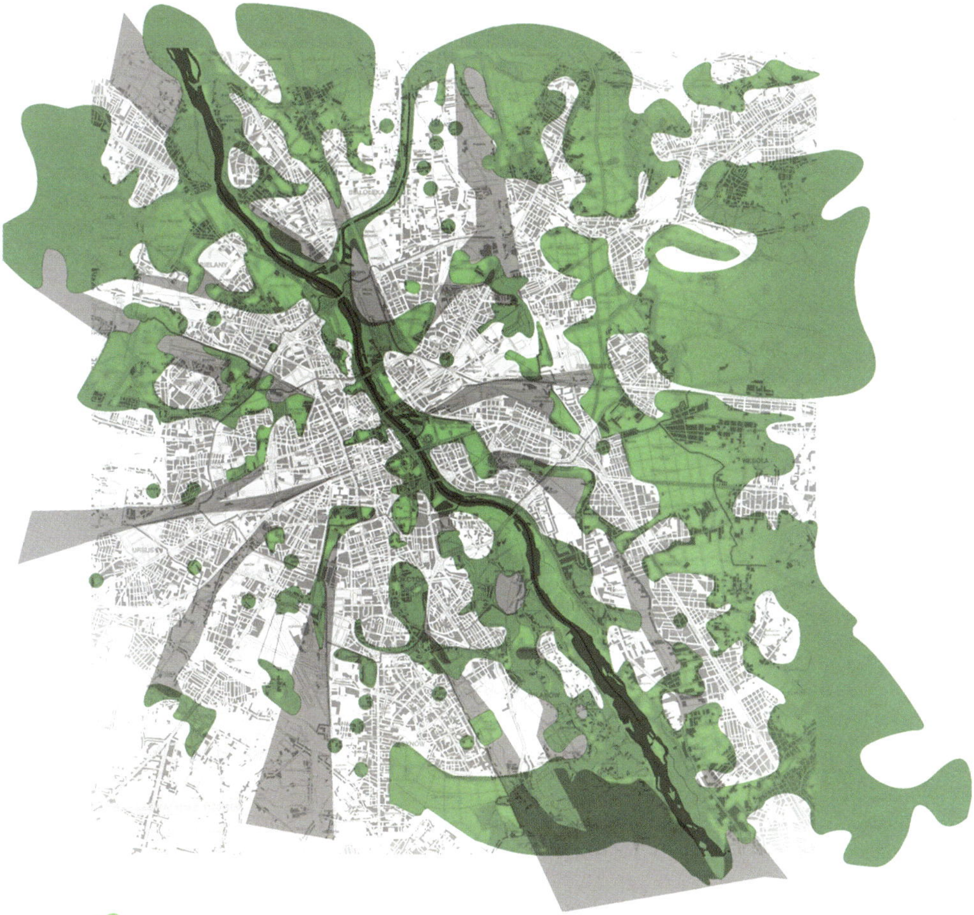

EXISTING AND DESIRED GREEN AREAS

NON BUILT-UP AREAS TO PRESERVE

BERLIN

BRATISLAVA

BUDAPEST

209

LJUBLJANA

PRAGUE

VIENNA

WARSAW

CITY MATRIX - detailed analysis of space relations in reference to existing and desired attractions for several districts

Analysis conducted on selected city quarters:

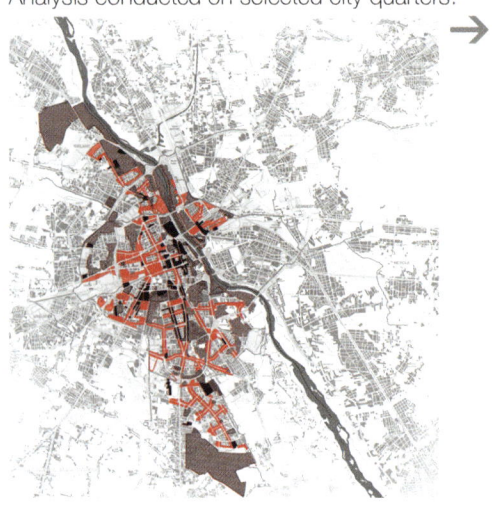 

■ **EXISTING LOCAL ATTRACTORS**
- RETAIL/ EDUCATION/ CULTURE/ SPORT/ TRANSPORT NODES

■ **DESIRED LOCAL ATTRACTORS**

POSSIBLE NETWORK OF CONNECTIONS

CITY MATRIX - possible analysis applied to the whole city:

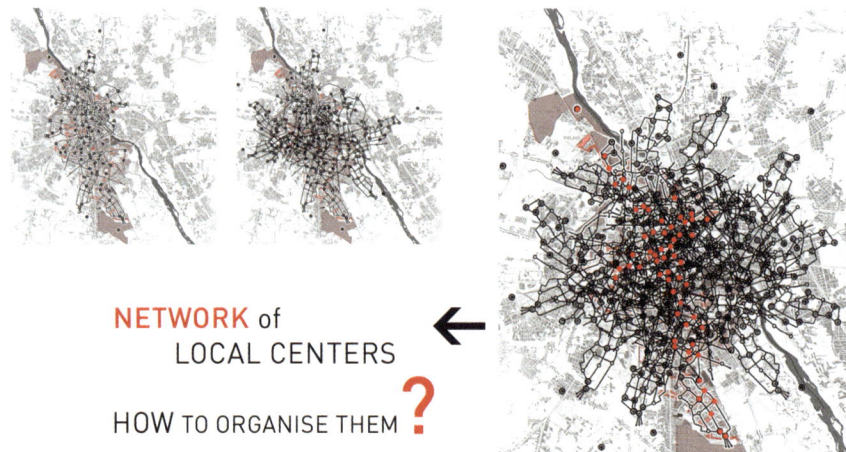

NETWORK of **LOCAL CENTERS**

HOW TO ORGANISE THEM **?**

Students: Piotr Kilanowski | Joanna Koszewska | Aleksandra Melion
Dorota Nagowska | Marcin Brzeski

Analysis of further City-LAYERS

Analysis of the city's most important layes as a clue to the final concept.

TRANSPORTATION:

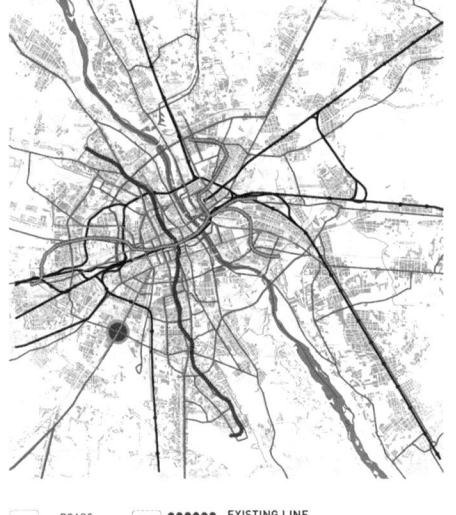

HISTORICAL SITES:

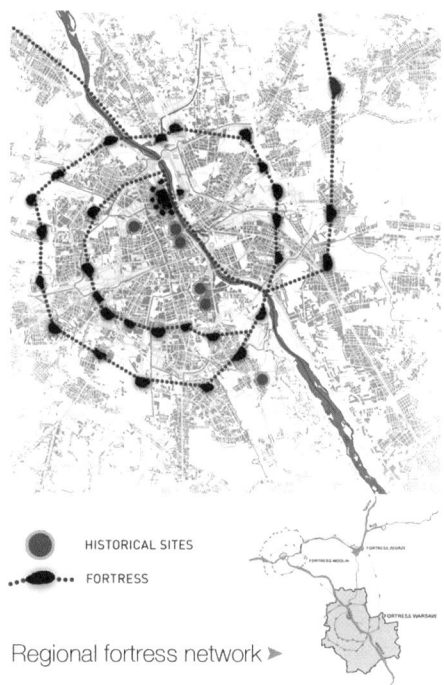

Regional fortress network ➤

City-LAYERS: pattern of all layers merged together

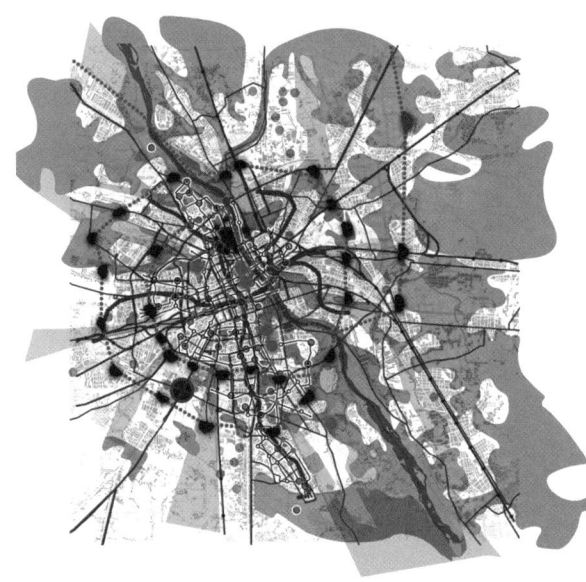

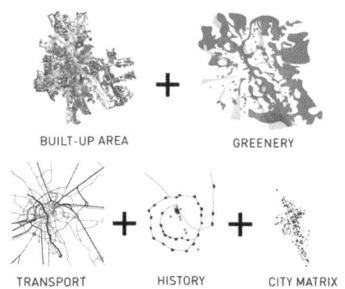

The solution: Warsaw needs some extra layer
 - a new public space layer LINKING the whole city

Alternative City - Axes:

LET'S **PARKOUR**
WARSAW!

Parkour is the physical discipline of training
to overcome any obstacle within one's path
by adapting one's movements to the environment.

HIT WARSAW RUNNING!

PARKOUR WARSAW
IS A SYSTEM OF STRAIGHT **AXES**
RUNNING THROUGH THE CITY.

→ EACH AXIS CONTAINS **3 PATHS**
CUSTOMIZED TO 3 DIFFERENT TYPES OF **ACTIVITIES**

→ PARKOUR CREATES **NEW PUBLIC SPACES**
FULLY ACCESSIBLE FOR EVERY CITIZEN

EXTREME TRACK
PAHT FOR ALL
SLOW ALLEY
+ **GREEN BAND**

Following the parkour paths through….

…HOUSING ESTATE
PARKOUR **WAKES UP** SLEEPING HOUSING QUARTERS IN THE CITY

… THE VISTULA RIVERFRONT
PARKOUR BRINGS THE RIVERSIDE AREA **BACK INTO LIFE**

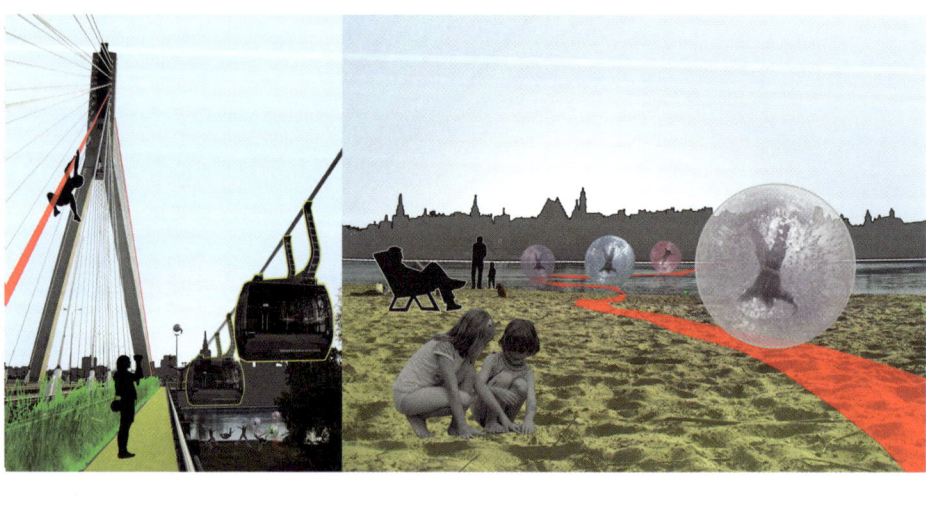

Following the parkour paths through....

...THE GREEN BAND
OF FORMER FORTRESS OF WARSAW

PARKOUR TRANSFORMED INTO
THE PARK LINE RUNNING AROUND THE INNER CITY CORE

...POSTINDUSTRIAL AREA OF THE 'URSUS' FACTORY

PARKOUR GIVES **THE SECOND LIFE**
TO THE OLD ABANDONED PLACES IN THE CITY

BERLIN

BRATISLAVA

BUDAPEST

215

LJUBLJANA

PRAGUE

VIENNA

WARSAW

The knots on the parkour axes:

ON THE CROSSROADS OF PARKOUR LINES
THERE ARE MULTIFUNCTIONAL **KNOTS**
WHICH ARE TO
ACTIVATE THE LIFE AROUND

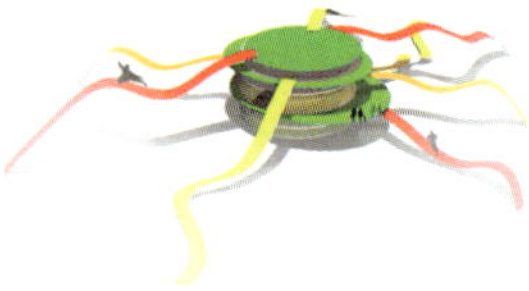

The parkour knots' typology:

TOWER KNOT

- THE CENTRAL ENCOUNTER SPOT

IN A DENSE CITY AREA/
HIGH-RISE STRUCTURE/
MULTIFUNCTIONAL/
MUNICIPAL

SQUARE KNOT

- OUTER RING CENTER

ON THE EDGE OF INNER CITY CORE/
MID-SIZED STRUCTURE/
FOCUSED ON LOCAL NEEDS/

PARK KNOT

- OUTER RING LANDSCAPE CENTER

ON THE EDGE OF INNER CITY CORE/
LANDSCAPE STRUCTURE/
EVENT SPACE/

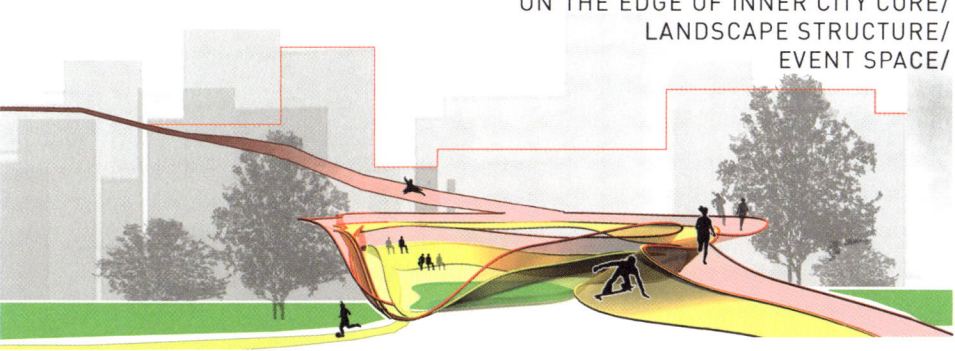

GYÖRGY ALFÖLDI
----
is an associate professor at
Technical University of Budapest
Faculty of Architecture Department of
Urban Planning & Design. He was
the urban planner and the project
manager of two urban regeneration
projects in Budapest; both were
the first engagement of integrated
approach in the field of the urban
development in Hungary.

THOMAS ARNOLD
----
is principal of workspheres
architects in Berlin. He also teaches
a design studio and
a postgraduate master studio together
with David Greene and Andrew Holmes
at Oxford Brookes University. Before
coming to Oxford he was assistant
professor at the TU-Berlin. He has
taught and exhibited architecture
worldwide. He is the author of
Architektur Rausch, a position on
architectural design (2005) and the
Design Manual for Office Buildings
(2001). His latest publication is
Thaumatography or The Use of Wonders
in ADIP Magazine (2010).

IRENA FIALOVÁ
----
is a member of the Czech Chamber of
Architects, as well as a co-founder
of the architectural journal and
publisher Zlatý řez. She lectures on
theories and trends in architecture
and urban design at the Faculty of
Architecture at the Czech Technical
University in Prague, is the Czech
expert representative for
the European Union Prize for
contemporary architecture, and is
the (co)author of several books.

STEFAN GRUBER
----
is principal of STUDIOGRUBER
a Vienna-based design practice for
architecture, urban strategies and
research. He is a professor of
Architecture and Urbanism and
the Deputy Head of the Institute for
Art and Architecture at the Academy
of Fine Arts Vienna. In the past
three years he has run urban design
studios following an approach of
Acupuncture Urbanism. Acupuncture
Urbanism entails the physiological
understanding of an urban milieu
leading to strategic local
interventions that have an impact on
a region, the city or
a neighbourhood as a whole.

MARTIN GSANDTNER
----
is a Bratislava based architect. In
the collaborative Imro Vasko studio
he is working on architecture and
exhibition projects. He is teaching
at the Academy of Fine Arts & Design
Bratislava in the studio Laboratory
of Architecture.

SŁAWOMIR GZELL
----
teaches at Warsaw University of
Technology, Faculty of Architecture.
He cooperated at many housing and
commercial estates, urban studies and
master plans in Poland and abroad.
He is interested in architectural
conservation and reconstruction
and he wrote 3 books and numerous
articles on urban society and
development. For his work he was
awarded many times.

BALINT KADAR
----
is teaching and doing his Phd at
the faculty of Urban Design of
the Technical University of Budapest
(BME). He runs a small architectural

studio and is curator of Kék (Centre for Contemporary Architecture). He teaches and organizes conferences regarding soft rehabilitation methods of historical urban cores. His PhD research topic focuses on the usage of urban space by tourists and locals.

BIRGIT KLAUCK
----

studied architecture at the RWTH Aachen, AA London and the Bartlett School of Architecture and Planning London. Since 1995 "Akademische Rätin" and since 2008 Dean of Studies at the TU Berlin. She has been collaborating with Thomas Arnold on workspheres.com. Author and Editor of Design Manual for Office Buildings (2001 Birkhäuser). Latest publication ADIP MAGAZINE: Rethinking Berlin (2010 TU Verlag).

MICHAL KOHOUT
----

taught in the Architecture Department of Prague Technical University first between 1989 and 1994. In the past three years he became the head of the school Housing and Planning teaching and research programme. Since 1995 he has been a partner in the architectural practice Jiran Kohout Architekti, Prague. He also works for the architectural publishing house Zlatý řez (Golden Section) where he co-edits an architectural revue of the same name and published two guide books on Czech 20th Century architecture.

UROŠ RUSTJA
----

is a Ljubljana based architect. In collaboration with various architecture offices he is working on projects for housing and public buildings. As assistant at the Faculty of Architecture in Ljubljana he collaborated in

the architecture design studio and in workshops where students focused their attention on the quality of public space in contemporary city.

LISA SCHMIDT-COLINET
----

is a Vienna-based architect. In the collaborative schmidt-colinet. schmoeger she is working on architecture and exhibition projects. She is Deputy Head of Institute for Art and Architecture at the Academy of Fine Arts Vienna, where she teaches design and courses in the platforms Geography/Landscapes/Cities and History/Theory/Criticism.

IMRO VAŠKO
----

founded Institut for Visionary Architecture as conceptual architecture platform and Laboratory of Architecture as an experimental and research -teaching architecture studio at Academy both in Bratislava. As an architect, Imro Vaško is author of conceptual architecture and urbanism, experiments in architecture, interior creation, installations and exhibitions.

MARUŠA ZOREC
----

is a senior lecturer at the Faculty of Architecture in Ljubljana and running her own architectural practice based in Ljubljana. Area of her work is mainly public buildings including numerous renovations of historical heritage. She is co-author of valorisation of Slovene modern architecture buildings from 1945 to 1970 and author of publication on architect Oton Jugovec. In last years she has run urban design and architecture studio with various workshops where students focused their attention on quality of public space in the contemporary city.

LEARNING FROM FUTURE

BERLIN

BRATISLAVA

BUDAPEST

223

LJUBLJANA

PRAGUE

VIENNA

WARSAW

DEANS

—
Deans' thoughts on identity, history, cooperation and future.

The release of a book with seven contributing faculties of Architecture is a rare case. Therefore Centre for Central European Architecture took this opportunity to ask deans of participating faculties to share their thoughts about history, cooperation and identity of Central European territory by answering the identical answers.

Johannes Cramer
Berlin Institute of Technology School VI, Planning Building Environment, Institute for Architecture

Peter Gabrijelčič
University of Ljubljana, Faculty of Architecture

Pálfy Sándor
Technical University of Budapest, Faculty of Architecture, Department of Urban Design

Nasrine Seraji
Academy of Fine Arts Vienna, Institute for Art and Architecture

Imro Vaško
Academy of Fine Arts and Design Bratislava, Department of Architecture

Zdeněk Zavřel
Faculty of Architecture, Czech Technical University in Prague

HOW IMPORTANT IS THE ARCHITECTURAL IDENTITY IN THE CONTEXT OF CENTRAL EUROPE CITIES?

Johannes Cramer

Specific identity is one of the most remarkable characteristics of the European city. Other continents are suffering from the lack of architectural identity in the urban context. Therefore European urbanism should concentrate on conserving and developing an architectural identity in terms of historic fabric, architectural heritage, public space and new architecture.

Peter Gabrijelčič

Space is the most objective reflection of society and social processes. Signs of the past and present are concentrated in its layout which, in a specific physical space, permeate into a characteristic example which we describe by the term "space identity". The existing need for flexibility and recycling of urban elements is part of the new social reality however we often try, by economic, often false or distorted indicators, to devalue the existing spatial qualities in order to prepare the place for new investments. Such an emptied space can no longer provide material evidence about the continuity of a certain culture and loses contact with the city's identity and causes the impoverishment of the human environment. Culture which loses the physical track of time becomes dumb in the historical space of cities. We discover that the historical nuclei of cities lose the leading position of the carriers of the development of a city and the colour

of city life. Business activities have been moved to the city outskirts where modern centres appear which, to a greater extent, are also centres of city events. Many city administrations have not been able or could not prevent this spontaneous process. Therefore we are the witnesses of the gradual demise of city centres. Modern cities resemble one another and look like great chaotic suburbs. In this urban chaos, in this huge sea of uniformity and in our mental appearance the historical nuclei of cities remain the more important points for the identity, anchorage and axis of urban regions. Hence, if we talk of Prague, Vienna or Ljubljana, we do not mean an endless space of anonymous urban tissue, but their historical nuclei. It is, according to them, that Central European cities are distinguished on the European or global map, and so have comparative priority in global economic competition. This is a view which the city administrations of Central European cities neglect too often.

Pálfy Sándor

Identity, such as architectural identity, is of great importance and actuality in the post-socialist countries of Central Europe. After 40 years of forced conformity in the ideological, social, economical and cultural sense, each country seeks to find and declare its own traditions and culture, and also its unique architecture. This is a moment to clarify if these countries could find an appropriate architectural language, and how it would fit into the contemporary architectural trends of Europe.

Nasrine Seraji

Central Europe is one of many agents that define our general culture. The question here is not how to instrumentalize identity, but to ask how Central Europe can contribute to the specificity of architecture in our cities.

Imro Vaško

The identity of Bratislava is like a smeared spot, a permanently rolling atmospheric cloud consisting of regional fumes of the topographical region of Central Europe. Communism and Austria-Hungary, Prague, Vienna and Budapest, west and east, the Mediterranean and the north are environments in which Bratislava is always on the boundary line. The late identification of the "Slovak cloud" is our present identity in view of its "delayed (late) creation".

Zdeněk Zavřel

Central European cities have their own architectural identity, which is unique and is associated with their rich common history. It is important to know this and teach the new generation about it.
How far will this identity function as a common value in the new conditions of 21st century is a big question… all the countries involved have their own very different interests. Further European integration will probably have more of an impact than "Visegrad…" sympathies.

WHAT ARE THE POSITIVE HISTORICAL EXAMPLES OF INTERNATIONAL COOPERATION BETWEEN ARCHITECTS IN YOUR COUNTRY?

Johannes Cramer

The international movement has been created in Germany and from here there was quite a number of built exhibitions in architecture such as Stuttgart-Weissenhof (1927), Interbau Berlin (1957) or IBA Berlin (1987) (=International Building Exhibition) with the participation of numerous famous architects from all over the world. Not only this has encouraged international contacts and exchange.
Beyond this many exiled German architects with outstanding qualifications have contributed to the urban and architectural development during and after the Nazi-regime all over Europe, in the USA and beyond.

Peter Gabrijelčič

I would like to mention the international project "Re Urban Mobil" on the subject of the restoration of city centres in which Ljubljana cooperated with the cities of Leipzig, Bologna and Leon which was launched in 2002 and officially ended in 2005.
The name of the project indicates the acute condition of city centres and the adjacent districts, and there is talk here of mobilisation to re-urbanise these centres.
The project was mostly financed by the European Commission and took place as part of the "Improvement of Life Quality" programme. It was conceived as being multidisciplinary because architects, urbanists, economists, sociologists, geographers and other experts from nine universities and research

institutes as well as from the Faculty of Architecture, from the Faculty of Economics and for the Urbanist Institute in Slovenia cooperated on the project. We wished to draw up a methodology within the project for elaborating projects of renovation and revitalisation of city centres; the main objective of the project involved preparing a "toolbox", i.e. draft measures and tools to stop dilapidation, or reverse the trend of the development of city centres to a positive direction. The project took place by each city selecting two historical areas to work on as so-called "Case Study Areas" to analyse the adequacy of the methodology.

Pálfy Sándor

Hungarian architecture and its actors were often latched into international movements by European connections: French in medieval times, Italian with the Renaissance, German and French during the Eclecticism of the 19th century. Hungarian Secession at the turn of the century won great European attention, and many Hungarian professionals made great contributions to international Modernism at its birth in Weimar.

Nasrine Seraji

The Academy of Fine Arts Vienna has historically proven to be a link for international exchange between architects of Central Europe. Think of Jože Plečnik who, amongst many others, came to study at the Academy in Vienna and went on to significantly contribute to transforming Prague and Ljubljana. Today the Institute for Art and Architecture with its Bachelor and Master Programmes and an international faculty still

attracts talented students from across Central Europe and beyond.

Imro Vaško

The architectural cloud of Slovakia consists of vectors of the fate of architects migrating from Hungary and the south at the start of the century. Afterwards, the Czech interwar wave helped build the emerging Slovakia and at the time of communist isolation a "Slovak steam roller" was created with the coming together of all energy from all over Slovakia to Bratislava, though physically isolated from the surrounding world, however a culturally constant part of the "western boundary line". The 20th century of Slovak architecture is characterised by the triangle between Prague, Bratislava and the High Tatras (Slovak-Polish Borderland) and the distinct north-western-south-eastern axis between Berlin, Prague and Budapest which was stronger as vectors between Bratislava and Vienna.

Zdeněk Zavřel

There are many – Central European space was open to common activities in the past.
Examples – 1920's: Loos in CZ, Plecnik in Prague, pupils of Bauhaus form CZ, PL, H, A etc.
Nowdays: Strong traditional ties between Prague and Bratislava, collaboration between TU Prague-TU Dresden, monument conservation collaboration with Poland and a lot of individual connections such as Jano Stempel's with Budapest…

HOW DO YOU SEE THE COOPERATION ON AN EDUCATIONAL LEVEL IN CENTRAL EUROPE IN THE CONTEXT OF THE URBANITY PROJECT?

Johannes Cramer

There have been many efforts and a lot of opportunities but not enough time and limited resources for the students as well as the teachers to extend these activities. Our department has a strong focus on projects and cooperation with developing countries such as Mexico or in the Himalayan region.

Peter Gabrijelčič

Only several decades ago we lived with the conviction that all things in the world happen in accordance with the logic of development which is built on the foundation of continuity, that these things are completed, that they are improved as a consequence of historical experience and that this experience must be constantly incorporated into all areas of our social, economic and cultural life. Today, when we are witnesses of the telecommunication revolution, we are, on the contrary, convinced that only changes are this constant in the development of human society which allows its long-term survival. However, today's system of education is still directed above all at the past, and for this reason are also such noticeable contrasts between planned objectives and their implementation in space. We talk of a crisis in the field. Today is a period of pluralism and co-existence of various spatial models of identity. The contemporary moral views of the field must therefore be based on the need to respect various cultures and subcultures together with respect for their various spatial expectations. We must search for new, complementary forms of the organisation of space, or new epistemological tools by which it will be possible to control the dynamic processes in contemporary urban structures. Besides the modernist concept of "less is more", the validity will also have to be recognised of the ecological concept of "more is less" which is based on the recognition that complex ecological systems are more vital than simple in nature, and therefore they adapt better to the interpretations of contemporary social and spatial organisation which is complex, dynamic and variable. This can be the axis of future academic projects in Central Europe.

Pálfy Sándor

It is a great opportunity - and also our duty - to exchange knowledge and experience in higher education establishing close connections among European institutions, especially inside our Central European region. This is affirmed by the demand for mobility during university studies made possible by the three cycles of the Bologna Process. The Urbanity project is the first example in the Central European region for real academic collaboration in architecture and urbanism, and it is a successful one in my opinion.

Nasrine Seraji

Twenty years after the fall of the iron curtain the Urbanity project has highlighted a condition that we already tend to take for granted: It is remarkable that 70 students from seven different countries could engage in intense discussions and work together on developing visions for the future of Central European cities.

Imro Vaško

Bratislava is still the least distinguishable architectural point in the Central European architectural network. It does not possess the power and architectural strength of Berlin, Prague, Vienna and Budapest, or the national and topographical exclusivity of Warsaw and the cultural exceptionality of Plečnik's Ljubljana. In this region Bratislava is an unknown and unattractive territory and therefore is perhaps its new catalyst and fuse of its new strategies. Each Central European locality has its specifics and characteristics and the mutual mental differences are striking. The Urbanity Workshops have shown the differences - precise and contextual Vienna, open and speculative Berlin, pragmatic Prague and Ljubljana, broadminded Warsaw, sociological Budapest and abstract Bratislava. The hybrid coexistence of the various educative entities in the Urbanity Project was its strength.

Zdeněk Zavřel

Very interesting work experience, network of interested teachers and students established - important for further collaboration. The work should be more focused on specific problems, less on superficial comparisons and statistics.

IS THERE ANYTHING MISSING IN THE EXCHANGE OF IDEAS AMONG WORLDWIDE ARCHITECTURE?

Johannes Cramer

Technical means and possibilities are sufficient and there are international exchange programmes, but financial resources are limited and, moreover, have been reduced further by our government in recent years so that actual mobility among students and teachers is declining.

Peter Gabrijelčič

In my opinion we need objective reflection in architecture and urbanism which will evaluate, regulate and popularise our activity. In the field of architecture we are also witnesses of a serious crisis as such, as well as what the critic should do. A crisis of identity and reason has currently affected criticism because the fact remains that neither the method nor a specific subject of an essay about criticism can define the activity. Unlike traditional criticism, which formulates its standpoint with a critical aloofness and with the help of analysis and evaluation of a specific subject, today's criticism is not satisfied only with a former interpretative role. We can say that almost the opposite applies, that criticism wishes to relinquish the former role of interpreter and evaluator. The criticism no longer has its specific subject and has also relinquished its former public. The way it has subjected its former subject of an essay and so has become assimila-ted into creative activities, it has become its equal. In place of the traditional subject its own activity will become the new final objective of criticism. We can

describe the meta-talk as
a para-discourse, i.e. discourse
which is included in the work
itself, however in such a way that
most often it will not say anything
fundamentally new, nor help us to
evaluate it, but only attempts to
use it above all as a springboard
for itself. This new subject of
critici-sm has reached a new internal
and self-reflective nature with
interpretations which are limited
only to understanding from within
the environment of criticism itself.
The activity which was developed with
the intention to explain the work of
other creative activities itself
becomes an artistic discipline which
is expressed in the area of pure
textuality. The critical text becomes
a work which is equal to other
creative works which used to be
a subject of criticism.

Pálfy Sándor
In Central Europe we must collaborate
to find our own thoughts and
common voice in contemporary world
architecture. If not this region
will loose its valuable and unique
architectural character:
the insensitive forms of property
development frequently backed up by
international star architecture are
more often changing even
the historical core of our cities.
These alarming signs should make us
act together, let us hope it is not
too late!

Nasrine Seraji
Today it seems of little interest
to search for what we all share in
common. It is more essential to
investigate respective specificities
and find ways of turning the mutual
understanding of our differences into
vehicles for producing knowledge and
significant architecture.

Imro Vaško
The common language is a problem
of the present. Even if we coexist
in a common Europe and in a global
European space, we are confronted by
our individual differing problems,
unequal initial conditions,
unequal hierarchical positions and
differentiated local ambitions.
The problems may be common but are
clearly individualised. The mistake
of the greater ability to understand
the subtleties of dialects, feel
the lack of senstivity to
differences is small opportunity for
understanding foreign humour.

Zdeněk Zavřel
There is enough information about
everything that happens anywhere.
What is missing is direct
involvement and personal experience.
Educational exchange programmes help
to fill this gap. But don't forget:
"think global - act local"!

_

WHAT ARE THE FUTURE POSSIBILITIES FOR CENTRAL EUROPEAN EXCHANGES IN THE ARCHITECTURAL AND URBAN PLANNING FIELD?

Johannes Cramer
Better exchange of information will
contribute to building up a European
spirit and even more an European
architectural identity, which will
much more include the awareness of
the extended European Community,
namely in its south-eastern parts.

Peter Gabrijelčič
The accession of the former eastern
European countries to the EU meant
that the Central European region
came face to face with systemic
measures by which Europe wants to
enforce more intensive economic,
social and spatial development on
its entire territory. Although
individual member countries regard

some of the measures as
an unauthorised interference in
their integrity and a loss of
certain economic potentials (above
all in the sphere of agriculture),
however the policy and interests of
Europe are directed at
the development of the economically
strong and stable European regions
with the help of which Europe will
be able to effectively compete
with strong world regions. Hence,
each of the European countries
and regions must objectively ask
where it sees its own comparative
merits within the EU which it will
develop according to the principle
of the complementarity of functions
and will enable long-term stable
economic and social development.
Here I see the future of cooperation
between architects and urbanists.
Cooperation on an academic and
cultural level is always a prelude
to later more intensive economic
connection.
Hence it is the obligation of
universities to continue in
intensive cooperation in the form
of various partnership projects
which will involve both economic
and social entities. Once air
flights between Berlin, Budapest,
Bratislava, Ljubljana, Prague,
Warsaw and Vienna will be just as
frequent and full as they are to
London, Rome, Amsterdam or Paris,
we will be satisfied with
the results of our cohesive
activity.

Pálfy Sándor
We must use all tools to collaborate
here in Central Europe for our
common history, similar potentials
and possibilities, but also for
the possibility and obligation to
get to know and use each others
achievements. In the field of
urbanism cooperation is also
essential because of big structural
correspondences, regions extending

along borders, and cities slowly
growing together. Working together
might result in a new common
identity in Central European
architecture. The Urbanity project
is good promotion for this.

Nasrine Seraji
Only if architects renounce
the reiteration of global ideas
and focus on the articulation of
manifold specificities instead, will
architecture succeed as an ecology
that instigates and proliferates
difference and vitality.

Imro Vaško
Daily apocalyptic news about
the volcanic ash over the Atlantic,
the oil slick in the Gulf of Mexico,
fires and smog over Russia and
the floods in Europe and Asia are
connected. It does not depend on
whether events are local or global,
but on the current nature of
the problems which we as architects,
urbanists and sensitive people
have the opportunity to deal with.
Perhaps we will have to deal more
with the consequences or processes
activated outside our cloud
epicentre in Central Europe than
we have so far wanted to admit to.
Our localisation and historical
experience is a permanent reminder.
The constant vibration and migration
of the vectors of our "geo
-architectural-climatic" cloud is
the hope that it will "rain" from
this cloud.

Zdeněk Zavřel
There are many - schools could
collaborate on educational and
research programmes. In the form
of common projects, symposia,
workshops, lectures, excursions etc.
At a practical level, professional
bodies and municipalities could show
more initiative in the accessibility
of mutual competitions.

BERLIN

BRATISLAVA

BUDAPEST

LJUBLJANA

PRAGUE

VIENNA

WARSAW

TEAM

–

Zuzana Bodnárová
Bostjan Bugarič
Nóra Bürger
Václav Cimbál
Michal Dioszegi
Zuzana Duchova
Milan Hanuš
Svea Heinemann
Luba Hledlová
Michaela Janečková
Karolina Jírová
Igor Kovačević
Monika Lacková
Lenka Lednická
Alexandra Machacova
Marta Mlodozeniec
Zuzanna Skoczek
Lucie Stejskalová
Nelin Tunc
Yvette Vašourková
Ladislav Zikmund

TUTORS

–

György Alföldi
Thomas Arnold
Irena Fialová
Stefan Gruber
Martin Gsandtner
Sławomir Gzell
Jan Jehlík
Bálint Kádár
Birgit Klauck
Michal Kohout
Radek Kolařík
Uroš Rustja
Lisa Schmidt-Colinet
Imro Vaško
Maruša Zorec

LECTURERS

–

Lieven De Cauter
Mariusz Czepczynski
Jiří Hrůza
Miroslav Marcelli
Christian Teckert
Tomáš Valena
Elia Zenghelis

SOCIOLOGISTS

–

Ľubomír Falťan
Peter Gajdoš
Albrecht Göschel
Blaž Križnik
Janos Ladanyi
Krysztof Nawratek
Martin Ouředníček
Reinhard Seiss
Jana Temelová
Matjaž Uršič

STUDENTS

–

Anna Anděrová
Stefan Aursulesei
Alisha Baker
Adnan Balcinovic
Miriam Barona
Sebastian Bauer
András Beke
Anna Beránková
Káča Blahutová
Andrej Blatnik
Marcin Brzeski
Peter Buday
Anna Cséfalvay
Adriana Debnárová
Matej Delak
Isabella Domanska
Nagowska Dorota

Florentine Dreier
Attila Fábri
János Fekete
Ajda Fortuna
Christian Friess
Matthias Frimberger
Mojca Gabrič
Agnieszka Gaczkowska
Eliška Gálová
Valéria Gašparová
Terézia Grešková
Anna Háblová
Clemens Hasler
Wesley Ho
Filip Hodulík
Christiane Hütter
Roland Icking
Christiane Irxenmayer
Urban Jeriha
Teo Kajzer
Irina Khamidulina
Piotr Kilanowski
Richard Kilo
Zoltán Kincses
Mariedl Kleemann
Sarah Köck
Júlia Kolláthová
Veronika Kommová
Joanna Koszewska
Kristína Králová
Alenka Kramer
Tomáš Kučera
Hannes Langguth
Jasmin Leonhard
Tomáš Letenay
Tomáš Lindovský
Marek Lüley
Suoyi Ma
Katarína Mačková
Nina Majoranc
Daniela Majzlanová
Katarína Martonová
Aleksandra Melion
Peter Mihaľák
Staš Mitrovič
Daniela Mitterberger
Vladimír Mrázik
Maximilian Müller
Anja Neupert
Veronika Parteľová

Ania Pas
Gunita Pavlovica
Lukas Pazmandy
Haris Piplas
Ajda Primožič
Adina Radway
Žiga Ravnikar
Lukas Rückerl
Uroš Rustja
Borg Sarah
Frank Schwenk
Daniel Silva
Sara Slivnik
Philipp Soeparno
Martin Stára
Roland Stolz
Moritz Stork
Zsolt Szendrei
Veronika Škof
Adrián Švec
Jyri Tartia
Eva Taučar
Andrea Teierlová
Lucie Tomaštíková
Szilvia Tóth
Teresa Traunsteiner
Veronika Trnovská
Aron Tsang
Alena Týfová
Martin Václavík
Martin Varga
Petr Vavřina
Rok Velikonja
Ana Vogelfang
Pavel Vrzala
Mechtild Weber
Katalin Wéber
Marc Werner
Isabell Wolke
Michaela Wonisch
Linda Wortmann
Vid Zabel
Martin Zaiček
Klara Zalokar
Janka Zatlukajová
Ivan Zuliani
Klemen Zupančič

BERLIN

BRATISLAVA

BUDAPEST

233

LJUBLJANA

PRAGUE

VIENNA

WARSAW

Under the auspices of the Mayors

Mr. Pavel Bém
-mayor of the Capital City of Prague

Mr. Klaus Wowereit
-mayor of the Capital City of Berlin

Mr. Andrej Ďurkovský
-mayor of the Capital City of Bratislava

Mrs. Hanna Gronkiewicz-Waltz
-mayor of the Capital City of Warsaw

Mr. Michael Häupl
-mayor of the Capital City of Vienna

Research partners

Berlin Institute of Technology

Technical University of Budapest

Academy of Fine Arts Vienna

Academy of Fine Arts and Design
Bratislava

University of Ljubljana

Czech Technical University in Prague

Warsaw University of Technology

Organizer

| | | | |
centre for central european architecture
| | | |

Initiator

MOBA

Support

 Visegrad Fund

 PRAGUE PRAGA PRAG

ČESKO-NĚMECKÝ FOND BUDOUCNOSTI
DEUTSCH-TSCHECHISCHER
ZUKUNFTSFONDS

 MINISTERSTVO KULTURY

 european cultural foundation

City partners

 PRAGUE PRAGA PRAG

StaDt Wien

 Berlin

 BRATISLAVA

 City of Ljubljana

BUDAPEST

Project partners

 METROSTAV

 GOETHE-INSTITUT PRAG

 rakouské kulturní fórum

 A10 new European

Co-organizers

 miasto siela

 OSSA

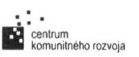 centrum komunitného rozvoja

 KUD C3

 Deutsches Architektur Zentrum

 DAZ

 SOHO IN OTTAKRING 09

Publisher:
Centre for Central European Architecture
U Půjčovny 4
110 00 Praha 1
Czech Republic

Initiated and directed by:
Igor Kovačević, Yvette Vašourková (MOBA)

Editors:
Igor Kovačević, Yvette Vašourková

Coeditor:
Urban Jeriha

Editorial assistants:
Lenka Lednická, Lucie Stejskalová

Authors:
György Alföldi, Thomas Arnold,
Irena Fialová, Stefan Gruber,
Martin Gsandtner, Sławomir Gzell,
Bálint Kádár, Birgit Klauck,
Michal Kohout, Igor Kovačević,
Uroš Rustja, Lisa Schmidt-Colinet,
Imro Vaško, Yvette Vašourková,
Maruša Zorec

Graphic design:
Ado Juraček

Print:
PBtisk
Czech Republic, EU

1st Edition

September 2010

ISBN 978-80-254-8170-7

Distributed by ACTAR

www.urbanityproject.eu
www.ccea.cz